RELIGION BY ~~~~~~

Religion and Public Life
in the Pacific Northwest

RELIGION BY REGION

Religion by Region Series
Co-published with the Leonard E. Greenberg Center for the Study of Religion in Public Life at Trinity College
Mark Silk and Andrew Walsh, Series Editors

The United States is a nation of many distinct regions. But until now, no literature has looked at these regional differences in terms of religion. The Religion by Region Series describes, both quantitatively and qualitatively, the religious character of contemporary America, region by region. Each of the eight regional volumes includes overviews and demographic information to allow comparisons between regions. But at the same time, each volume strives to show what makes its region unique. A concluding volume looks at what these regional variations mean for American religion as a whole.

Religion and Public Life in the Pacific Northwest:
The None Zone

Edited by
Patricia O'Connell Killen
and
Mark Silk

Published in cooperation with the Leonard E. Greenberg
Center for the Study of Religion in Public Life at
Trinity College, Hartford, Connecticut

ALTAMIRA
PRESS

A Division of
ROWMAN & LITTLEFIELD PUBLISHERS, INC.
Walnut Creek • Lanham • New York • Toronto • Oxford

Published in cooperation with the Leonard E. Greenberg Center for the Study of Religion in Public Life at Trinity College, Hartford, Connecticut

ALTAMIRA PRESS
A division of Rowman & Littlefield Publishers, Inc.
1630 North Main Street, #367
Walnut Creek, CA 94596
www.altamirapress.com

Rowman & Littlefield Publishers, Inc.
A wholly owned subsidiary of The Rowman & Littlefield Publishing Group, Inc.
4501 Forbes Boulevard, Suite 200
Lanham, MD 20706

PO Box 317
Oxford
OX2 9RU, UK

British Library Cataloguing in Publication Information Available

Library of Congress Cataloging-in-Publication Data

Religion and public life in the Pacific Northwest : the none zone / edited by
    Patricia O'Connell Killen and Mark Silk.
        p.   cm. — (Religion by region ; 1)
    Includes bibliographical references and index.
        ISBN 0-7591-0624-X (alk. paper) — ISBN 0-7591-0625-8 (pbk : alk. paper)
        1. Northwest, Pacific—Religion.   I. Killen, Patricia O'Connell.   II. Silk, Mark.
    III. Series.
    BL2527.N95R45 2004
    200'.9795—dc22   2004000859

Printed in the United States of America

⊗ The paper used in this publication meets the minimum requirements of American National Standard for Information Sciences—Permanence of Paper for Printed Library Materials, ANSI/NISO Z39.48–1992.

CONTENTS

Preface

Geographical diversity is the hallmark of religion in the United States. There are Catholic zones and evangelical Bible Belts, a Lutheran domain and a Mormon fastness, metropolitan concentrations of Jews and Muslims, and (in a different dimension) parts of the country where religious affiliation of whatever kind is very high and parts where it is far below the norm. This religious heterogeneity is inextricably linked to the character of American places. From Boston to Birmingham, from Salt Lake City to Santa Barbara, even the casual observer perceives public cultures that are intimately connected to the religious identities and habits of the local population.

Yet when the story of religion in American public life gets told, the country's variegated religious landscape tends to be reduced to a series of monochrome portraits of the spiritual state of the union, of piety along the Potomac, of great events or swings of mood that raise or lower the collective religious temperature. Whatever the virtues of compiling such a unified national narrative—and I believe they are considerable—it obscures a great deal. As the famous red-and-blue map of the 2000 presidential vote makes clear, region has not ceased to matter in national politics. Indeed, in this era of increasing federalism, regions are, state by state, charting ever more distinctive courses.

To understand where each region is headed and why, it is critical to recognize the place of religion in it.

Religion by Region, a project of the Leonard E. Greenberg Center for the Study of Religion in Public Life at Trinity College in Hartford, represents the first comprehensive effort to show how religion shapes, and is being shaped by, regional culture in America. The project has been designed to produce edited volumes (of which this is the first) on each of eight regions of the country. A ninth volume will sum up the results in order to draw larger conclusions about the way religion and region combine to affect civic culture and public policy in the United States as a whole.

The purpose of the project is not to decompose a national storyline into eight separate narratives. Rather, it is to bring regional realities to bear, in a systematic way, on how American culture is understood at the beginning of the twenty-first century. In line with the Greenberg Center's commitment to enhance public understanding of religion, these volumes are intended for a general audience, with a particular eye towards helping working journalists make better sense of the part religion plays in the public life—local, statewide, regional, and national—that they cover. At the same time, I am persuaded that the accounts and analyses provided in these volumes will make a significant contribution to the academic study of religion in contemporary America.

The project's division of the country into regions will be generally familiar, with the exception of what we are calling the Southern Crossroads—a region roughly equivalent to what American historians know as the Old Southwest, comprising Louisiana, Texas, Arkansas, Oklahoma, and Missouri. Since we are committed to covering every state in the Union (though not the territories—e.g., Puerto Rico), Hawaii has been included in a Pacific region with California and Nevada, and Alaska in the Pacific Northwest.

Cultural geographers may be surprised to discover a few states out of their customary places. Idaho, which is usually considered part of the Pacific Northwest, has been assigned to the Mountain West. In our view, the fact that the bulk of Idaho's population lives in the heavily Mormon southern part of the state links it more closely to Utah than to Oregon and Washington. To be sure, we might have chosen to parcel out certain states between regions, assigning northern Idaho and western Montana to the Pacific Northwest or, to take another example, creating a Catholic band running from southern Louisiana through south Texas and across the lower tiers of New Mexico and Arizona on into southern California. The purpose of the project, however, is not to map the country religiously but to explore the ways that politics, public policies, and civil society relate—or fail to relate—to the religion that is on the ground. States have had to be kept intact because when American laws are not made in Washington, D.C. they are made in statehouses. To understand what is decided in Baton Rouge, Louisiana's Catholic south and evangelical north must be seen as engaged in a single undertaking.

That is not to say that the details of American religious demography are unimportant to our purpose. That demography has undergone notable shifts in recent years, and these have affected public life in any number of ways. To reckon with them, it has been essential to assemble the best data available on the religious identities of Americans and how they correlate with voting patterns and views on public issues. As students of American religion know, however, this is far from an easy task. The U.S. Census is prohibited by law from asking questions about religion, and membership reports provided by religious bodies to non-governmental researchers—when they are provided at all—vary greatly in accuracy. Most public opinion polling does not enable us to draw precise correlations between respondents' views on issues and their religious identity and behavior.

In order to secure the best possible empirical grounding, the project has assembled a range of data from three sources, which are described in detail in the Appendix. These have supplied us with, among other things, information from religious bodies on their membership; from individuals on their religious identities; and from voters in specific religious categories on their political preferences and opinions. (For purposes of clarity, people are described as "adherents" or "members" only when reported as such by a religious institution. Otherwise, they are "identifiers.") Putting this information together with 2000 census and other survey data, the project has been able to create both the best available picture of religion in America today and the most comprehensive account of its political significance. The North American Religion Atlas website, www.religionatlas.org, includes maps and tables specifically developed for each volume in the Religion by Region series.

Religion by Region does not argue that religion plays the same kind of role in each region of the country; nor does it mean to advance the proposition that religion is the master key that unlocks all the secrets of American public life. As the tables of contents of the individual volumes make clear, each region has its distinctive religious layout, based not only on the numerical strength of particular religious bodies but also on how those bodies, or groups of them, function on the public stage. In some regions, religion serves as a shaping force; in others it is a subtler conditioning agent. Our objective is simply to show what the picture looks like from place to place and to provide consistent data and a framework of discussion sufficient to enable useful contrasts and comparisons to be drawn.

A project of such scope and ambition does not come cheap. We are deeply indebted to the Lilly Endowment for making it possible.

Mark Silk
Hartford, Connecticut
January 2004

INTRODUCTION

PATTERNS OF THE PAST, PROSPECTS FOR THE FUTURE: RELIGION IN THE NONE ZONE

Patricia O'Connell Killen

The defining feature of religion in the Pacific Northwest is that most of the population is "unchurched." Fewer people in Oregon, Washington, and Alaska affiliate with a religious institution than in any other region of the United States. More people here claim "none" when asked their religious identification than in any other region of the United States. And, unlike any other region, the single largest segment of the Pacific Northwest's population is composed of those who identify with a religious tradition but have no affiliation with a religious community.

What's more, this is not a late-breaking trend. The Pacific Northwest has pretty much always been this way, to the longstanding frustration and bewilderment of its religious leaders. In 1914, for example, a symposium was convened to address such regional problems as Sunday amusements, the arrival of "untold thousands of foreigners," and unemployment.

"The people that builded [sic] this empire . . . [left] the Golden Rule beyond the Rockies, and they proceeded to do others before others could do them," lamented Professor E.J. Klemme of the Washington State Normal School in Ellensburg. "In the East they were faithful church members; now they are not even church [at]tenders." According to Klemme, the fault lay with the geography itself: "The ascent of the Great Divide seemed too steep for church letters. The air of the Northwest seemed too rare for prayer. We have hurried forth to conquer the wilderness, but we have been conquered by it."

Or as B.F. Kumler, superintendent of the largest Methodist Sunday School in the Columbia River Annual Conference, put it, "The very vastness of the resources of the Northwest, the preponderance of mountains, rivers, and forests tend to increase the problems. Nowhere in the United States in a like area are found such a variety of industry and natural resources of every conceivable type. This fact brings men of every kind and social condition."[1]

Employing the optimistic language of Progressive Era reform, Klemme and Kumler challenged their audience to greater effort in the saving and civilizing work they believed was rightly the province of Protestant Christianity in the Pacific Northwest. But underneath their rhetoric lay a deep anxiety about whether it was possible to create a proper human community in a place of seemingly infinite resources and opportunity that also was, to borrow language from the contemporary Northwest writer Bruce Barcott, the "catchbasin for washed-up westering dreams."[2]

That question remains central. Today, as in the past, answers are forged by people within and beyond religious congregations at the confluence of theological heritage, history, and present experience in this place. Understanding how these facts matter for public life in the Pacific Northwest requires an extended look at the region's religious environment and its characteristic ethos or style.

The Pacific Northwest is an open religious environment. This place is alternately indifferent or inviting to religion, an obstacle or opportunity, a refuge or revelation. Here, more than in other regions of the United States, weak religious institutions and the absence of a dominant institutional religious reference group allow for a highly elastic religious reality. This is a religious environment where boundaries and identities are fluid, where energy and movements coalesce and then dissolve. In the Pacific Northwest there are simultaneous tendencies, at a different and sometimes the same moment, to cooperation across and beyond religious institutions, to almost sectarian religious conflicts and extremes, and to religious indifference. In this environment the question of boundaries—physical, social, and human—is constantly present. Here theological heritage, creative imagination, fascination with the new, and the promise of unlimited possibility coalesce to make religion present in both conventional and unconventional ways.

Key features of the Pacific Northwest's religious environment have contributed to the development of a style of individual and institutional religiousness that profoundly shapes how religion is present in the region's public life. Throughout the region's history most people have not participated in institutional religion, and the few who have are divided among many different groups. No single denomination or religious community has been present for any period in numbers sufficient to constitute a dominant public force with which all must contend. This absence of a single, persistently dominant, strongly institutionalized religious reference group colors all individual and institutional religiousness in the region. The region also has a long history of geographic, social, and psychic mobility. Mobility offers options and severs social relationships. In addition, the region's unsurpassed physical grandeur and topographic variety pervade people's experience, overwhelming and awing them. In the Pacific Northwest topography dwarfs human communities.

Because the boundaries of individual and social identity in the Pacific Northwest are fluid, and because religious institutions are relatively weak, religion has never been a strong mechanism of social control. With minimal social pressure to affiliate with a religious institution, individuals are free to pursue or abandon a spiritual quest as they will. Individuals and groups develop belief, practice, and sensibility under little pressure to conform and with considerable freedom to experiment and innovate. This physical and spiritual environment confronts all who enter the region with a set of religious tasks that involve clarifying individual religious identity, constructing social relationships, and making sense of the land itself. As they negotiate these tasks, individuals both adopt and exhibit the Pacific Northwest's religious ethos or style.

Low levels of religious "adherence," (i.e., affiliation with an organized religious community), coupled with the lack of a dominant denomination, render religious identity, commitment, and long-term belonging within a religious organization an on-going problem. High levels of religious adherence provide social support for institutional religious participation. A clearly recognizable religious reference group functions as a social mirror, alongside or against which an individual can define herself or himself. The Pacific Northwest has neither, and so each individual's religious identity and organizational affiliation can be a life-long project. Everyone who comes into the region must negotiate his or her own religious identity, because the meaning and style of religious belonging changes in a context where commitment, experimentation, and indifference are equal.

On-going religious commitment takes explicit, regularly re-affirmed choice. A pastor of one Seattle congregation with over 1,000 members recently put the average span of an individual's membership in his congregation at five years. Histories of Christian denominations in the region describe heroic ministers overcoming both a wild land and "indifferent" people in wrenching the church into existence.[3] Those who believe and practice must put energy into re-enforcing their belief and practice.

The need to make religious belief, activity, and institutions significant is part of the region's historic pre-occupation with size of congregations, buildings, or programs. It helps to explain why First Presbyterian Church in Seattle being the largest congregation in the denomination during the early twentieth century mattered so much; why in the second decade of that century the *Catholic Sentinel* of the Archdiocese of Portland claimed to be the largest Catholic weekly in the world, when Catholics made up less than 10 percent of Oregon's population; why

Protestants and Catholic built and maintained church-related colleges and universities in numbers disproportionate to their segment of the population; and why
today congregations and judicatories battle city and county governments over
restrictions placed on the size of their physical plants by growth management laws.

Absent strong social re-enforcement for religious identification and affiliation with religious communities, religious institutions that offer intense emotional and physical experiences of the divine, that make the "supernatural" real, have
been attractive to people in the region in ways that more moderate Protestant
denominations have not. It takes a robust experience of the supernatural to hold
its own against a backdrop of snow-capped mountains capable of eliciting human
devotion. Catholics and Mormons historically did this by emphasizing the church
as the medium of salvation. Pentecostal churches, which from their inception
have had a greater portion of the adherent pie here than elsewhere, have done it
by offering a portable, visceral, self-verifiable experience of the divine.

The ambiguity of this macro religious environment, with no clearly dominant
institutional religious reference group and expansive natural surroundings, has
fed an individual and institutional religious style that is alternately expansive and
self-absorbed. Individual religiousness tends to be private and episodically
intense. Many pursue a spiritual quest on their own, drawing from multiple traditions and practices on a journey of religious experimentation.

But for others the ambiguity of the larger religious environment propels them
toward commitment that is clearly defined, emotionally significant, and often
inflexible because it has been hard won, and thus is in need of protection. For these
people, highlighting boundaries between one's religious community and others
helps to re-enforce identity and commitment. Hence, the same environment that
provides space for wide-ranging religious experimentation feeds a sectarian
impulse. It also has inspired creative innovations in leadership and cooperation
across organizational boundaries. What the region's religious environment seems
to work against is sustaining a large population of sturdy religious moderates.

The hold of formally designated institutional religious leaders over the lives
of their members in the Pacific Northwest has been more a matter of the leader's
charisma and persuasiveness than of designated office or position. In a situation
of demographic thinness, institutional religious leaders are keenly aware that the
existence of a congregation and its educational or social service outreach depend
on the good will of members and the sympathetic support of persons beyond the
congregation's doors. The fact that churches, synagogues, temples, and mosques
survive only if the people want them lies very close to the surface in the religious
life of the region. This drives lay ownership and lay autonomy.

Throughout the region's history individuals have acted with marked independence in relation to religious institutions. Even in 1860, A.M.A. Blanchet,

Roman Catholic Bishop of Nesqualy, cautioned his priests against refusing to perform mixed marriages lest the Catholics choose to be married by a judge.

The tendency of people to act independently in matters religious has created an ongoing challenge for faith communities in which history and theological heritage are significant. It is difficult to transmit traditions of belief, practice, and sensibility to people on the move, disconnected from larger social networks, and often disinterested in historic theological traditions and skeptical of institutional authority.

Most people who come into the region do not come seeking to replicate what they left behind. They come for better opportunity or to escape hardship elsewhere. One thing they seek to escape is social pressure to conform. At the 1914 symposium E.L. Blaine noted, "Many of these newcomers have either become so cold or so cloyed in their old church that they frequently do not identify themselves with the church in their newly chosen home."

Each person who enters the region must choose whether, if, and how to reconnect. That choice is part of a larger question of community in the Pacific Northwest, a question about how an individual can be fully free, in nature, and part of society. People seek community, often through churches, and yet feel ambivalent about the constraints that community entails. This ambivalence leads some out of churches and drives others toward intense commitment and ownership.

For most of the region's history, however, people supported religious institutions for the services they provided and as signs of civilization and progress. A widely shared view of religious institutions as a social utility, coupled with institutional religious leaders' realization of the fragility of their enterprises, contributed to ecumenical cooperation in the region. Cooperation between Protestants and Catholics, and inter-faith cooperation between Christians and Jews, was practiced in the West for a century before it began in the Midwest, South, and East.[4]

In 1866 Caroline Leighton commented on a Scotch Protestant stage depot manager of such "liberal attitudes" that he maintained a collection box for funds to support a school run by Roman Catholic sisters.[5] And in 1924 a coalition of prominent Protestant, Catholic, and Jewish businessmen headed the campaign to defeat the Ku Klux Klan-sponsored Initiative 49 that would have outlawed parochial schools in Washington State, by arguing that it was bad for business. This pragmatic appreciation for conventional religious institutions, however, did not curb people's interest in new religious movements and modes of religious organization in the Pacific Northwest.

Throughout the region's history individuals have joined, dropped out, and switched organizational affiliation. While this practice is not unique to the Pacific Northwest, it has been more common here and historically has had a greater impact because of the small population within religious organizations.

In many ways the same is true of religious institutions. The environment that renders them weak also provides impetus for innovation and experimentation. Successful religiously motivated public campaigns in the Pacific Northwest must be ecumenical, inter-faith, and couched in language that resonates with those beyond church, synagogue, temple or mosque. Demographics do not allow any other option. Creativity in religious organizations has been part of the region's religious environment. At the same time, however, religious institutions, like individuals, become concerned with boundaries of identity and exhibit the same alternation between expansiveness and self-absorption.

The final major challenge with which the religious environment of the Pacific Northwest confronts individuals and communities is the region itself. The expanse and grandeur of the region dwarfs the human. While Romantic writers considered this uplifting and some have found nature a place of mystical union, many who came experienced it as did the character Hank Stamper in Ken Kesey's *Sometimes a Great Notion*, "And for *another* thing, there was nothing, *not a thing*, about the country that made a man feel Big And Important. If anything it made a man feel dwarfed, . . . Important? Why, there was something about the whole blessed country that made a soul feel whipped before he got started."[6]

The region is itself an actor in any story about life in the Pacific Northwest. As a result, individuals and communities must find a metaphor by which to incorporate the region into their experience here. Variant metaphors pervade religious histories and the literature of the region, the Pacific Northwest as an obstacle to be overcome, a challenge to greatness, an opportunity or stage for action, a space of refuge and anonymity, a site of revelation. Every individual or group finds a metaphor by which to write the region—the place—into its story.

The metaphor chosen to "story" this place profoundly affects how it is perceived in an individual's or group's religious history. To mainline Protestants, Catholics, and Reform and Conservative Jews the place challenges people to build a society that is equal to the region's grandeur and promise of opportunity. To religious entrepreneurs, the region's low adherence rates constitute an opportunity; its unchurched are a vast untapped market, souls in need of salvation. To an immigrant refugee community of Vietnamese Buddhists the region's low levels of religious adherence make it a more welcoming space, one where they are free to practice their religion with less concern about public response. To artists and writers the region inspires creativity and offers a project worth giving their lives to, protecting its wilderness in order to protect their very souls.

To refer to the Pacific Northwest as an open religious environment implies many things about how individual and institutional religion are composed and lived. *The None Zone* argues that four clusters of religious communities, each joined by theological, historical, and social affinities—and all reflecting the region's characteristic religious style—have emerged. Each brings religion into the region's public life. Cumulatively, their story explains how religion is a public presence that matters in the Pacific Northwest, where most people do not participate in religious institutions and where the single largest denomination, the Roman Catholic Church, claims barely 11 percent of the total population.

The first cluster includes mainline Protestants, Catholics, and Reform and Conservative Jews. These three groups share theological visions that impel their members to action on behalf of the broader common good. Those visions have motivated experiments in providing social services, innovations in worship, self-critique, civic leadership, and prophetic political involvement. Though not equally powerful or prominent throughout the region's history, these three groups have cooperated in civic life and brought the resources of their members to bear on social problems. They have been most influential when able to offer a compelling vision of the public good characterized by tolerance, fair play, and social responsibility toward the less fortunate that resonated with the general population. To the extent that there has been a "religious establishment" in the Pacific Northwest, these groups have constituted it.

By 1980 broader social changes had begun to render these communities' vision of the public good less compelling. While larger regional and national social forces and internal tensions have in various ways continued to erode their power and status, they remain important both numerically—making up nearly 20 percent of the region's population and 47 percent of adherents—and for their vision. These three groups continue to keep broader social concerns before the public in a region where commitments are often tentative and the dominant preoccupations are individualistic or familial. Mainline Protestants, Catholics, and Reform and Conservative Jews will continue to be important in the region's public life.

But the extent of their future influence will depend on several factors, including the growth of other religious clusters, internal conflicts within each community, and their ability to motivate their members to political action based on historical theological principles in a context in which people increasingly are disconnected from the teachings of historic faiths and uncritically receptive to economic market metaphors for conceptualizing and organizing public life.

The second cluster, sectarian entrepreneurs, includes some older evangelical denominations and newer post-denominational groups that have embraced with renewed energy the entrepreneurship that always has been a feature of the Pacific Northwest's more open religious environment. This cluster may soon rival the first in size and perhaps influence. Today's sectarian entrepreneurs wed an exclusivist, evangelical theology with skillful use of modern communication technology and organizational structures borrowed from the information economy.

Contemporary worship, emphasis on small group experiences that meet members' needs, and an entrepreneurial ethos directed toward expansion and success contribute to their growth. Some, viewing the supernatural as palpably present in angels and demons, promote spiritual warfare and promise ample material blessings to the faithful. These groups are benefiting from the congruence between their emphasis on family, individual responsibility, and entrepreneurship, and a currently dominant national social ideology that echoes the same themes. Individual congregations have exerted power locally around issues they deem important. The unresolved question is whether, and how, they will organize into a more concerted public political presence.

The third cluster is people of the Pacific Rim. The earliest and longest-present Pacific Rim people in the Pacific Northwest are Native Americans, who make up 2.3 percent of the regional population. They are most dominant in Alaska, where they are 15.6 percent of the population. The region's Native Americans, in continuity with their historic cultures, pursue spiritual journeys by drawing on the resources of a range of indigenous and Christian teachings and practices. These include an array of European-American Christian churches, the Indian Shaker Church, the Native American Church, shamanistic rituals, sweat lodges, and longhouse meetings.

Native Americans do not structure religious identification and belonging in ways readily amenable to conventional European-American categories. Their religious practices have been misunderstood and at times targeted for eradication. Over the past half century, Native American religious freedom has been intimately intertwined in conflicts over Indian cultural preservation and tribal autonomy. Struggles over Native American religious freedom test the limit of the openness of the Pacific Northwest's religious environment.

Other Pacific Rim populations for whom the Pacific Northwest is home include ethnic communities from Oceania and East and South Asia. Some have been present in the region since the early nineteenth century; many more arrived after 1965 and 1990 revisions in immigration laws. In the region's more open religious environment newer immigrants have both reflected long-standing patterns of assimilation and self-definition, and faced racial and religious persecution at the hands of European-Americans. At certain moments, the region's fluid social and religious environment has contributed to ethnic minorities being perceived as dangerous and threatening. This has made these communities cautious and reluctant to attract attention from others. Newer immigrants' presence and participation as citizens in the public life of the region often go unnoticed. These communities' presence becomes most public through "ethnic festivals" and when their members or worship sites are attacked.

Some Pacific Rim immigrants are Christian, but many are not. They have brought other religions, especially Buddhism, Hinduism, and Islam, which are beginning to shape the Pacific Northwest. Religious seekers from many backgrounds join communities of these traditions. Others encounter them when they adopt yoga, Tai Chi, or meditation for stress relief. Combined, followers of Eastern religions and Islam, including immigrants from Africa and the Middle East as well, constitute the seventh largest slice of the Pacific Northwest's religious adherents, 4.1 percent, a larger segment than that of most of the mainline Protestant denominations taken individually.

The extent of this cluster's influence is only beginning to be studied, making it difficult to characterize. The presence of the communities that compose it significantly increases religious pluralism in the region and so counters efforts at regional definition based on a single religious narrative.[7] As well, the sizeable presence of Pacific Rim communities and religions in the region highlights the complex interrelationships of ethnicity, religion, and social change in the twenty-first century.

The fourth cluster, the "secular but spiritual," constitutes most of the region's population. It includes two groups, both outside of conventional religious institutions. The first is those individuals who identify with a religious tradition but do not belong to one of its congregations. The second is the "Nones" proper, those who in response to the question "What is your religious tradition, if any?" answer "None." Neither group is without religion. Even among the "Nones" only a small minority identify as atheist or agnostic. In fact, the vast majority of "Nones" claim beliefs and attitudes more like than unlike those of persons inside churches, synagogues, temples, and mosques.

Those who identify with a religious heritage but do not belong to one of its institutions are the larger of the two groups. It is not clear whether these people:

- continue a long-standing American practice of identifying with a religious heritage but resisting institutional constraints;
- constitute a prime, untapped market for enterprising religious entrepreneurs;
- are on a path toward some new constellation of religious identity and belonging, including the option of a totally naturalistic or materialistic understanding of existence.

It is clear that their identification with a religious heritage is sufficiently deep and meaningful that when asked their religious tradition, if any, they respond with the name of a recognized religious community. That identification may be a residue of family history or ethnic heritage, both of which the region quickly leaches out of many. It may be a lingering element in a much larger process of disaffiliation in which the region leads the nation. In this process post-modern global trends in individual motivation and social organization coalesce with the region's religious fluidity and with internal tensions in religious communities to erode individuals' connections to religious institutions. If so, those who identify with, but do not belong to, an institution of a religious tradition may be moving toward full "None" status. Given the size of this population, whether this group moves and in what direction—toward "None" status with its complete de-identification from an historic faith or toward affiliation with a faith community—may significantly influence the region's future.

The "Nones" make up a slightly smaller segment of the unchurched. Not only have they moved beyond religious institutions, they have moved beyond identifying themselves in any way with a religious tradition. They may be one step beyond those who identify with a tradition but do not belong to one of its institutions. They may be fully engaged in a larger process of religious disaffiliation and de-identification. They also may be exemplars of a developing new mode of religiousness.

The "secular but spiritual" do experience the sacred and bring spiritual convictions and practices into the public life of the region, but often in ways that, at first glance, do not appear religious. Central to their religiousness is the project of defining this place and its meaning for the human person. Three regional expressions of this religiousness beyond conventional institutions are "New Age" seeking, anti-government and property rights associations, and, most prominently, nature religion and commitment to environmental protection. More explicitly than any of the other clusters, the "secular but spiritual" population grapples with what it means to be fully human and part of the region's ecosystem. In doing so they throw into sharp relief ideas and impulses present across all the clusters.

The four clusters represent four dominant modes of public religious presence—religiously civic oriented, sectarian entrepreneurial, immigrant pluralist, and religiously non-institutional. As will become clear in this volume, the particular concerns and commitments of each cluster, as well as alliances and conflicts across clusters, emerge most clearly in debate over public issues such as assisted suicide, drilling in the Arctic National Wildlife Refuge, protecting salmon, urban growth management, Native Americans' religious freedom, poverty, and welfare reform.

Around these issues the different ways that the clusters have forged theological heritage, history, and present experience with this land into a mode of public presence become apparent. Like magma from below the region's volcanoes, religion in the Pacific Northwest is an energetic, viscous fluid that is capable of altering the public landscape, galvanizing citizens for action, but not in ways easily predicted or directed by leaders of religious organizations.

Religious politics in the Pacific Northwest centers on the environment—on natural processes, how in the largest sense the ecosystem works. Each of the four clusters described in this volume emphasizes different dimensions of the region's ecosystem, physical, biological, social, and cultural. Each, in its own way, answers the question of what it means to be human while situated on the northern edge of the Pacific Rim. Framed in this manner, religion's presence and its power for good and for ill in shaping the Pacific Northwest's future become clear.

To situate the four clusters, this volume first sketches the lay of the land in Alaska, Washington, and Oregon—comparing the region to the nation on dimensions of the U.S. census, describing patterns of religious adherence and identification as well as key moments in each state's religious history, and considering the current array of religious groups and their recent fortunes in the region. After four essays that describe in depth each of the four religious clusters, the themes captured in this introduction are revisited in a brief concluding essay.

Acknowledgement Note

Several individuals contributed information, expertise, and insight to this volume. Janet Hauck, Archivist at Whitworth College, Spokane, Washington, brought the 1914 symposium to my attention. The Inter-library loan staff of the Mortvedt Library, Pacific Lutheran University, efficiently processed numerous requests. Katie Pfister served ably as a research assistant. Dr. Regina Bosclair, Alaska Pacific University, provided material on Alaska's religious situation from her work for the Pluralism Project. Dr. Kristen Hanson, University of Alaska-Anchorage, and Dr. Laura Klein, Pacific Lutheran University, shared expertise concerning Alaska's indigenous peoples and village life. Dr. Suzanne Crawford, Pacific Lutheran University, answered numerous questions about Native American religions. Dr. Anna Leon-Guerrero provided expert advice on statistical matters. The project benefited from robust discussion with Dr. David McCloskey, Seattle University, about the region's religious demography. Steve Maynard of *The News Tribune* in Tacoma and Shelby Oppel of *The Oregonian* in Portland served as journalist advisers for the volume. Thank you.

Endnotes

1. E.J. Klemme & B.F. Kumler, in *The Pacific Northwest Pulpit,* compiled by Paul Little (New York: The Methodist Book Concern, 1915).

2. Bruce Barcott, *Northwest Passages: A Literary Anthology of the Pacific Northwest from Coyote Tales to Roadside Attractions* (Seattle: Sasquatch Books, 1994): xviii, quoted in Nicholas Brown O'Connell, "On Sacred Ground: The Landscape Literature of the Pacific Northwest" (Ph.D. thesis, University of Washington, 1996): 8.

3. Jeffrey M. Burns, "Building the Best: A History of Catholic Parish Life in the Pacific States," in Jay P. Dolan, ed. *The American Catholic Parish: A History from 1850 to the Present* Volume 2 (New York: Paulist Press, 1987): 15; Erle Howell, *Methodism in the Northwest* (Nashville, TN: The Parthenon Press Printers, 1966).

4. Ferenc Szasz, *Religion in the Modern American West* (Tucson, AZ: University of Arizona Press, 2000): 100.

5. Caroline C. Leighton, *West Coast Journeys, 1865-1879.* Introduction and notes by David M. Buerge (Seattle: Sasquatch Books, 1995): 72-73.

6. Kesey quoted in O'Connell, 92.

7. Robert S. Ellwood has argued that since the 1960s the entire nation has faced a post-modern situation, where no single narrative and certainly not the Heberw/Christian mythos or Enlightenment faith in science proves compelling. See his *The Sixties Spiritual Awakening: American Religion Moving from Modern to Postmodern* (New Brunswick, NJ: Rutgers University Press, 1994).

RELIGIOUS AFFILIATION IN THE PACIFIC NORTHWEST AND THE NATION

The charts on the following pages compare two measures of religious identification: self-identification by individuals responding to a survey and adherents claimed by religious institutions. The charts compare regional data for the pacific Northwest and national data for both measures. The sources of the data are described below.

On page 22
Adherents Claimed by Religious Groups

The Polis Center at Indiana University-Purdue University Indianapolis provided the Religion by Region Project with estimates of adherents claimed by religious groups in the Pacific Northwest and the nation at large. These results are identified as the North American Religion Atlas (NARA). NARA combines 2000 Census data with the Glenmary Research Center's 2000 Religious Congregations and Membership Survey (RCMS). Polis Center demographers supplemented the RCMS reports with data from other sources to produce estimates for groups that did not report to Glenmary.

On page 23
Religious Self-Identification

Drawn from the American Religious Identification Survey (ARIS 2001), these charts contrast how Americans in the Pacific Northwest and the nation at large describe their own religious identities. The ARIS study, conducted by Barry A. Kosmin, Egon Mayer, and Ariela Keysar at the Graduate Center of the City University of New York, includes the responses of 50,283 U.S. households gathered in a series of national, random-digit dialing, telephone surveys.

Adherents Claimed by Religious Groups
Pacific Northwest Region

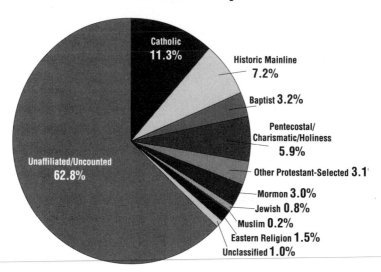

- Catholic 11.3%
- Historic Mainline 7.2%
- Baptist 3.2%
- Pentecostal/Charismatic/Holiness 5.9%
- Other Protestant-Selected 3.1
- Mormon 3.0%
- Jewish 0.8%
- Muslim 0.2%
- Eastern Religion 1.5%
- Unclassified 1.0%
- Unaffiliated/Uncounted 62.8%

Adherents Claimed by Religious Groups
National

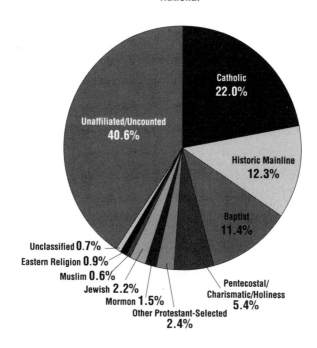

- Catholic 22.0%
- Historic Mainline 12.3%
- Baptist 11.4%
- Pentecostal/Charismatic/Holiness 5.4%
- Other Protestant-Selected 2.4%
- Mormon 1.5%
- Jewish 2.2%
- Muslim 0.6%
- Eastern Religion 0.9%
- Unclassified 0.7%
- Unaffiliated/Uncounted 40.6%

Religious Self-Identification
Pacific Northwest Region

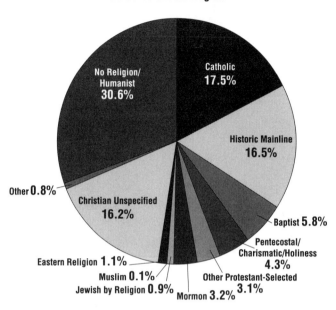

Religious Self-Identification
National

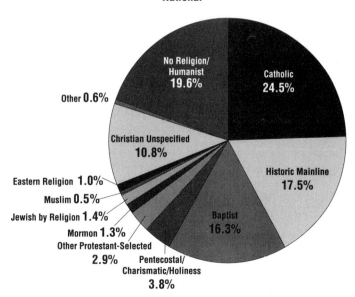

CHAPTER ONE

SURVEYING THE RELIGIOUS LANDSCAPE: HISTORICAL TRENDS AND CURRENT PATTERNS IN OREGON, WASHINGTON, AND ALASKA

Patricia O'Connell Killen and Mark A. Shibley
with assistance from Kellee Boyer and Kellie A. Riley

The Pacific Northwest is a vast and relatively unpopulated landscape. It represents more than one-fifth of the nation's total land base, yet contains only 3.5 percent of the population. Among the 50 states Alaska ranks first, Oregon tenth, and Washington twentieth in size. Hence the Pacific Northwest has far fewer people per square mile than any other region of the country (13.5 in the Northwest compared to 416.4 in the mid-Atlantic), as shown in Table 1.1 (page 27).

Despite this expansive geography and a frontier ethos, a higher percentage of the population of the Pacific Northwest is urban than in the South or Midwest. Four of five Northwesterners live in a city, though they have easy access to snow-capped mountains, remote forests, fast-flowing rivers, and a magnificent coastline. In all, nearly 10 million people live in this region; about half reside in the Puget Sound and Willamette Valley areas, a wet and fertile corridor between the Cascade and Coast mountain ranges. While the nation's population more than tripled during the twentieth century, population in the Northwest increased 10 fold. In 2000 Washington had 5,894,121 residents, Oregon 3,421,399, and Alaska 626,932.

On many demographic variables, this region closely mirrors the nation. For instance, the age and gender composition of the population is nearly identical to the rest of the country, and more than half of all Northwesterners over 15 are married. Slightly more than one-quarter never have married. The Pacific Northwest has a higher level of divorce than any other region of the country, but it also has a lower level of separation while married. One notable difference is the average household size (2.6 persons in the Pacific Northwest), lower than elsewhere.

In other respects, the Pacific Northwest differs significantly from the rest of the country. The region is whiter than the nation as a whole, but not as white as New England or the Midwest. In fact, the popular image of a racially homogeneous region is inaccurate. A smaller percentage of the Northwest population is African American than in other regions, but a larger percentage is Asian, Native American, and multi-racial than in most other regions. A smaller percentage of the Northwest population is Hispanic than in the nation as a whole, and a smaller percentage is foreign born. Yet, like most regions of the country, the Pacific Northwest is moving inexorably in the direction of more racial and ethnic diversity, which reflects the region's Pacific Rim location.

The Pacific Northwest has the lowest level of illiteracy in the nation (13.5 percent of adults without a high school degree), and a relatively high level of advanced education (26.6 percent with at least a bachelor's degree). A larger percentage of the work force is employed in professional and managerial occupations than in the nation as a whole, and the blue-collar and white-collar service sectors are smaller. But the Pacific Northwest still has a larger percentage of the workforce in farming, fishing, and forestry than any other region. This educational and occupational profile explains a higher median annual household income in the Pacific Northwest ($44,413) than in the nation as a whole ($41,949), and a lower percentage of people live in poverty (10.8 percent compared to 12.3 percent in 2000).

This favorable socio-economic profile, however, masks persistently higher unemployment than in the rest of the country. The transition to a "new" economy (away from agriculture and resource extraction toward high-tech and tourism) has been painful for rural Northwesterners whose livelihood depends on working the land.

The story of religion and culture in the Pacific Northwest includes recognizable players and cultural patterns from New England, the Midwest, and the South. It also includes indigenous Native American religions, and religious communities from all around the Pacific Rim, as well as India, Africa, and the Middle East. The interactions of these varied groups with the physical and social space that defines the Pacific Northwest has created a regionally distinctive religious environment.

The remainder of this chapter provides a broadly framed picture of religious participation and identification in the region, surveys major religious groups and traditions, examines briefly patterns in the three states, and concludes with a brief discussion of the region's religious public presence.

Table 1.1   Population Characteristics of the Northwest Compared to the Nation

		Northwest	Nation
Population count		9,942,452	281,421,906
Land-base (square miles)		734,492	3,537,440
Population density (per square mile)		13.5	79.5
Percent living in a different state in 1995		24.3	19.5
Percent living in urban areas		79.8	79.0
Percent that are	Less than age 18	25.5	25.7
	18 – 44	39.8	39.8
	45 – 64	23.0	22.0
	65 and Over	11.4	12.4
Percent male		49.8	49.1
Percent over age 15 that are	Married	56.9	56.5
	Never married	25.9	27.0
	Divorced	11.5	9.7
	Widowed	5.5	6.6
	Married but separated	2.9	3.8
Average household size (persons)		2.6	2.7
Percent that are	Caucasian	82.6	75.1
	Asian	4.5	3.6
	African American	2.6	12.3
	American Indian	2.3	0.8
	Hawaiian/Pacific Islander	0.3	0.1
	Other Race	3.8	5.5
	Multi-racial	3.5	2.4
	Non-Hispanic	92.5	87.5
	Hispanic	7.4	12.5
	Foreign born	9.4	11.0
Percent over age 25	Without a High School degree	13.5	19.6
	With at least a Bachelor's degree	26.6	24.4
Percent employed in	Management/Professional	34.6	33.6
	Sales/Office	25.9	26.6
	Service	15.0	14.8
	Production/Transportation	13.2	14.6
	Construction/Maintenance	9.4	9.4
	Farming/Fishing/Forestry	1.6	0.7
Median Household Income		$44,413.00	$41,949.00
Percent living in poverty		10.8	12.3

Religious Adherence and Identification in the Pacific Northwest—the Broad Picture

Three basic facts stand out when looking at religion in Oregon, Washington, and Alaska today.

First, the Pacific Northwest has the lowest affiliation with religious institutions of any region in the United States. In 2000 Oregon ranked lowest with 35.2 percent of its population affiliated with a religious group, followed by Washington with 38.1 percent and Alaska with 39.8 percent. Together these states have a 37.2 percent adherence rate in contrast to the nation's 59.4 percent rate, according to the North American Religion Atlas (NARA). With nearly two-thirds of its population "unchurched" the Pacific Northwest states frequently are described as secular and godless. As one former Catholic archbishop reportedly put it, "There are no Christians here, they are all pagans."

A second basic fact complicates this assessment and points to the complexity of the region's religious environment. More than two-thirds of adults in Oregon and Washington identify themselves with a religious denomination or tradition, according to the American Religious Identification Survey (ARIS), which did not include survey data from Alaska. ARIS asked adults, "What is your religion, if any?" Seventy-one percent of adults in Oregon and 69 percent in Washington identify with a religious group. By this second measure of religiosity, most adults in the region are religious.

Assuming that Alaska is congruent with Oregon and Washington on religious self-identification, and recognizing that ARIS surveyed adults while the NARA data on adherents did not control for age, an intriguing picture emerges from the two major studies provided for this project. In the Pacific Northwest nearly two-thirds of the adult population is "unchurched" and slightly more than two-thirds of adults identify with a religious group. This gap between adherents (those who both identify with a religious tradition and participate in a religious congregation) and self-identifiers (those who identify with a religious community of some kind but do not participate) is larger in the Pacific Northwest than anywhere else in the United States. Regionally, those who identify with a religious tradition but do not participate in a religious community make up a population larger than those who both identify and participate. This "gap group," those who identify but do not affiliate, is the wild card in any assessment of the role of religion in the public life of the region.

The third basic fact about religion in the Pacific Northwest today also emerges from the ARIS study. Together, Washington and Oregon lead the nation in the number of adults who report that they have no religious identification, 25 percent. The national figure is 14.1 percent. In the Pacific Northwest, these "Nones" constitute a group twice as large as the single largest denomination in

Table 1.2   Number of Adherents in the Pacific Northwest by Religious Family

Religious Family, Rank Ordered	# of Adherents	% of Total Population	% of all PNW Adherents
1. Catholic	1,118,731	11.3	30.2
2. Holiness/Wesleyan/Pentecostal	465,611	4.7	12.6
3. Other Conservative Christian	394,371	4.0	10.7
4. Mormon	301,331	3.0	8.1
5. Baptist	263,294	2.6	7.1
6. Lutheran (ELCA)	186,004	1.9	5.0
7. Historically African-Amer. Protestant	182,813	1.8	4.9
8. Eastern Religion	151,475	1.5	4.1
9. United Methodist	115,882	1.2	3.1
10. Presbyterian U.S.A.	114,608	1.2	3.1
11. Confessional/Reformed Non-UCC Cong.	106,836	1.1	2.9
12. Jewish	78,650	0.8	2.1
13. Episcopalians	72,653	0.7	2.0
14. Orthodox	35,798	0.4	1.0
15. Other Mainline Prot/Liberal Christian	26,060	0.3	0.7
16. Christians (Disciples)	25,121	0.3	0.7
17. UCC	22,247	0.2	0.6
18. Muslim	22,158	0.2	0.6
19. Pietist/Anabaptist	15,431	0.2	0.4
Total	3,699,074	37.2	100.0
Unaffiliated	6,243,378	62.8	

the region. The "Nones," are discussed more fully below and in Chapter 5. From the beginning, however, it is important to note that this group contains only a minority of atheists and agnostics. The overwhelming majority of people in this category exhibit religious beliefs similar to those of individuals who identify with a denomination or religious tradition.

These three facts provide the broad contours of the region's religious environment. A bit more than a third of the population identify and participate institutionally, a slightly larger portion identify but do not participate, and a quarter or more of adults neither identify nor participate. These three facts suggest the regional milieu within which all individuals construct and understand their religious identity, opt into and out of institutional participation, develop their thinking in relation to the historic beliefs of their religious heritage, and interact with others within and beyond their immediate religious peers.

Through most of the history of European-American presence in the region, doing these things has been complicated by what these three basic facts add up to. In the Pacific Northwest, more than elsewhere in the nation, religious identity and belonging are composed and enacted without benefit of a strong, clearly visible "social mirror." The region has never had a single religious reference group consistently large enough and influential enough to be recognized by all as that group against which individuals must work out their religious identity and belonging.[1]

The minority of the population, those who are affiliated with a denomination or religious community, belong to many different groups. At moments some groups, often with historical ties or theological affinity, have coalesced for specific purposes. For example, Methodists, Congregationalists, and Presbyterians did so in the mid-nineteenth century, and mainstream Protestants, Catholics, and Reform and Conservative Jews in the 1950s and 1960s. Each time, however, the affinity group has wielded a fragile and short-term majority. Emerging religious affinity groups, like those in the past, must reckon with a regional history of low religious adherence rates, marked religious independence, fluid alliances, and tentative claims to political power and cultural influence. This religious environment influences whether, how, and when religion plays a role in the public life of the Pacific Northwest.

Historic Patterns of Institutional Religious Adherence in the Pacific Northwest

Most people in the Pacific Northwest do not participate in religious institutions and never have. In 2000, the Pacific Northwest reached the institutional religious adherence rate of the nation at 1890.[2] Focusing on the region's low rate, however, obscures the fact that the percentage of the population involved in religious institutions did increase in Oregon, Washington, and Alaska from 1890 until today. Most of that growth occurred before 1970. Subsequently adherence rates in these three states have remained relatively stable.

The pattern of increase in participation in religious institutions differs only slightly for the three states. Oregon provides an example. In 1890, Oregon had a 22 percent adherence rate in a total state population of 317,704, while the national rate was 34.4 percent. In 1952 Oregon had reached a 26.4 percent adherence rate, and by 1971 it had an adherence rate of 33 percent in a population of 2,091,385. In 1980 the rate was 36.5 percent; currently it is 35.2 percent. Today Oregon's adherence rate lags behind the nation's by 24 percentage points, putting it farther behind than in 1890.

Washington presents a slightly different picture. In 1890 its 16.4 percent adherence rate lagged farther behind the national rate than Oregon's. In 1971 its 35.1 percent rate had reached the nation's 1890 rate. Today Washington's adherence rate is 38.1 percent, which leaves it lagging behind the national rate slightly less than Oregon.

Comparable figures are available for Alaska beginning in 1971. In that year Alaska too had reached the nation's 1890 institutional religious adherence rate of 34.4 percent. Today Alaska's rate is 39.8 percent out of a total population of 626,932, half of which resides in Anchorage. Alaska's population doubled between 1970 and 2000, but its adherence rate, like that of Oregon and Washington, remained relatively stable.

While institutional religious adherence rates have remained steady in the Pacific Northwest for the past thirty years, population has not. The region experienced a significantly higher rate of population increase than the nation. Between 1970 and 2000, the Pacific Northwest's population grew by 4,139,725, a 70 percent increase, most of which occurred in Washington State. The large number of in-migrants during this period, as in the past, brought national religious trends with them into the Pacific Northwest. Whether and how they contributed to stability in the region's adherence rates since 1970 is a question that remains to be explored. One thing, however, is clear. Any religious body that did not increase its number of adherents by at least 70 percent between 1970 and 2000 has a thinner slice of the total adherent pie today than it did thirty years ago.

The Pacific Northwest's slow increase in adherence rates over the past century and the persistence of relatively lower rates presents an intriguing question to historians, sociologists, and geographers, especially when considered in light of comparative studies of other regions that show a very different pattern. Various explanations, singly and in combination, are put forth to explain the Pacific Northwest's situation. Among these are high levels of mobility, a frontier mentality, individualism, higher levels of education, the urban character of most of the region's population for most if its history, the absence of a dominant Christian denomination at first effective settlement, the smaller presence of nationally predominant denominations, national patterns of disaffiliation from historic Protestant denominations, and the size and beauty of the region's natural environment.

Dividing the Adherent Pie: The Prevalence and Relative Strength of Religious Traditions

Today the established religious traditions claim only 37.2 percent of the region's population, leaving 62.8 percent "unaffiliated." This is the opposite of the national pattern: 59.5 percent of all Americans participate in organized religion and only 40.5 percent are unaffiliated. To facilitate regional comparisons,

NARA grouped more than 150 denominations into 19 "religious families" based on theological and historical kinship. The following discussion of the prevalence and relative strength of various religious families in the Pacific Northwest draws primarily on data reported in Tables 1.2 (page 29) and 1.3 (page 35).

As those tables make clear, the religious picture of the region looks quite different depending on whether one considers a group as a percentage of the region's total population or as a percentage of the adherent pie. For public life the former is significant. The latter, however, is important for understanding the dynamics of people who are in church, synagogue, mosque, or temple.

As in most regions of the country, Catholics are the largest single religious group in the Pacific Northwest, although Catholicism is not a dominant tradition as it is in New England or the southwestern United States. Only 11.3 percent of Northwesterners are Catholic compared to 22 percent of all Americans.

Most notably, Holiness/Wesleyan/Pentecostal and "Other Conservative Christians," which rank second (4.7 percent of all who affiliate in the region) and third (4.0 percent) respectively in the Northwest, rank only fifth (2.8 percent) and sixth (2.8 percent) nationally. Mormons are fourth (3.0 percent) in this region, and tenth (1.5 percent) nationally. Baptists are the fifth largest group in the Northwest (2.6 percent of the population), but second nationally (8.5 percent). Taken together, these data show that the Pacific Northwest is the only region outside the South and the "Southern Crossroads" with as many conservative Protestants as Catholics. But within the South those conservative Protestants are mostly Baptist, in the Northwest the bulk are Pentecostal and nondenominational Christian.

Since there are comparatively few blacks in the Northwest, Historically African-American Protestants represent only 1.8 percent of the region's population (ranked seventh), while 7.4 percent of all Americans affiliate with that tradition (ranking it third nationally). Remarkably, Eastern Religion ranks higher (eighth) in the Northwest than does Methodism (ninth), Presbyterianism (tenth), Confessional/Reformed (eleventh) or Judaism (twelfth). In the country as a whole Eastern Religion ranks lower than these four traditions. While only 1.5 percent of Northwesterners participate in Eastern Religion, each Mainline Protestant tradition captures less than 2 percent of the region's population (Lutheran—1.9 percent; Methodist—1.2 percent; Presbyterian—1.2 percent; Episcopalian—0.7 percent; Christian Disciples – 0.3 percent; United Church of Christ—0.2 percent). Finally, Muslims are less prominent in the Northwest (ranking eighteenth) than in the nation (fifteenth).

Another distinctive feature of institutional religion in the Pacific Northwest is pluralism. All other regions are more homogeneous; that is, fewer groups control a larger share of the religious marketplace. In the Northwest, two-thirds of all religious adherents affiliate with the top five groups. In other regions, the top five groups capture 75 to 85 percent of all adherents.

Are there important differences within the region? Alaska, Oregon, and Washington are far more alike than different in religious demography, with a few notable exceptions. One exception is that Orthodox Christians are the fifth largest group in Alaska, constituting 8.5 percent of all adherents in the state. Catholics represent 21.8 percent of Alaska's adherent pie and there are roughly equal proportions (about 11 percent) of Baptists, Pentecostals, and Other Conservative Christians. This makes Alaska the most heterogeneous state in the region. The top five groups capture only 62 percent of the state's religious adherents. Another important difference between states is the low number of African-American Protestants in Oregon. That group makes up 5.9 percent of the adherents in Washington and 6.6 percent in Alaska, but only 2.8 percent in Oregon.

Historically and Demographically Significant Religious Groups in the Pacific Northwest

Roman Catholics As noted above, the Catholic Church is the largest religious body regionally and in each of the three states. It has more than kept pace with regional population increase, primarily through in-migration from the East and Midwest, and a growing Hispanic presence. Native Americans, African Americans, Filipinos, Vietnamese, Chinese, and Koreans add to the diversity of the Catholic population in the region.

Orthodox Christians Orthodox Christianity entered North America through Alaska with the arrival of Russian Orthodox missionaries in 1794. Alaska remains the center of the Orthodox Christian population in the region today, with 21,256, more than three times the number in Oregon and nearly three times the number in Washington. Indigenous Alaskan peoples make up the bulk of the Orthodox Christians in the region.

Lutherans For the Religion by Region project, the Lutheran category was limited to the Evangelical Lutheran Church in America (ELCA). The Lutheran Church—Missouri Synod (LC-MS), the second largest Lutheran body in the region, as well as the smaller Wisconsin Evangelical Lutheran Synod and the Association of Free Lutheran Congregations were placed in the Confessional/Reformed/non-UCC Congregational category.

In the unchurched Pacific Northwest the ELCA and the LC-MS historically have sensed their shared identity and cooperated in educational and ministerial projects more than in other regions with higher demographic concentrations of both churches. When combined, the ELCA and LC-MS constitute a body slightly smaller than the Mormons in each of the three states. The ELCA ranks as the sixth largest distinct denomination in Alaska, the fourth largest in Oregon, and the third largest in Washington.

All Lutheran groups have lost ground in the region since 1971, but not as rapidly as other moderate and liberal Protestant groups, having been protected longer by the strong ethnic identifications of Lutherans. As ethnic identification erodes, Lutheran patterns in the region may come to resemble more closely those of other moderate Protestant denominations.

Presbyterians The Presbyterian Church U.S.A. is tenth regionally and eleventh nationally in size. Like the Lutherans, Presbyterians have lost members since 1971, but at a slower rate regionally than nationally. The denomination here, as elsewhere in the nation, is stressed by conflicts between evangelical and more progressive or liberal wings, illustrated by the different historic and theological trajectories of Whitworth College in Spokane and Lewis and Clark College in Portland, both denominationally established.

Episcopalians Since 1971 the Episcopal Church has lost members more rapidly in the Pacific Northwest than nationally. Never a large denomination regionally, for most of the region's history it counted wealthy and influential leaders among its members. Since 1990 the Church has grown, but not at a rate equal to the population, in Alaska, where it accounts for 1.1 percent of the population and 2.7 percent of adherents. It has lost members in Oregon and Washington, where it now accounts for 0.7 percent of the population in each state, but 2 percent and 1.9 percent of adherents respectively.

Methodists For the Religion by Region project Methodists includes only the United Methodist Church. The two smaller Methodist bodies in the region, Free Methodists and The Wesleyan Church, were placed in the Holiness/Wesleyan/Pentecostal category. The Methodists were central in the development of Oregon and Washington, but played less of a role in Alaska. Today this denomination ranks fourth nationally and ninth regionally. The United Methodist Church has declined steadily in the region since the 1960s, especially in Oregon, where it originally was the strongest. The United Methodist Church has lost a greater percentage of membership regionally than nationally.

Christian (Disciples of Christ) This frontier religious body has lost ground steadily since 1970. In 1980 this group accounted for 2.4 percent of all adherents, today it accounts for 0.7 percent. The denomination struggles with internal tensions between those who would move it in a more evangelical and confessional direction and those who want to maintain its historic biblical and rationalist traditions, emphasizing the believer's freedom.

United Church of Christ (U.C.C.) This denomination has declined more than any other in the Pacific Northwest over the past century and has lost ground faster regionally than nationally since 1971. It did not report at all from Alaska in

Table 1.3 Number of Adherents in the United States by Religious Family

Religious Family, Rank Ordered	# of Adherents	% of Total Population	% of all Adherents
1. Catholic	62,035,042	22.0	37.0
2. Baptist	23,880,856	8.5	14.3
3. Historically African-Amer. Protestant	20,774,338	7.4	12.4
4. United Methodist	10,350,629	3.7	6.2
5. Other Conservative Christian	7,934,198	2.8	4.7
6. Holiness/Wesleyan/Pentecostal	7,764,756	2.8	4.6
7. Jewish	6,141,325	2.2	3.7
8. Lutheran (ECLA)	5,113,418	1.8	3.1
9. Confessional/Reformed Non-UCC Cong.	4,374,743	1.6	2.6
10. Mormon	4,224,026	1.5	2.5
11. Presbyterian U.S.A.	3,141,566	1.1	1.9
12. Eastern Religion	2,560,243	0.9	1.5
13. Episcopalian	2,314,756	0.8	1.4
14. UCC	1,698,918	0.6	1.0
15. Muslim	1,559,294	0.6	0.9
16. Orthodox	1,449,274	0.5	0.9
17. Christians (Disciples)	1,017,784	0.4	0.6
18. Pietist/Anabaptist	698,897	0.2	0.4
19. Other Mainline Prot/Liberal Christian	418,098	0.1	0.2
Total	167,425,161	59.5	100.0
Unaffiliated	114,165,080	40.5	

2000. In Oregon it has 7,817 adherents and in Washington 1,084.

Other Mainline Protestant or Liberal Christian This category includes the Community of Christ, Friends (Quakers), Universal Fellowship of Metropolitan Community Churches, and the Unitarian-Universalist Association of Congregations. Of these groups the Unitarian-Universalist Association is the largest regionally with 9,650, followed closely by Friends, with 9,233. The Community of Christ is considerably smaller, 6,450, and the Metropolitan Community Churches the smallest, with 734. Quakers are largest in Oregon. Unitarian-Universalists are considerably larger in Washington, (5,828), than Oregon, (3,365), or Alaska (457). Most Quakers regionally belong to the more evangelical branch of that tradition. The region's Unitarian-Univeraslists are noted within their denomination for their forward thinking and innovative style.

All of the historically moderate and liberal Protestant denominations have lost ground in the Pacific Northwest since 1970, which is true nationally as well. Given the smaller population base that each had here compared to other regions of the country, the consequences of decline became visible sooner.

Confessional/Reformed/non U.C.C. (Congregational) Of the twenty-seven bodies included in this category, only eleven are present in the Pacific Northwest, and these are dominated by historically ethnic denominations. The largest is the Lutheran Church-Missouri Synod, with 42,110 adherents across all three states. The second largest is the Christian Reformed Church in North America, with 12,737 adherents, the vast majority of whom are in Washington. The third largest is the Wisconsin Evangelical Lutheran Synod, with 6,592 adherents across the three states. Fourth is the Reformed Church of America, with 3,559 adherents, all in Washington. Fifth is the National Association of Congregational Christian Churches, with 1,695 adherents, primarily in Washington and Alaska. Next in size is the Association of Free Lutheran Congregations, with 1,260 adherents, the vast majority of whom are in Washington.

Historically African-American Protestant This category includes the African Methodist Episcopal Zion Church, Christian Methodist Episcopal, Church of God in Christ, Fire Baptized Holiness Church, an estimate for Black Baptists, and the African Methodist Episcopal Church. Of these groups, Black Baptists and Church of God in Christ are the largest in the region, with a smaller A.M.E. Zion presence. Though African-Americans were present in the region considerably earlier, the first African-American churches in the region were organized in the late 1880s and early 1890s by black in-migrants from the South and Midwest. Growth in the presence of historically black Protestants accelerated during and after World War II.

Baptists Of the thirty-eight groups in this category, ten are present in the region. The largest is the Southern Baptists, with 117,701 adherents; followed by the Conservative Baptists, with 53,531; American Baptist Churches USA, with 46,866; Baptist General Conference, with 20,134; General Association of Regular Baptist churches, with 14,072; North American Baptist Conference, with 5,030; and American Baptist Association, with 2,216 adherents. The remaining Baptist bodies together comprise about 2,000 adherents.

Overwhelmingly, then, Baptists in the region are Southern or Conservative, which is a shift from the region's earlier history. When the comity agreement between American Baptists and Southern Baptists regarding evangelization in the West ended in 1953, Southern Baptists began extensive evangelization efforts, which together with in-migration rebalanced Baptist power in the region. The transformation was significant in Oregon where, historically, American Baptists had formed part of a moderate Protestant power group that influenced politics and culture. Over the past decade Southern Baptists in the region have lost ground in the competition with Pentecostal and newer non-denominational conservative Protestant groups. Conservative Baptists did not provide data for the 1990 study of church membership, but between 1980 and 2000 lost ground in the three states. American Baptists have lost more ground than either Southern or Conservative in the last decade.

Other Conservative Christian This category ranks third regionally and fifth nationally. Ten of the twenty-five groups in this category are present in the Pacific Northwest. The largest is the Seventh-day Adventists, with 77,992 adherents, the majority of whom are in Washington (43,222), followed by Oregon (30,929), with a much smaller number in Alaska (3,841). The next largest is Christian Churches and Churches of Christ, with 64,105. Most are in Oregon (39,011) followed by Washington (21,521) and Alaska (3,473). The third largest within this category is Independent Non-Charismatic, with 61,720. Again, most are in Washington (33,070), followed by Oregon (21,050) and Alaska (7,600). The top three make up half of the regional adherents in this category.

The next largest group is Churches of Christ, with 28,630 adherents, most in Washington (14,803), followed by Oregon (11,544) and Alaska (2,283). The Evangelical Covenant Church follows, with 15,895 adherents, with Washington leading (9,801) followed by Oregon (4,124) and Alaska (1,970). Next comes the Evangelical Free Church, with 7,781 adherents. Most are in Washington (5,648), followed by Oregon (1,898) and Alaska (235). Vineyard Christian Fellowship follows, with 7,246 adherents. Again most are in Washington (3,874), followed by Oregon (2,854) and Alaska (518). The region also has at least seventy-seven Calvary Chapel congregations.

Pietist/Anabaptist This is the smallest of all the religious groups in the Pacific Northwest. Of the twenty-four religious bodies that make up this category, nine are present in the region. The largest body is the Mennonite Brethren Churches, with 4,187 adherents; followed by the Mennonite Church USA, with 3,050; the Moravian Church—Alaska Province, with 2,562; Other Mennonite, with 2,237; Church of the Brethren, with 1,778; Hutterite Brethren, with 600; and Church of God in Christ Mennonite, with 579. None of the remaining bodies in this category has as many as 300 members. Of these groups only the Mennonite Church USA is present in all three states. The Moravians are present only in Alaska and primarily among indigenous peoples. Adherents of Church of the Brethren are found overwhelmingly in Washington. All of these bodies are historic peace churches and historically all have strong ethnic identification.

Holiness/Wesleyan/Pentecostal This group of religious bodies is second largest in the region and sixth largest nationally. It would account for more adherents regionally if the Church of God in Christ, a predominantly African-American denomination, were included with this family on theological grounds.

Of the twenty-three groups clustered into this category, thirteen are present in the Pacific Northwest. The largest is the Assemblies of God, with 166,681 adherents. This denomination is two and one-half times larger in Washington (105,692) than in Oregon (49,357), with a much smaller presence in Alaska (11,638). Following in size is the International Church of the Foursquare Gospel, with 78,628 adherents. Most are in Oregon (44,826), followed by Washington (33,434) and Alaska (368). The third largest body in this category is Church of the Nazarene, with 63,462 adherents, most in Washington (37,085), followed by Oregon (22,707) and Alaska (3,670). Fourth is Independent Charismatic, with 50,230, over two-thirds of which are in Washington. Fifth is the Christian and Missionary Alliance, with 30,416, again with over two-thirds in Washington.

Together these five account for the vast majority of people in this category regionally. They are followed in order by Church of God (Anderson, Indiana), with 14,025; Salvation Army, with 13,748; Free Methodist Church of North America, with 13,292; Church of God (Cleveland, Tennessee), with 11,615; Wesleyan Church, with 4,757; Pentecostal Church of God, with 4,161; International Pentecostal Holiness Church, with 2,407; and Church of God of Prophecy, with 1,543.

Both the Assemblies of God and the International Church of the Foursquare Gospel are highly overrepresented in the region compared to the nation and both have experienced considerable growth since 1971. The Assemblies of God experienced massive grown between 1980 and 2000, especially in Washington. Both denominations have expanded significantly in suburban metropolitan areas since 1980. The Foursquare Gospel Church during this period did better than the Assemblies of God at maintaining adherents in rural areas while expanding in suburban areas.

Mormons Mormons (members of the Church of Jesus Christ of Latter-day Saints) are the second-largest single denomination in the region following Roman Catholics. Within the ranking of religious families used for the Religion by Region project, Mormons are a stronger regional (fourth) than national (tenth) presence. In all three Pacific Northwest states they constitute 3 percent of the total population, but constitute 7.6 percent of adherents in Alaska, 7.9 percent in Washington, and 8.7 percent in Oregon. The Church of Jesus Christ of Latter-day Saints experienced sustained growth between 1971 and 2000, increasing by 172,000 (fastest in Alaska, followed by Washington and then Oregon). This church's regional growth is part of the expansion by Mormons out of Utah and across the West.

Mormons regionally, as well as nationally, are now more likely to be in urban or suburban centers than in agricultural communities, their historic cultural base. Mormon missionaries are active throughout the Pacific Northwest. They do not engage in ecumenical or inter-faith cooperative alliances. They share many values with conservative Christians of several denominations, especially emphasis on the importance of family, which they communicate through radio and television advertisements. At the same time, their distinctive theology sets them apart and makes them an object of suspicion and for some Christians a target of evangelization.

Jews As noted previously, Jews are under-represented in the region, where they rank twelfth, as opposed to seventh in the nation. The 78,650 Jews affiliated with congregations are present across all three states. They make up a larger percentage of the population (0.9 percent) and of adherents (2.6 percent) in Oregon than in Washington (0.7 percent and 1.9 percent) or Alaska (0.6 percent and 1.4 percent). Reform, Conservative, and Orthodox Jewish Congregations are present in all three states.

Jews in the Pacific Northwest, as elsewhere in the West, appear to be more observant than in regions of the country where they are a larger presence. As in the rest of the West, Ashkenazic Jews were the first to enter the Pacific Northwest, primarily as merchants. The earliest Jewish organization in the Northwest was Portland's Mount Sinai Association, a burial society that was followed shortly by the founding of Portland's Congregation Beth Israel in 1858, which built the region's first synagogue. Jews were present in Washington at the same time, but did not organize into a group to build a synagogue until 1889. By 1900 separate ethnic Jewish synagogues had been established for German, Polish, and Russian Jews.[3]

In the early 1900s a wave of Sephardic immigrants into the region became the nucleus for Seattle's Congregation Ezra Bessaroth and Congregation Sephardic Bikur Holim, made up of Jews from the Island of Rhodes and from Turkey. Russian Jews organized Congregation Keneseth Israel in Spokane around this time. Temple de Hirsch in Seattle became the leader in Americanizing by offering services in English. From 1942 until 1969, Rabbi Raphael Levine led Temple De Hirsch, and even after his retirement remained a major regional religious and civic leader until his death in 1985.

This sketch of historically and demographically significant bodies makes clear that moderate and liberal Protestant denominations have lost adherents regionally over the past thirty years while Catholics, Pentecostals, conservative Christian bodies, and the Church of Jesus Christ of Latter-day Saints have grown. This has led to shifts in the size of segments of the adherent pie in the Pacific Northwest, but the long-term consequences of that shift remain to be seen. It is important not to lose sight of the fact that the adherent pie is small in the Pacific

Northwest. The public power of any one of these groups of like traditions depends in large part on their ability to attract allies from among other religious bodies, and even more importantly from among those who are not affiliated with a church, synagogue, temple, or mosque.

Making Sense of Identifying but not Belonging

The single largest religious group in the Pacific Northwest is made up of persons who identify with a religious tradition but do not belong to a religious institution or community of that tradition. These people share with religious adherents identification with a religious tradition, yet they share and with the "Nones" nonparticipation in institutional religion. The size of this population in the Pacific Northwest makes identifiers significant for public life, but available research does not reveal much about this population beyond its existence. More research is needed to understand the meaning of identifying but not participating, how long continued identification without participation goes on, and whether it is a step in a larger process of secularization. No empirical study has measured the character or depth of these people's emotional connection to a religious heritage or its consequences for voting or other public activity. No study has explored why this population is larger in the Pacific Northwest than elsewhere.

There are a number of plausible explanations for the size of this population in the Pacific Northwest, including:
- such identification reflects the vestige of eroded connections to family or ethnic community;
- for various reasons people in the Pacific Northwest are more likely to abandon institutional religious connections than people in other regions;
- many people who move into the region are not interested in building institutional religious connections;
- it is simply a reflection of the fate of churches of the magisterial Reformation in the wake of late industrial capitalism.

Behind all these plausible explanations lie theories about how mobility influences religious participation, the relationship between the fortunes of religious institutions and larger economic changes, the fate of religious institutions on frontiers and in cities, and the power of the region's natural grandeur and beauty to satisfy religious sensibilities.

Whatever the causes, those who identify with a religious tradition but do not participate in a religious community have some kind of tenuous connection to institutional religion. Whatever that connection, be it deeply ingrained religious sensibility, fleeting emotional attachment, or readiness to be recruited into a religious institution, its potential as a reservoir of religious commitment that can be mobilized around public causes has an influence on religion in the region's public life.

Who Are the "Nones"?

As noted earlier, most Northwesterners do not affiliate with religious institutions; but most adults, according to ARIS, do identify with religious traditions. While there is little information about those who identify with a religious group but do not participate, the opposite is true for the "Nones," those who neither self-identify with a religious tradition nor participate in a religious community.

This group, those who claim no religious identity, accounts for one quarter of the region's adult population, which is the highest percentage of "Nones" anywhere in the country. In 2001, according to ARIS, about 14 percent of all American adults (29.4 million) were in this group, up from 8 percent (14.3 million) in 1990.[4] Thus "Nones" are the fastest growing "religious" group in the United States. Over the last decade of the twentieth century, "Nones" grew from 17 to 21 percent of the adult population in Oregon and from 14 to 25 percent of the adult population in Washington.[5]

Who are these people claiming no religious identity, and how do "Nones" in the Northwest compare with "Nones" nationally?

According to ARIS, most "Nones" in the U.S. are neither agnostic nor atheist. As Chapter 5 explores, most "Nones" in the Northwest and elsewhere are spiritually inclined, despite lacking meaningful ties to an established religious tradition. We also know that "Nones" in the Northwest are mostly white; slightly more than half are married and at least forty years old; relatively few have children under age seventeen; a majority are men and employed full-time; seven in ten own their home; and fewer than one in ten are without a high school degree. A demographic composite of a "None" in the Northwest would yield a well-educated, white, middle-class, male baby-boomer living in a metropolitan area with a wife and no young children. In other words, the prototypical Northwest "None" is rather conventional, according to ARIS estimates shown in Table 1.4 (page 43); "he" is not a grungy Generation-X refugee from the East Coast. In this sense, not to identify with established religion is an ordinary rather than a countercultural practice in the Northwest.

"Nones" also are important to understanding the region's political character. Another important ARIS finding is that all adults in the Northwest are more politically independent than in the nation, but no less politically engaged. Thirty-six percent of all adult Northwesterners indicate their party preference is "Independent," for example, compared to 30 percent nationally. About four in five Northwest "Nones" are registered to vote, according to ARIS, no different from anyone else living in the region. But they are disproportionately registered as Independent (46 percent) and tend to be politically liberal. Only 14 percent of "Nones" in the Northwest claim Republican party registration, and only 28 percent supported George W. Bush in the 2000 presidential election (see Table 1.5, page

43). Data not presented here show that "Nones" in the Northwest are more independent than "Nones" nationally, more engaged, and more likely to have opposed Bush. In short, "Nones" in the Northwest are demographically conventional but politically as well as religiously irreverent. Why they are growing in number and how they are shaping regional culture will be explored in subsequent chapters.

Religion in Oregon, Washington, and Alaska as a Time Series

While the religious profiles of Oregon, Washington, and Alaska are similar, their differences today reflect something of a time series in settlement. Among the states Oregon was settled first, formally organized as a territory in 1849 and admitted to the Union in 1859. Saving the Oregon Territory for a "Christian nation" (i.e., Anglo-Protestant) was one of the projects of the Second Great Awakening. Protestant missionaries quickly became involved in agriculture, land speculation, and other business enterprises. Settlers from the eastern United States headed west to the rich land of the Willamette Valley.

With the end of joint occupancy of the Oregon Country in 1846 and increased immigration from the United States, a fur trading culture of Native Americans and heavily Catholic French Canadians and Métis was eclipsed by growing Yankee Protestant dominance. Power in politics and culture belonged primarily to citizens whose religious identification was Methodist, Congregationalist, Presbyterian, and northern Baptist. While they bequeathed middle-class Protestant habits and sensibilities to the Oregon Territory, especially cities and towns in the Willamette Valley, they did not succeed in keeping their constituent immigrant populations in church.

Nor were they able to bring into their orbit others who entered Oregon in pursuit of economic dreams that did not require church membership or Yankee habits. Territorial leaders also had to contend with the on-going presence of Catholics. Territorial legislation, driven by racist attitudes and fear of conflict, limited African-American presence in Oregon. In 1849 the first territorial governor, Joseph Lane, cited race to explain his refusal to give voting rights to Kanakas (Hawaiians). And what disease did not accomplish in destroying or containing indigenous Native American populations, force did. Force also worked as well to rid Portland, (as well as Seattle and Tacoma) of Chinese in the mid-1880s.

Beneath and around a fragile mainline Protestant establishment that by the early twentieth century accepted the partnership of Jews and Catholics in most civic causes flourished an array of metaphysical and theosophical religions as well as smaller, isolated ethnic religious groups and conservative sects. Oregon has been a strong center of Christian Science and home to some utopian experiments.

Oregon's open space and relatively moderate culture has made it attractive to groups seeking a home. The state became notorious in the 1980s after the

Table 1.4   Population Characteristics of "Nones," Pacific Northwest
             Compared to the Nation[1]

	Costal Northwest	Nation
Percent white	88.1	73.1
Percent age 40 or older	53.4	44.8
Percent married	56.5	48.4
Percent with children under 17	16.7	18.5
Percent female	45.9	41.4
Percent living in non-metro areas	20.2	18.4
Percent employed full-time	55.7	62.8
Percent who own their home	69.6	66.0
Percent with less than a high school degree	6.4	10.0

1 ARIS website.<http://www.gc.cuny.edu/studies/key_findings.htm>

Table 1.5   Political Behavior in the Pacific Northwest, "Nones" Compared to all Others

		Nones (Percent)	All Others (Percent)
Party Preference[1]	Republican	14	28
	Democrat	31	27
	Independent	46	36
	Other	9	9
Registered to vote[2]		79	79
Vote in 2000	Gore	62	48
Presidential Election[3]	Bush	28	45
	Nader	9	6
	Buchanan	1	0
	Other	1	1

1 ARIS data.
2 Ibid.
3 John Green's exit poll data; the group he calls "secular."

Rajneeshpuram group purchased the Big Muddy Ranch near Antelope in 1981. The group's efforts to establish its ideal ashram in the high desert of Oregon unraveled through a series of events that led to criminal prosecution of leading members and deportation of the group's guru and leader, Bhagwan Shree Rajneesh. Today the Big Muddy Ranch is a Christian Camp.

In Oregon even more than in Washington and Alaska, the erosion of numbers and influence on the part of historically moderate and liberal Protestant bodies and the emergence of new modes of religiousness in an open religious environment are most visible. Among the moderate Protestants, the Presbytery of the Cascades provided leadership for the Presbyterians nationally and for the Ecumenical Ministries of Oregon on social policy documents showing the connection between environmental protection and social justice, exemplifying an appropriation of that theological tradition for the twenty-first century.

Washington became a territory in 1853 but did not become a state until 1889. When separated from Oregon in 1853 its European-American population was quite small, 1,201 compared to 12,093. Though something of a Protestant establishment wielded power in territorial government through the Civil War, it was not as strong economically and culturally as Oregon's. In part this was because of continued large population movement within the Washington Territory between Vancouver, Puget Sound, Walla Walla and Spokane. As well, a rapidly increasing foreign-born population in Washington in the early twentieth century, militant labor activity, population centers east and west of the Cascades, and a wealthy Catholic cadre of ranchers and businessmen impeded the growth of a Protestant establishment.

Puget Sound came to dominate the state by 1890, with Tacoma, not Seattle, the major city until the 1898 Alaska Gold rush. By 1890 Washington had achieved a slight edge over Oregon in population (357,232 to 317,704). In the post-World War I and especially the post-World War II periods, Washington's population outstripped Oregon's, so that the former had 800,000 more people in 1950. Between 1870 and 1950 Washington's in-migration of all population exceeded that of Oregon during all but two decades. Today Washington's population exceeds Oregon's by more than two million.

From the beginning of its territorial period Washington has had a larger population of Catholics than Oregon. During the late nineteenth and early twentieth centuries, it received a larger portion of Scandinavian and German immigrants, which fed Lutheran numbers. As well, Washington received a larger share of in-migrants from the South than did Oregon, especially during the later nineteenth and the twentieth centuries. Washington's in-migrants then, were culturally inclined to identify, if at all, with historically ethnic churches and with newer, American-born sectarian groups, especially the Holiness and Pentecostal churches that emerged in the late nineteenth and early twentieth centuries.

In both Oregon and Washington, population increase and economic development after World War II influenced the religious picture. During the two decades after the war mainline Protestant denominations achieved membership and financial resources that allowed them to be self-sufficient and independent of denominational headquarters located elsewhere. The experience of World War II, from development of nuclear weapons to internment of the Japanese and racism against newly arrived black workers and Hispanic agricultural workers informed the imagination of denominational leaders and inspired leadership and innovation in ministry.

African-American churches became increasingly important for public life during and after World War II as large numbers of African-Americans who had entered the region as soldiers or to work in defense industries settled in the Pacific Northwest. Settlement in the region after the war brought more members for Pentecostal and Holiness churches. Members of these churches experienced a rise in educational and economic status. Mormons also began to enter Oregon and Washington in much larger numbers. Refugees from Europe brought new waves of European Christians and Jews to the region.

During these years Washington's economy diversified more and faster than Oregon's. Washington has more and larger military bases, and more defense-related companies, including Boeing. It also participated earlier than Oregon in the computer and biotechnology industries. Oregon, on the other hand, remained more reliant on agriculture and extractive industries. Patterns of in-migration and economic development, then, influence the religious environment and so patterns of participation and religious adherence rates. As a result of in-migration and economics, Washington experienced a larger growth in evangelical and Pentecostal church membership than did Oregon from 1970 on.

While empirical data for tracing the development of religious adherence in Alaska is less readily available than for Oregon and Washington, history provides the contours of the state's religious development. Alaska was a land of indigenous Native practice and belief until after Russian Orthodox missionaries arrived in 1794, introducing Orthodox Christianity to North America. Some shamans encouraged their people to adopt Orthodox Christianity, especially since the missionaries challenged the Russian fur traders' practice of forcing indigenous peoples to slaughter large numbers of animals. When Alaska became a territory in 1867 most Russians left, but not the Russian Orthodox Church. Russia continued to support the Orthodox mission in Alaska until the Russian Revolution of 1917. Orthodox Christianity has continued in Alaska, primarily among indigenous peoples. Today Alaska has 90 parishes under the jurisdiction of the Orthodox Church of America (headquartered in New York), and a new cathedral was built in Anchorage in the 1990s. In 1890 Russian Orthodox still dominated the population of religious adherents (excluding indigenous traditions), but steadily lost its share of the adherent pie through the twentieth century.

When Alaska became a U.S. territory an Ashkenazi Jew raised the flag. Jews came into the territory as traders, and later as prospectors. They first celebrated a Passover Seder in Sitka in 1869. Anchorage today has two synagogues, Juneau and Fairbanks one each. Jews are more observant in Alaska than their confreres in the lower forty-eight states.

Roman Catholic missionaries entered Alaska in 1871. Four Sisters of St. Ann arrived in 1886, signifying the first stable Catholic presence. The Jesuit Volunteers, now an international program, grew out of a strategy devised in the 1950s for staffing Copper Valley schools. Today the Catholic Church in Alaska is divided among the Dioceses of Fairbanks and Juneau and the Archdiocese of Anchorage.

Other religious presence from the lower forty-eight states began to enter Alaska after Sheldon Jackson arrived in 1880 and founded the Presbyterian mission. Jackson saw that the area was too vast for a single denomination. In 1885, then General Agent for Education in Alaska, Jackson recruited other Protestant churches to send missionaries, with wives to serve as schoolteachers. Alaska. Under a "comity plan," different groups entered different areas. The Moravians set up missions in the Kuskokwim region and the Baptists in Cook Inlet. The Episcopalians continued an earlier Anglican mission to the Yukon. The Methodists took the Aleutian and Shumagin Islands, the Congregationalists Cape Prince of Wales, the Swedish Evangelicals Unalaklett, the Quakers Kotzebue and Juneau, the Lutherans and Covenant Churches Nome. Presbyterians continued in the southeast and northern Artic. Today, the Christian affiliation of Alaskan natives reflects where their families lived when the "comity plan" was in effect. (Jackson did not provide areas for Catholics or Russian Orthodox because he considered them "foreign" religions.)

Alaska achieved statehood in 1959. Since then most churches from the United States have become established in the state. With half the population located in and around a single city, Anchorage, Alaska presents a picture of recent religious development but primarily in an urban context. So in Alaska today one finds Orthodox Christians, Catholics, mainline Protestant denominations, Episcopal/Holiness and Pentecostal churches, independent non-denominational groups, and more. It is home to ethnic Christian communities including Korean churches, Samoan churches, and major African-American denominations.

Buddhism was institutionally established in Alaska in 1979, though Buddhist presence began in the nineteenth century with Japanese immigrants. Today Alaska is home to a Theravada community of Thai immigrant families, as well as to Korean and Japanese Zen, Sokka Gakkai, and Jodo Shinshu. In May each year the Buddhist communities in or near Anchorage participate publicly in the national annual "Change Your Mind" day.

Most villages around Alaska have an Orthodox Church, a Catholic Church, a mainline Protestant church, and one or more newer Pentecostal, Holiness, or non-denominational churches. Some are staffed full-time, others are served on circuits. Indigenous peoples often belong to one or more of these churches. In addition, there has been a resurgence of indigenous belief and practice, in part in response to the Alaska Native Claims Act of 1971.

Anchorage has some very large congregations. Catholics, Lutherans, Baptists, and Jews, among others, have congregations of 1,000 to 3,000.

Baha'is organized in Alaska in 1939. Islam and Hinduism are more recent. Alaska also is home to neo-pagan and spiritual movements.

Across Alaska today, religious affiliation is tied to political and economic disagreement among indigenous peoples and between indigenous peoples and the government. One anthropologist has proposed that rapid growth of Holiness, Pentecostal and non-denominational groups among indigenous peoples since 1971 is an expression of disagreement about the unsatisfactory consequences of economic initiatives taken in villages in the wake of the Alaska Native Claims Act.[6]

Because of its large urban population—half its entire population is in Anchorage—massive increases in population through in-migration, vast natural spaces with scattered small villages, a large indigenous population, and its immense natural resources, Alaska today is the site of religious dynamics from frontier to post-modern global urban life.

Religion's Public Presence

Religion's public presence in the Pacific Northwest is both complex and elusive. With a minority of the population in religious institutions and those divided among many different religious communities, no single religion or denomination is sufficiently large to assure the outcome on any public issue. In this context religious communities have had to develop alliances with other religious bodies and with those outside of religious institutions in order to influence public life. In the Pacific Northwest's more open and fluid religious environment, these alliances have required tending and have been influenced by broader social trends and change.

In the 1980s, for instance, the Christian Right succeeded in organizing conservative Protestants of various denominational and nondenominational stripes around a set of cultural issues. The Oregon Christian Alliance (OCA—an affiliate of Pat Robertson's Christian Coalition) drew considerable media attention and had some success in setting the agenda for public debate over "family values." Those cultural themes did resonate with some church-going Oregonians (conservative Protestants are a relatively large piece of the state's adherent pie), but because that cultural reservoir was demographically small, the OCA won nothing significant in the long run and has largely withered away.

About the same time, however, and under the radar of most news media, mainline and liberal Protestant denominations, liberal Catholic parishes, and Reform and Conservative Jews in the Northwest began addressing a different set of moral issues—ecological and social sustainability—in interfaith coalitions with pantheistic, neo-pagans and secular environmental organizations. Earth Ministry in Seattle and Interfaith Network for Earth Concern in Portland exemplify religion's public presence in the region in two important ways. First, these groups are *not* sectarian, and second, they explore the question at the heart of what it means to be a Northwesterner: How shall we live in this place?

The contest to redefine the culture of Southern Oregon's fabled "State of Jefferson" exemplifies the poles of contemporary public religious debate in the region. In the struggle to protect of the Klamath-Siskiyou bio-region, a place the World Wildlife Fund identified as one of the world's most significant, old time residents who lament the "erosion of tradition Christian values" and whose livelihood depends on using the land clash with newer residents who prize its natural beauty and recreational amenities and for whom wilderness protection is a spiritual quest.

Conflict in the State of Jefferson came to a head with President Clinton's designation of the Cascade-Siskiyou National Monument in 2000, followed in 2001 by the Klamath Basin water crisis in which the federal government withheld irrigation water from local farmers to protect endangered fish. Similar land use and resource management issues with comparable dynamics played out all over the Pacific Northwest in the last two decades of the twentieth century. The conflict over logging and spotted owl habitat was the pivotal event in the culture clash between the old and the new Pacific Northwest. This was followed by the "salmon crisis" and widespread debate over the breaching of four Snake River dams. Then came the restoration of whale hunting in the Puget Sound by the Makai Indians, and for several years now, the prospect of oil drilling in Alaska's Arctic National Wildlife Refuge has generated heated public debate.

Environmental advocates on all these issues make arguments for the preservation of nature that put forth scientific claims, but their pleas hinge on striking a resonant moral and spiritual chord in the populace, and increasingly they do. These conflicts are cultural struggles about the nature of nature and what it means to live in the Pacific Northwest. In the contest over the fate of this place and the culture that will define it, current and emerging religious clusters are visible. The next four chapters use the frame of these religious clusters to explore how religion is visibly present in the public life of the Pacific Northwest today.

Endnotes

1. Eldon G. Ernst, "American Religious History From a Pacific Coast Perspective," in Carl Guarneri and David Alvarez, *Religion and Society in the American West: Historical Essays* (Lanham, MD: University Press of America, 1987): 3-39.

2. This discussion uses figures from NARA (Dale E. Jones, et al. *Religious Congregations and Membership in the United States* [Nashville, Glenmary Research Center, 2002]. U.S. Religious Census, 1890-1936, National Council of Churches of Christ in the United States of America. Bureau of Research and Survey's *Churches and Church Membership in the United States; an Enumeration and Analysis by Counties, States, and Regions*, 1952; Douglas W. Johnson, *Churches and Church Membership in the United States: An Enumeration by Region, State, and County*, 1971; Bernard Quinn, et al, *Churches and Church Membership in the United States*, 1980; Martin B. Bradley, et al, *Churches and Church Membership in the United States 1990*; U.S. Census Bureau *Statistical Abstract of the U.S.; Historical Statistics of the United States Colonial Times to 1970*. Adherent figures are based on self-reporting by religious bodies and in some cases by estimate.

3. David M. Buerge and Junius Rochester, *Roots and Branches: The Religious Heritage of Washington State* (Seattle: Church Council of Greater Seattle, 1988): 145-146, 194-197, 210-212, 218-221.

4. ARIS Website. *http://www.gc.cuny.edu/studies/key_findings.htm*. ARIS did not include Alaska.

5. Ibid; Barry Kosmin and Seymour Lachman, *One Nation Under God: Religion in Contemporary American Society* (New York: Harmony Books, 1993): 88-89.

6. Kirk Dombrowski, *Against Culture: Development, Politics, and Religion in Indian Alaska* (Lincoln, NE: University of Nebraska Press, 2001).

Chapter Two

Contesting for the Soul of an Unlikely Land: Mainline Protestants, Catholics, and Reform and Conservative Jews in the Pacific Northwest

Dale E. Soden

In February 2002 thirty-seven leaders from Jewish and Christian traditions in Washington State signed a statement urging United States senators to implement proposals for "energy conservation, fuel efficiency, and alternate energy development to protect God's creation and God's children." Calling on senators to increase vehicle fuel efficiency, to prevent drilling in the Arctic National Wildlife Reserve, and to invest more in renewable energy resources, these religious leaders attempted to leverage their cooperation on behalf of an important social issue.

The Catholic bishops of the Pacific Northwest had already issued a pastoral letter in January 2001 that encouraged an ethic of stewardship, ecological responsibility, conservation, and pursuit of the common good. While that letter had not made specific policy recommendations regarding such issues as the breaching of dams along the Columbia and Snake rivers, it nevertheless established a context for Catholics and other Christians to move toward more regulation of activity within the watershed.

In many ways these efforts by mainline Protestants, Catholics, and Reform and Conservative Jews to influence public policy regarding the environment are a continuation of efforts that began over 170 years ago. From the onset of Anglo-European settlement in the Pacific Northwest in the 1830s, individuals representing these religious traditions have exerted extraordinary energy in hopes of shaping the common life of all people in the region. While at first glance one might assume that their impact has been minimal, given the fact that Oregon,

Washington, and Alaska are overwhelmingly unchurched, the actual story is much more complex.

Mainline Protestants, Catholics, and Reform and Conservative Jews have played critical roles in the public debate over policy issues. From statutes affecting social behavior and social services to the establishment of educational and health care institutions, they have helped shape the character of life in the Pacific Northwest. At the beginning of the twenty-first century, even as they compete with spiritual alternatives in the region, mainline Protestants, Catholics, and Reform and Conservative Jews continue to form an important component of the religious landscape. Today, they remain actively involved on a number of political fronts, including issues related to war and peace, economic justice, race, gender, and class discrimination, and the environment. Equally importantly, they deliver social services to hundreds of thousands of people throughout the region.

Mainline Protestants, Catholics, and Reform and Conservative Jews have shaped public policies, social ethos, and the cultural landscape in the Pacific Northwest even though they never achieved a cultural hegemony comparable to Lutherans in the upper-Midwest or Baptists in the South. They overcame a paucity of resources, a population largely disinterested in institutional religion, and competition from alternative religious and spiritual movements to make their contributions.

At their worst, Catholics and Protestants played a major role in the subjugation of Native Americans and fought bitterly among themselves. At their best, along with the region's Jewish community, they shaped an emerging urban culture and established a significant number of educational, health care, and social service agencies and institutions. These religious groups succeeded in extending protection to those most vulnerable in the society. Single women and children, non-Caucasians, recent immigrants, and the laboring poor have all been served by professional and volunteer efforts, ministries, and financial resources dedicated to resolving significant social problems.

Mainline Protestants, Catholics, and Reform and Conservative Jews have provided schools, hospitals, and orphanages; they have worked for the homeless, the mentally ill, sexually abused, the migrant worker, and other victims. On issues related to the environment and poverty, mainline Christians and Jews cooperate through ecumenical organizations in an effort to influence policy at the local, state, and national levels.

As the twenty-first century begins, these communities and their organizations, from judicatories to congregations, parishes, and synagogues, face significant challenges to their efforts to continue influencing the public policy and social ethos of the region. Ongoing political and social debates framed along liberal and conservative lines reinforce tensions within local congregations and parishes, and between local bodies and regional and national denominational leaders. That tension contributes to declining financial support from congregations and parishes for ecumenical activity, national programs, and denominational infrastructure. So too does the current intense debate within most mainline Protestant denominations over ordination of homosexuals.

Sub-regional differences also play a role. The cultures of eastern Washington and Oregon are considered more conservative than the cultures of western Washington and Oregon; this creates differences of opinion between the east and west regions of Oregon and Washington on issues ranging from sexual orientation to the environment.

This chapter focuses on these mainline religious groups that identify with and contribute to the "definition of society's core values."[1] Mainline Protestant refers to denominations that emerged from the Reformation in the sixteenth century and subsequent expansions from those churches in the seventeenth and eighteenth centuries. In the United States, these include the Episcopalian, Presbyterian, Lutheran, Methodist, American (Northern) Baptist, Congregationalist (United Church of Christ), Christian (Disciples of Christ), Unitarian, Reformed Church in America, and African American Baptist churches, as well as African Methodist Episcopal churches. Also included in this analysis are ecumenical bodies that emerged primarily in the twentieth century and draw heavily on the mainline denominations but which also include participation from historic peace or Anabaptist churches such as Mennonites and Quakers.

For most of the nation's history, Catholicism was regarded as foreign and dangerous, not as mainline. After World War II, however, Catholics entered the middle-class in overwhelming numbers and became part of mainstream society, and since the 1960s the Catholic Church has been considered part of mainline Christianity. Likewise, Reform and Conservative Jews since World War II have been considered part of mainstream of society and partners with mainline Christian groups.

Though Catholics and Reform and Conservative Jews only more recently have been recognized as part of the main stream, historically both groups have shared with Protestants in the United States and the region a theological vision that impels attending to the common good of the broader community and to practices of civic leadership as a religious duty.

Statistically, 20 percent of the population in Washington and 14 percent in Oregon identify as Catholic, according to the American Religious Identification Survey (ARIS). Only those people not identifying with any religious tradition (25 percent in Washington and 21 percent in Oregon) outnumber Catholics. In addition, 6 percent identify as Lutheran, and an additional 6 percent identify as Baptist in Washington, 3 percent in both Washington and Oregon identify with the Presbyterian tradition, and 4 percent in both states identify as Methodist. Two percent in Oregon and 1 percent in Washington identify themselves as Episcopalian, approximately 1 percent in both states named the United Church of Christ (Congregational) as their religious tradition, and approximately 1 percent in both states identify themselves as Jewish.

Compared with other parts of the country, the number of those who self-identify as mainline Protestants, Catholics, or Reform and Conservative Jews is thin, about 50 percent in Washington and 45 percent in Oregon. Even fewer are affiliated with an institution of one of these traditions. Despite this, these religious traditions constitute something of a religious establishment in the Pacific Northwest.

While there are significant differences within these expressions of the Jewish and Christian traditions, these groups share a commitment to transforming the political and social ethos of the world. Catholics have a long history of work on behalf of social justice. Reform and Conservative Jews have engaged issues of social justice for themselves and for other oppressed minorities. Presbyterians, Episcopalians, Methodists, and Congregationalists, among others, all have long traditions of social engagement. Even Lutherans since World War II have devoted resources and intellectual energy to issues of public policy. Despite membership loss among mainline Protestant denominations over the last three decades, all three groups remain influential in the public squares of the Pacific Northwest.

The nature of these communities' public influence has differed in each of four historical periods in the region, as individuals brought their religious values to bear on cultural conflicts.

In the first period, from the 1830s to the 1880s, Protestants, Catholics, and Jews established religious institutions in the region. Protestants and Catholics participated with the United States government in efforts to isolate and/or assimilate Native Americans, an activity some associated with the triumph of Christian culture and Western civilization. Christians also engaged the issue of slavery and migration of African-Americans to the Pacific Northwest, particularly in Oregon.

The second period, from the 1880s through the 1920s, was marked by a concerted effort on the part of mainline Protestants, Catholics, and Reform and Conservative Jews to thwart the establishment of an emerging urban culture. This culture, which focused on alcohol consumption, gambling, and prostitution, catered to young men and women through inexpensive recreational activities ranging from unregulated theatre and movies to dance halls, racetracks, and amusement parks. Religious reformers fought to mold the culture in more constructive directions and tried to mitigate its effects on women and children.

The third era began with the Great Depression and ended in the early 1970s. An unusual period of consensus in American society emerged from the Great Depression, World War II, and the Cold War. Mainline Christians and Jews participated in a larger social effort to bolster normalcy through strengthening families, citizenship, and decency. They increased cooperation around social issues and projects, including intermittent ecumenical efforts challenging racial discrimination. This last effort signaled a more critical perspective on society.

The present era began in the latter part of the 1960s and early 1970s.[2] In the Pacific Northwest, as across the United States, the high expectations and hopes of the later 1950s met the intransigencies of racism, sexism, and the Vietnam War and produced a pervasive disillusionment with and distrust of institutions. The seemingly broad social consensus of the 1950s unraveled into bitter divisions over the nature of American society, the role of institutions, and the place of the United States in the world. Mainline Protestant and Catholic churches, and to a lesser extent Reform and Conservative Jewish synagogues, experienced the growing disregard for institutional authority and the growing independence of individuals' quest for the sacred. Mainline Protestants and Catholics saw their communities split along liberal and conservative lines, where liberal meant expanding individual freedoms and conditions for social justice and conservative meant respect for traditional authority, individual initiative, and purity in personal morals.[3] As congregations divided sharply between proponents of liberal and conservative social philosophies, both lay leadership and clergy within mainline Christianity and Judaism moved toward more liberal social and political positions, increasing tensions.

Despite the internal difficulties and challenges, for the past 30 years mainline Protestants, Catholics, and Reform and Conservative Jews in the Pacific Northwest have collaborated on many social and political issues out of a common theological commitment to justice. They have focused energies and resources on behalf of race relations, poverty, hunger, homelessness, and the environment. Several issues related to war and peace, as well as U.S. foreign policy, have motivated thousands to challenge the policies of the American government.

Issues such as abortion, the death penalty, gay and lesbian rights, and physician-assisted suicide have been bitterly contested. On issues of sexual morality and control of the body, not only are mainline Protestants, Catholics, and Reform and Conservative Jews divided, the public debate is also complicated by the active involvement of more conservative Christian groups. Congregational and parish-level analysis presents an even more complicated picture because of the number and diversity of those churches. While there are exceptions, parishioners tend to express more conservative social values than church leaders at the national level. In addition, in both Oregon and Washington, the eastern side of each state is generally more conservative than the western side.

Despite internal tensions, and even as mainline Protestant groups are losing "market share," the commitment of mainline religious communities to shaping the public square is reflected in virtually every important public debate. That commitment likely will continue well into the twenty-first century. Whether historic mainline religious expressions will continue to exercise the most significant influence on the public square in the Pacific Northwest, or whether more evangelical or entrepreneurial varieties of religious expression will push mainline churches to the sideline is the intriguing question.

On the one hand, mainline Protestant religious groups have lost considerable numbers of members since the 1970s. The Catholic Church currently is in an enormous crisis with the clergy-abuse scandal. Further, the challenge to define perhaps a new role within a region that is generally hostile to institutional religion makes it difficult to predict what the future holds. On the other hand, the long history of cultural engagement and adaptation, as well as the considerable number of educational, health care, and social service institutions that have been established by mainline religious groups, suggest that they will remain a significant force well into the twenty-first century. However, if mainline religious groups fail to educate subsequent generations into the rich theological resources of their respective heritages, these groups' cultural influence may decline precipitously.

1830s – 1880s

Mainline Protestants, Catholics, and Jews have been in the region for nearly 175 years. Beginning in the 1830s, Protestants and Catholics sent missionaries to the Northwest for the purpose of converting Native Americans.

While hopeful in the beginning, early missionaries experienced more failure than success. In 1834, Methodists Jason Lee and his nephew Daniel settled in the Willamette Valley, but for a variety of reasons fell well short of expectations regarding the conversion of Native Americans.[4]

Missionaries Marcus and Narcissa Whitman also met resistance among the Cayuse from the Walla Walla River Valley in 1836 until their deaths in 1847. In that year, Native Americans, driven by frustration over disease and death as well as fear regarding future white settlement in the region, murdered the Whitmans and 12 others. Throughout the region, Protestant Christians struggled to persuade Native Americans to reject traditional beliefs and, failing, began to rely increasingly on coercion and military force to achieve their objectives.[5]

Catholics fared slightly better. Associated with the Hudson's Bay Company rather than Yankee settlers and armed with a theology and worldview seemingly more compatible with Native spirituality, Roman Catholic priests arrived in the region in 1838 in response to requests from Canadian *voyageurs* and traders. Fathers Francis Norbert Blanchet and Modeste Demers arrived at Fort Vancouver (Washington) with the primary intent of evangelizing Native Americans. Catholics did better than Protestants over the next 30 years, but competition between the two groups produced considerable ill will and often confusion among Native Americans.[6]

In the wake of increased Yankee settlement and the seeming impossibility of cultural co-existence, after the Civil War Protestants, notably Methodists, and Catholics cooperated with the United States government in the forced assimilation of Native Americans. Informed by world-views that considered non-Western civilizations inferior, they participated in a process that stripped Native populations of their land, culture, language, and religion. Beginning in 1869, under President Ulysses S. Grant's Peace Policy, Protestant missionary societies, and for some reservations the Catholic bishop, provided agents who theoretically ensured that reservation schools, churches, mills, and farms were built and maintained.[7] In the end, the Peace Policy failed to achieve its principal objectives, but that did not discourage Christians from establishing regional Indian boarding schools. Congregationalists founded the most famous of the Northwest schools, Chemawa, on the model of Richard Pratt's Carlisle school in Pennsylvania. It continues to operate.[8]

Settlers and the government, with the help of churches, successfully overwhelmed a culture that had been present in the region for at least 12,000 years. Disease, military force, religious conversion, and forced assimilation took their toll. But beginning in the 1930s, and gaining momentum by the 1970s, Christians regionally expressed deep regret over the role of their churches in this near cultural genocide. The impact of this guilt on the current state of Indian-white affairs remains to be analyzed but is certainly a factor in everything from Native fishing rights, the breaching of Columbia River dams, compensation for boarding school abuses, and policies that regulate gambling on local reservations.

Mainline Christians also played a significant role in shaping public discourse over racial issues. In the years surrounding the Civil War, residents of Oregon Territory confronted the questions of whether to prohibit the introduction of slavery into the territory and whether to prohibit the settlement of free African-Americans. Reverend Obed Dickinson, a Congregational minister sent to Salem, Oregon in 1852, exemplified the courage with which some Protestant ministers and parishioners spoke out against slavery and supported the right of black Americans to move into the region. However, many Christians failed to support Dickinson and actively opposed racial integration within the state.[9]

1880s – 1920s

The subjugation of Native Americans, the struggle to determine the nature of race relations, and the task of establishing religious institutions in the region did not end the challenges Christians faced in the region. Well before the final treaties were signed, a frontier culture emerged that threatened the middle-class mores identified with "civilization" by Protestant Christians and Americanized Catholics and Jews. The building of railroads, the mining of silver and gold, the harvesting of timber, the nascent industrial activity in the late nineteenth century, and massive immigration (the population of Oregon and Washington increased from 249,884 to 2,095,758 between 1880 and 1930) produced its own cultural dynamics. The utilization of cheap labor, including miners, farm workers, loggers, and fishermen—mostly young males between the ages of 16 and 30—created the demand for cheap amusements and psychological escape. The saloon, gambling den, dancehall, and bordello became staples of many budding communities.[10]

In this second era, mainline Protestants, Catholics, and the newly established Reform and Conservative Jewish movements, battled together to tame this frontier culture. The struggle proved difficult; the region itself remained far from the home offices of religious denominations, and the people were often indifferent. Yet Protestants in particular were not lacking in entrepreneurial effort and hope for cultural influence. Mainline Protestants publicly embraced the values of capitalism, ran for public office, and stepped into leadership roles in both public and private education. Catholics and Reform and Conservative Jews also founded numerous educational, health care, and social service organizations and institutions. They exerted extraordinary effort to build what they believed were civilized and, on occasion, utopian communities.[11]

Though religiously motivated people in the Northwest failed to dominate the emerging culture, they succeeded in altering it in significant ways. In particular, religious individuals and organizations changed the nature of life for vulnerable members of the community. The health and protection of women and children proved a major concern for Christian and Jewish clergy and lay people. Appealing to tenets of the Social Gospel and often adopting agendas and strategies associated with Populism and Progressivism, Christians worked actively on behalf of numerous social causes. Jews, now sufficiently numerous to become effectively organized, and motivated by their own religious teaching, worked to improve the quality of life in the community. Together they advocated for unemployment bureaus, kindergartens, rescue homes for single women, laws restricting child labor, juvenile courts, libraries, hospitals, and the establishment of various other social-service agencies.[12]

The work of several individuals and organizations is illustrative. George Whitworth was one of the earliest Protestant ministers to come to the region with an eye toward influencing its culture. Traveling west on the Oregon Trail in 1853, Whitworth headed north to Puget Sound. He founded as many as 20 churches and also became superintendent of public schools in Thurston County (Olympia) and Seattle. He served as chief clerk of the Indian Department, participated in several business ventures, and was so well respected as an educator that he was named president of the University of Washington twice in the 1870s. By the 1880s he had helped found another institution that would eventually bear his name, Whitworth College. George Whitworth believed in democracy, common school education, capitalism, and non-sectarian Christianity. He spearheaded early efforts at Prohibition, which reflected his conviction that controlling the social behavior of young men would prove paramount to the well-being of the region.[13]

Mother Joseph proved to be Whitworth's counterpart from the Catholic community. Leading a group of Sisters of Providence, she worked to address health care in the region. These women started the first Catholic hospital in Portland, Oregon in 1875, and did the same in Spokane, Washington in 1886.[14] Italian immigration to the region provided impetus for the sisters of the Sacred Heart to begin similar work in Seattle in 1903. In that same year, Mother Francesca Cabrini, the first American citizen to be declared a saint by the Catholic Church, came to Seattle to start an orphanage and later, in 1916, to establish a hospital. The Catholic Church established an infrastructure of parishes, schools, hospitals, orphanages, colleges, and universities throughout the region.

Protestant denominations did the same. Methodists, Presbyterians, Episcopalians, Baptists, Congregationalists, and Lutherans all moved into the growing cities of the Pacific Northwest and established institutions to meet the needs of the urban poor.

Catholics and Protestants launched a bevy of colleges and universities in an attempt to shape the region's culture. Many failed, but those that endured pay witness to a significant religious commitment. These institutions produced community leaders at every level, from doctors and lawyers to teachers, nurses, businesspersons, and politicians, leaders whose political and social perspectives were directly influenced by a Christian understanding of the world.

Mainline Protestant organizations made a significant social impact in the Pacific Northwest in the late nineteenth and early twentieth centuries. Two of the most influential were the Young Men's Christian Association (YMCA) and the Young Women's Christian Association (YWCA). Established in Portland in 1868, in Seattle in 1876, and in Spokane in 1888, the "YM" concerned itself with the plight of young men who gravitated to the growing urban centers of the Pacific Northwest. Members of the "YM" met new arrivals at the railroad station and offered housing, Bible study, employment options, and athletic facilities. The YWCA was established in Seattle, Portland, and Spokane in 1894; the "YW" offered 10-cent lunches to women and a safe haven. The "Travelers Aid" program was started in 1900 in order to meet the needs of hundreds of women arriving alone at the city's docks and railroad stations.

But the organization that most symbolizes the late nineteenth and early twentieth century effort of Victorian Christian America to shape the culture of the region was the Women's Christian Temperance Union (WCTU). Established in 1874, the union spread throughout the country largely because of the indefatigable efforts of Frances Willard. In the summer of 1883 she visited Oregon,

Washington, and Idaho and helped organize chapters throughout the region. Alcohol reform motivated thousands of women (none of whom had the right to vote) to participate in the political system by lobbying legislatures, marching in front of saloons, and providing alternative activities.

While the WCTU was ecumenical by design, Methodists were particularly active. Thousands of women throughout the Pacific Northwest moved out of the domestic sphere and into the public realm in order to create some of the first town libraries, coffee houses, and refuge homes for single women with children. They demanded the presence of female matrons in local jails and prisons and succeeded in achieving curriculum reform in all three states by requiring education on the health effects of alcohol abuse. The anti-alcohol forces achieved significant success by 1916 when statewide prohibition went into effect in Washington, Oregon, and Idaho.

In addition to establishing institutions that molded the culture, mainline Protestants, Catholics, and Reform and Conservative Jews also wanted to shape the political tenor of the region. Progressive-era Christians sought to exercise social control over the working class. Prohibition was the most obvious issue, but Christians from most denominations, including Catholics, also succeeded on other issues, including raising the legal age required to purchase cigarettes. Communities passed ordinances that regulated motion pictures and dance halls and eliminated most forms of entertainment on Sunday—the one day that members of the working class did not have to work. Christians sought funds for Carnegie libraries and reading rooms and built museums in order to attract young men to more edifying pursuits. Protestant ministers throughout the Northwest, including itinerant revivalists like Billy Sunday, came through communities for the purpose of converting young working-class males to Christianity.

Most budding urban communities and many small towns could boast of ministers and priests who took the lead in shaping public discourse. Thomas Lamb Eliot, a Unitarian minister in Portland, publicly fought political corruption and advocated a variety of Progressive reforms. Roman Catholic Bishop Edward J. O'Dea was a major figure in Seattle circles from 1896 until his death in 1932. In Oregon Fr. Edwin Vincent O'Hara and Caroline Gleason, later Sr. Miriam Theresa, secured passage of the nation's first effective minimum wage law. In Alaska, the Presbyterian clergyman Sheldon Jackson shaped political and ecclesiastical structures.

The person who arguably best embodied the Protestant Progressive reform spirit, however, was Mark Matthews, pastor of Seattle's First Presbyterian Church for nearly 40 years. He built the congregation into his denomination's largest church, with nearly 9,000 members at its height. More importantly, Matthews became involved directly in the politics of his city; he spearheaded social projects that included night schools, unemployment bureaus, kinder-gartens, hospitals, and other institutions that served the poor and working class in Seattle. In 1909 his congregation established a day nursery, one of the first 50 child-care centers in the country, still operating today under the name Childhaven.

Envisioning Seattle in a way that might have suited John Winthrop, Matthews sought to foster religious orthodoxy and make the church the key insti-tution for determining public policy. A holy community was his goal. He believed in moral suasion from the pulpit and political activity in the community. He cam-paigned for prohibition and other laws that would shape social behavior; he pub-licly opposed mayors, police chiefs, and other public figures with whom he dis-agreed. Matthews and his allies understood themselves to be in a war for the con-trol of the culture of the Pacific Northwest.[15]

Reform and Conservative Jews also shaped the social ethos and public realm of the Pacific Northwest. Jewish women were particularly active in growing cities; for example, the Portland Chapter of the National Council of Jewish Women established a settlement house modeled loosely on Jane Addams' Hull House in Chicago. The historian of Oregon's Jewish community, Steven Lowenstein, wrote that Jewish women "simply eclipsed the men in their under-standing and organization of welfare, and they thereby gained a far greater civic role."[16] Nevertheless, philanthropists such as Ben Selling left their mark on the Portland community by creating institutions like the Working Men's Club, which by 1914 was serving 800 meals a day. Selling entered politics as a Republican and served as both president of the Oregon Senate and speaker of the Oregon House of Representatives.

Rabbi Stephen Wise served only six years in Portland but became exception-ally active in the city's political affairs. After visiting fish canneries on the Columbia River, Rabbi Wise became a leading advocate of child-labor legisla-tion. He vigorously supported women's suffrage while opposing the legalization of gambling and later emerged as one of the most powerful and respected leaders of the American Jewish community and a close advisor of President Franklin Roosevelt.

The bitterness as well as the complexity of the battle to influence the politi-cal culture of the Pacific Northwest during the 1920s was symbolized by the emergence of the Ku Klux Klan in Oregon and, to a lesser extent, in Washington. Although it is difficult to know how many Protestants joined the Klan, several prominent Klan leaders were Protestant ministers.

In 1922 the Klan sponsored a compulsory education bill in Oregon that would have required all students to attend public schools. Clearly aimed at destroying the Catholic school system, the bill was widely supported by

Protestants. During the campaign, an issue of the *Klamath Falls Herald* printed that at the birth of every male child in a Catholic family, a gun and ammunition were buried underneath the (Catholic) church to prepare for the day when government would be overthrown on behalf of the pope.[17] The bill passed by 12,000, but was ruled unconstitutional by the United States Supreme Court.

In Washington, a similar ballot measure was narrowly defeated, in an election where the campaign against the measure was spearheaded by an ecumenical coalition of businessmen. The school bill controversy suggests the degree to which Christians battled for cultural control—sometimes even against one another.

In spite of these periodic spasms of Nativism and mean-spirited intolerance, the era witnessed remarkable efforts by mainline Protestants, Catholics, and Reform and Conservative Jews on behalf of social and political reform. Often focused on education, health care, and the physical protection of women and children, these social reforms had significant impact on the culture of the region. Despite the extensive role that institutional religion played in the Northwest, compared with other regions its strength in terms of numbers and resources was comparatively thin. As a consequence, mainline religion continued to struggle to establish itself in the region.

1930s – 1970

The third period of regional cultural engagement began with the onset of the Great Depression and extended through the 1960s. This period is distinguished by efforts to influence a broader social consensus that began to emerge throughout the country. During this period much in mainline religious expression reinforced values associated with American civil religion. However, largely through ecumenical efforts, a more critical perspective emerged, particularly as mainline Christians and Jews challenged practices of racial discrimination.

Councils of Churches in major metropolitan areas emerged during the 1930s and 40s as the primary avenues by which Christians came together to influence regional public policy. The Federal Council of Churches, established in 1908, had helped establish local branches of the organization in both Portland and Seattle in 1919. In the beginning, both branches focused on traditional moral issues such as prohibition and prostitution. The councils issued statements supporting marriage and amendments to state constitutions to permit school credit for Bible study. However, beginning in the '30s, councils began to focus on broader social issues such as economic justice, racial reconciliation, and world peace.

During World War II this shift was reflected in the Seattle Council of Churches' reaction to the internment of Japanese-Americans. The Council pursued two campaigns intended to protect and support those of Japanese lineage as they endured tremendous hardships. First, it worked to halt, or at least to modify significantly, the expulsion of Nikkei (anyone of Japanese ancestry) from designated areas of the West Coast. Second, near the war's end, the council promoted the Nikkeis' return and integration into the city.

In March 1942 the Seattle Council of Churches, contrary to statements made by the mayor and governor, expressed opposition to evacuation and relocation. Clergymen were often present when officials investigated Japanese-Americans; clergy helped provide relief supplies and foodstuffs, and they often tried to shape public opinion more positively toward Japanese-Americans. Although the Seattle religious community failed to reach its overall goals, it seems that its role in this tragic episode was courageous and significant.[18]

Following World War II mainline Protestants, Catholics, and Reform and Conservative Jews cooperated on numerous fronts. One of the most intriguing joint religious efforts was the television show "Challenge" in Seattle. Originally conceived by Rabbi Raphael Levine of Seattle's Temple De Hirsch in 1952, the program brought local Protestant, Catholic, and Jewish leaders together to talk about timely issues from a religious perspective. Levine believed that having representatives from different faith traditions speak about common problems would effectively undermine religious intolerance and bigotry. He also hoped that together religious leaders could make a significant impact on public discourse in the Seattle community.

Initially, the Catholic Archbishop of Seattle, Thomas J. Connolly, refused to participate. However, with the accession to the papacy of John XXIII and his calling of Vatican Council II in 1959, Connolly revised his position and the program moved forward. Rabbi Levine, Father William Treacy, and Reverend Martin Goslin from Plymouth Congregational in Seattle began the show in September 1960, discussing the topic, "Can We Have a Catholic President?" The program on Palm Sunday, 1961, "Who Crucified Jesus?" received an award from the National Association of Christians and Jews. Father Treacy and Rabbi Levine participated in "Challenge" for the 14 years the program aired, while a number of different Protestant ministers rotated through. The program's 300,000 weekly viewers watched the clergymen discuss a variety of controversial subjects, from open housing to the celebration of Christmas in public schools.[19]

Primarily in the context of ecumenical organizations, mainline Protestants, Catholics, and Jews intensified their efforts on behalf of civil rights for minority groups between 1940 and 1970. While efforts were inconsistent and insufficient, they indicated a growing consensus that religious congregations should work more vigorously on behalf of racial integration. During the 1940s and 1950s in Seattle inter-racial groups such as the Christian Friends for Racial Equality organized to raise awareness and address issues of race relations.

As the civil rights movement gained momentum in the early '60s, mainline religious groups disagreed on strategy. In 1961, controversy emerged when the Reverend Samuel McKinney, the African-American pastor of Mount Zion Baptist Church in Seattle, arranged for Martin Luther King, Jr. to visit the city. Initially, McKinney had received assurances that First Presbyterian, Mark Matthews's former church, would host the event, since it seated roughly 3,000 people. When anonymous threats were made on King's life, several African-American leaders in Seattle questioned whether King's visit might trigger latent racial conflict within the city. Members of McKinney's church who worked for Boeing found anti-King material at their desks. Yet McKinney persisted in the project. In mid-October, however, just two weeks before the scheduled visit, First Presbyterian's pastor, Ralph Turnbull, withdrew from hosting the event. Eventually, organizers found a suitable place for King, but the fallout foreshadowed serious divisions between liberals and conservatives.

African-American religious leaders, as well as members of the NAACP, pushed the Seattle City Council to pass an ordinance that required homeowners and apartment managers to demonstrate that they did not discriminate. City Council delays prompted Seattle's first large-scale protest as the prominent black pastors Mance Jackson and Samuel McKinney led 400 on a march to City Hall in July 1963, while 300 more staged a sit-in at council chambers. Arrests led to larger demonstrations. The council finally passed an open-housing ordinance in October 1963 after intense lobbying by Seattle's only Asian councilman, Wing Luke. The following year, however, voters defeated a referendum on the measure by more than two to one. For the next four years religious leaders worked with other activists to lobby the council and educate the public. Finally, in the wake of King's assassination in 1968, an open-housing ordinance was passed—perhaps out of fear that without it, Seattle would erupt in major racial protest.

1970s to the Present

The contemporary period began at the end of the 1960s with disillusionment and distrust of institutions and authority. The emerging movement against the war in Vietnam, the counterculture, the continuing civil rights movement, and the beginning of feminist activity all sharply divided the middle class between liberal and conservative social philosophies, and this schism played itself out in religion. Sociologist Robert Wuthnow argues that Americans realigned themselves primarily by finding religious organizations that reflected their social and political views. Denominational switching increased significantly while denominational loyalty and respect for inherited religious traditions decreased.

National leadership in mainline denominations, including Episcopalian, Presbyterian, Methodist, Disciples of Christ, United Church of Christ, and Lutheran, moved noticeably to the left during the 1970s. While the picture at the local level was complex, many congregations reflected more conservative views, compared to their respective national church authorities.

With the exception of Catholics, most of these mainline denominations have lost membership, both nationally and in the Pacific Northwest, since the 1970s. How many lost members have gravitated toward more conservative churches and how many have dropped out altogether is difficult to ascertain. The cultural conflict between liberal and conservative religious expressions rages to this day, ebbing and flowing in both Washington and Oregon.

Several factors seemed to play important roles in the movement toward more liberal social, political, and theological positions on the part of mainline churches. One is education. By 1970 the constituency of most mainline religious groups was better educated than ever in their history. Further, most denominations required clergy to earn a master of divinity degree from an accredited seminary. After two decades of increased educational opportunity, the general intellectual tenor of church-related higher education, like the churches themselves, also moved in a liberal direction during the 1960s.

The civil rights movement, the Vietnam War, and the impact of the counterculture on the baby-boom generation all influenced religious activity. Additional impetus may have come from a degree of guilt triggered by Martin Luther King's *Letter from a Birmingham Jail* in 1963, which challenged Christians throughout the country to help fight for civil rights. One survey of California clergy revealed that by 1968 nearly a quarter of them had participated in a civil rights demonstration. Whatever the reasons, the net result was that throughout the country, and specifically in the Pacific Northwest, mainline Protestants, Catholics, and Reform and Conservative Jews devoted increased energy to engaging political and social issues and took stands that were identified as politically liberal. Those who opposed them did not see the connection these groups made between analyzing issues in terms of relationships of structural power on behalf of full, unfettered opportunity for every individual and their inherited theologies of God, the human person, and creation.

Since the 1970s mainline religious leaders and organizations have focused on combating what they perceived to be oppressive American social structures that generated imperialism, racism, poverty, sexism, exploitation, and environmental degradation. While mainline Protestant and Catholic clergy shared social consciousness with their laity, their strategies made little explicit connection between their work for justice and the theological teachings they espoused. Hence mainline Christian expressions have been criticized for disassociating social justice from a theology centered on belief in Jesus Christ.

Increased ecumenical activity in recent decades propelled mainline religious expressions toward liberal politics and away from public articulations of theology.

Urgency of need and ease in cooperative action eclipsed the difficult work of theological discussion. By the 1960s more evangelical partners in the Northwest began to withdraw from ecumenical relations, and such action became associated almost exclusively with liberal politics.

Renewed effort to influence public policy through ecumenical effort began in earnest in the 1970s. The Washington Association of Churches (WAC) organized itself in 1975. Consisting in 2002 of 10 Christian denominations and 12 ecumenical entities, the WAC remains a key organization in the Pacific Northwest for influencing legislative work and community development. Likewise, the Ecumenical Ministries of Oregon (EMO) organized itself in 1973 out of the old Portland Council of Churches. In 2002 the EMO claimed 17 Christian denominations and lobbied the Oregon legislature on a number of fronts. Associated Ministries of Tacoma-Pierce County was created in 1969, with roots in organizations going back to 1883. In eastern Washington the Spokane Council of Ecumenical Ministries reorganized in 1971 with roots in the Spokane Council of Churches. The Church Council of Greater Seattle, organized in 1919, continues to be very active in its efforts to shape public discourse on many issues. The Alaska Association of Churches first organized in 1956. It grew and was renamed the Alaska Council of Churches in 1959. In 1972 it was re-organized and expanded into the Alaska Christian Conference, an organization that includes 12 different denominations, from Quakers, Community Churches, the Salvation Army, and Roman Catholics to mainline Protestant bodies.

Over the last three decades of the twentieth century, mainline denominations employed lobbyists who, as Steven Lansing, former director of the Lutheran Public Policy Office in Olympia, said in a 2002 interview, "Advocate for issues in the context of Church social teachings." Congregationalists, Methodists, Episcopalians, American Baptists, and Quakers are generally supportive of both the Washington Association of Churches and the Ecumenical Ministries of Oregon. Catholics have maintained their own lobbying offices in both Oregon and Washington, but have at the same time worked very closely with ecumenical organizations. Lutherans have also established their own public policy advocacy offices in Salem and Olympia, and like their Catholic counterparts, have worked collaboratively with ecumenical organizations on behalf of the poor.

Synagogues are active in the Interfaith Council of Seattle. In both Oregon and Washington, they also have established networks of organizations and institutions designed to support the vitality of Jewish communities in the region, to assist immigrant Jews, especially from the former Soviet Union, and to contribute to the needs of the broader community in the region.

Over the course of the last three decades of the twentieth century, the presence of mainline religious groups in the public square was most evident on issues related to racism and hate groups, poverty or services for the poor, and American foreign and economic policy. Ecumenical organizations, supported primarily by mainline churches in Washington and Oregon, generally reflect a more liberal perspective and have led challenges to government, the business community, and the middle class, enjoining them to confront problems of the unemployed and underemployed, minorities, women, children, and refugees.

Specifically, mainline religious groups continued to fight various forms of discrimination and hatred against racial and ethnic minorities. Religious leaders at the grass roots worked to desegregate Seattle schools and to a lesser extent Portland schools in the 1970s. In the aftermath of the civil rights movement, white and black religious leaders began working together to achieve a greater level of racial integration within cities of the Northwest. In 1976, at the encouragement of Don Daughtry, a white pastor of the Beacon Avenue Church of Christ in Seattle, the Church Council of Greater Seattle formed a Task Force on Racial Justice in Education.

Bringing together a broad coalition of racial and ethnic groups, as well as clergy and lay people from the various churches, the task force and the council proved essential in formulating a philosophy of integration and applying pressure to the Seattle School Board to develop a plan for integration that has been considered a national model. Several black pastors, including Reverend Samuel McKinney, provided key leadership in formulating this integration plan.[20] In addition to the successful fight for a school desegregation plan in Seattle, other issues, such as discrimination in the work place and by lending institutions against African-Americans, occupied many church leaders from the 1970s into the 1980s.

By the middle of the 1980s issues shifted slightly to concerns about the emergence of white supremacist groups in the Pacific Northwest. In 1987 a Catholic priest, Father Bill Wassmuth, helped organize the Northwest Coalition Against Malicious Harassment in Coeur d'Alene, Idaho as a counter to the Aryan Nations, whose compound was located in nearby Hayden Lake. Wassmuth drew together churches, synagogues, law enforcement entities, grassroots community groups, and organized labor in order to work together against bigotry of all kinds. In 1999 the Northwest Coalition Against Malicious Harassment merged with another organization to become the Northwest Coalition for Human Dignity, currently headquartered in Seattle. The Coalition Against Hate Crimes was started by the American Jewish Committee in Portland in 1997, and has been supported by the Ecumenical Ministries of Oregon and other groups for much the same purpose. In 2000 with the aid of Morris Dees and the Southern Poverty Law Center, the coalition brought a successful lawsuit against Richard Butler and the Aryan Nation compound in Hayden Lake, Idaho and at least temporarily bankrupted the organization.

The problem of domestic violence also attracted the attention of mainline religious groups. In 1977 the Reverend Marie Fortune of the United Church of Christ (Congregational) established the Center for the Prevention of Sexual and Domestic Violence in Seattle after coming to the conclusion that religious leaders were not prepared to assist their parishioners with sexual or domestic abuse, and secular service agencies were not prepared to deal with clients' religious questions. By the 1990s the Center had grown into an inter-religious organization providing education and training to address sexual and domestic violence in communities throughout the world. In 2002 the Center was providing resources and counseling for those affected by the sexual abuse scandal within the Catholic Church.

By far the most visible impact and expression of mainline religion in the Pacific Northwest has been through providing services for the poor, the homeless, and the traditionally vulnerable—mentally ill, imprisoned, children, and single women. Historically, mainline churches and synagogues have exercised significant influence on public policies toward these groups throughout the Pacific Northwest. Ecumenical agencies in Oregon and Washington have consistently lobbied during the past two decades for causes that would be categorized as social justice issues, increases in minimum wage, the right to organize by migrant farm workers, and funds for poverty programs. Likewise, major social service agencies such as Catholic Charities and Lutheran Social Services (now Lutheran Community Services) among many other groups, have provided significant resources to address social needs in the Pacific Northwest.

Catholics, first through the work of women religious, have served the poor from virtually the beginning of their presence in the Pacific Northwest. Catholic Charities as an organization has exerted significant influence throughout the region. Formally organized in 1932 in Portland and Seattle, Catholic Charities focused its energies on serving those who were devastated by the Great Depression. By the 1950s, the organization broadened its efforts from caring for orphans and disadvantaged youth to working with the poor, the elderly, ethnic minorities, and refugees on issues of social services and housing. In these and other social welfare concerns, Catholic Charities has expanded significantly since 1975 in Oregon, Washington, and Alaska.

By 1988 Catholic Community Services of Western Washington (CCSWW) was incorporated as a separate institution, enabling the agency to receive government funding and engage in public-private partnerships. Michael Reichert, who has led CCSWW since 1979, has transformed an agency with a $4 million budget and fewer than 200 employees into the largest private non-profit agency providing human and social services in Washington, with an annual budget of over $60 million and over 3,000 employees. Catholic Charities in Spokane, Portland,

Yakima, and Anchorage all manage a wide array of housing opportunities for low-income individuals and families, homeless, and those with special needs living in the Pacific Northwest. These organizations provide refugee services, shelters, day centers, and transitional and permanent housing, along with other services necessary for people to live with dignity.

On the Protestant side, numerous churches have established congregationally based and cooperative programs to address the needs of the disadvantaged. Plymouth Congregational United Church of Christ in Seattle has led the way in addressing housing issues, an effort that began in 1980 when Rev. Dr. David Colwell challenged his congregation to end homelessness in downtown Seattle. Church members responded and founded Plymouth Housing Group (PHG) as an independent, non-profit organization to develop and operate housing for homeless and very poor people in Seattle. Under the leadership of its current pastor, Tony Robinson, the PHG has since grown into one of the largest providers of low-income housing in downtown Seattle, with more than 660 rental units and 17 retail tenants in 10 buildings, and an annual operating budget of $5.2 million.

The congregation was one of the first to participate in the Walk with Workers project, and in 2001 launched its Living Wage Ministry with a focus on low-wage workers in downtown Seattle. In addition, Plymouth has initiated Plymouth House, sometimes referred to as the House of Healing, where mentally ill individuals are treated in conjunction with Harborview Hospital. Plymouth Congregational's efforts have been the subject of a full-length book, *Seeking to Serve*, by Mildred Tanner Andrews.

Many of the more theologically conservative and evangelical congregations also have developed significant outreach ministries to the homeless in major metropolitan communities of the Pacific Northwest. For example, Seattle's University Presbyterian Church provides ministries for the mentally ill, homeless, teens living on the streets, and those who are in prison.

Lutherans have been particularly active in Oregon, Washington, and Alaska. In 1944 seven Lutheran synods from the Seattle/Tacoma area agreed to organize one Lutheran agency that would offer statewide welfare services. It was incorporated under the name Associated Lutheran Welfare, and later became Lutheran Family and Child Services, which provides programs for children and families in the region. Services have included foster care, adoption services, alcohol and drug abuse treatment, and community education. In 1974 Lutheran Social Services organized the Spokane Sexual Assault Center to provide counseling for those who had been sexually abused.

In recent years, one of the more dynamic faith-based efforts to meet community needs is the Emerald City Outreach Ministries (ECOM) program in Seattle. Organized in 1987 by an African-American, Harvey Drake, Jr., Emerald

City Ministries is modeled on principles of Christian Community Development established by Reverend John Perkins. During the last decade Drake and his staff have engaged thousands of youth and families in the Rainier Valley in programs that include academic mentoring, early childhood education, training in technology, small business development, job preparation, and peer support. ECOM is non-denominational and independent but partners with a number of Christian churches, including Mercer Island Presbyterian Church and Seattle Pacific University, a Free Methodist institution. In Portland, African-Americans churches have worked primarily through the Albina Ministerial Alliance to provide services to the urban poor.

Another widely supported effort among mainline Christians is Habitat for Humanity. In Seattle, Portland, Tacoma, Spokane, Anchorage, and a number of other communities throughout the region, Habitat for Humanity has mobilized Christians and non-Christians to create affordable housing for all people. In Seattle more than 70 homes have been built in the last 15 years, with plans for completing approximately 25 homes a year for the next several years. In Portland a similar number of homes have been constructed. College students frequently support the effort, as do local congregations.

In the mid-1990s, members of Washington's religious community, unions, and other advocates of low-income people joined to form the Washington Living Wage Coalition. Organized by the Washington Association for Churches (WAC), the Washington State Labor Council, and Washington Citizen Action, the coalition includes local Christian, Jewish, and Unitarian congregations, and the Church Council of Greater Seattle. Since forming, the coalition has worked with custodians on the east side and with hospital workers at Northwest Hospital. In 1998 it worked successfully to pass Initiative 688, which raised the state's minimum wage and adjusted it based on inflation. At $7.01 in 2003, Washington's minimum wage was the highest in the country. The federal minimum wage was then $5.15. In 2001 living wage supporters worked to link downtown development rules with quality of life issues for the city's low-wage workers. Ecumenical Ministries of Oregon has been particularly active over the last decade on behalf of migrant workers' right to organize, as well as their right to a living wage. Most recently, an Interfaith Task Force on Homelessness has been formed in Seattle.

Issues including social services for the poor, economic and environmental policies, access to health care, and matters concerning the end of life have all made their way into Oregon, Washington, and Alaska state legislatures since the 1980s. In addition to lobbying by major ecumenical organizations and other church bodies, individual state legislators have brought Christian and Jewish values into public debate surrounding these issues. In Oregon, for example, Avel Gordley, Margaret Carter, and Frank Shields are legislators who have brought their religious perspective to bear on issues of public policy.

Avel Gordley was the first African-American woman ever elected to the Oregon Senate. Prior to her election in 1996 Gordley served three terms in the Oregon House of Representatives after appointment to a vacancy in 1991. Active within the African-American religious community, Gordley advocated services for the mentally ill; she also supported the Minimum Wage Act of 1996, which raised Oregon's minimum wage to the then-highest in the nation.

In 1984 Margaret Carter became the first African-American elected to the Oregon House of Representatives. Active in her church, she served seven sessions in the House, where she helped create a permanent state Head Start program and helped found the Oregon Youth Conservation Corps. In 2000 she was elected to the Oregon State Senate.

State Senator Frank Shields, a Methodist minister, gained notoriety in the 1980s for establishing a homeless shelter in his church in Portland. The shelter became a model for other volunteer-intensive, church-based shelters in Portland and nationwide. Shields served on the House Committee on Human Resources, the Hunger Relief Task Force and the Commission on Black Affairs. In August of 1996 he was appointed to the Public Welfare Review Commission.

Perhaps the clash between liberal and conservative religious expressions is best reflected in Oregon in the work of Ellen Lowe and Lon Mabon. Beginning in the late 1980s Ellen Lowe became assistant director for legislative and governmental affairs of Ecumenical Ministries of Oregon. She actively fought for the Oregon Health Plan and opposed video poker, believing that it preys on the poor and ignorant. She has consistently advocated for increases in the minimum wage and has served as chair of the Oregon Hunger Relief Task Force. Her battle in 1992 against Lon Mabon threw into sharp relief the division between liberal and conservative perspectives on faith commitments and public policy.

Mabon had helped organize the Oregon Citizens Alliance, an attempt to rally conservative Christians in opposition to abortion and gay rights. In 1992 he supported an initiative that would have made homosexuality the equivalent of pedophilia. In a bitter campaign Mabon's initiative was defeated. Several times during the decade Mabon has brought additional measures for public debate; all have failed, but the underlying tension remains.

One area of concern that has consistently divided members of mainline congregations, parishes, and synagogues since the 1980s is American foreign policy. During the Cold War, American churches generally supported the fight against communism and frequently participated in refugee resettlement programs. In the years following the Vietnam War ecumenical councils, dioceses, and local congregations and parishes played major roles in resettling thousands of Southeast Asians who came to the Pacific Northwest.

However, by 1981 resettlement of refugees from Central America became more controversial and more politicized because of the Reagan administration's support for the Contras in Nicaragua and anti-leftist government forces in El Salvador. To reinforce Reagan's foreign policy, the Immigration and Naturalization Service began arresting and deporting thousands of Central American refugees.

In 1981 the Church Council of Greater Seattle asked that congregations offer sanctuary to Central American refugees. Seattle emerged as one of the most active communities in the nation in what became known as the Sanctuary movement. Twelve Christian, Unitarian, and Jewish congregations hid refugees from the INS and provided them food and shelter. In 1985 immigration agents arrested seven Salvadorans accorded sanctuary by the University Baptist Church in Seattle. Ultimately, the United States government chose not to challenge the work of these churches.

Another issue that clearly reflected the growing divide between liberals and conservatives was protest against nuclear weapons. Bill Cate, president of the Church Council of Greater Seattle, proposed that the Council join the protest against the Trident Submarine Base at Bangor, Washington. The Reverend Jonathan Nelson, a Seattle Lutheran pastor, had taken the lead in protesting the Trident as a symbol of the United States' instigation of the arms race. Nelson was jailed several times and, on one occasion, was joined by more than 400 people from the religious community who met him at the jail gate and marched with him to the First United Methodist Church for continued protest.

The Catholic archbishop of Seattle, Raymond Hunthausen, took protest against nuclear weapons and war a step further. In 1982 Hunthausen received national attention when he publicly admitted that he was withholding half of his income tax in protest against government foreign policy and defense spending. Bill and Jan Cate, and the head of the Seattle Council's Peace Task Force staff, Charles Meconis, joined Hunthausen in this act of protest.

That mainline religious leaders and congregants continue to address issues of American foreign and economic policy became clear to an international audience when the World Trade Organization met in Seattle from November 30 to December 3, 1999. Several mainline pastors and their parishioners became involved in events surrounding the meeting. While the sometimes violent protests received most media attention, in different parts of the city, hundreds of religious individuals and congregations found more peaceful ways to be involved in protest. Churches opened their sanctuaries as places of refuge while halls and church classrooms were lined with tables for position papers, posters, videos, and news releases. The First United Methodist Church provided a base of operation for many of the protest activities.

As part of these efforts, nationally known spokespersons, including Jim Wallis, editor of *Sojourners,* appealed to audiences to support Jubilee 2000, a worldwide religious movement to forgive the debts of the poorest nations. A march sponsored by the Washington Association of Churches ended with the crowd linking arms around a building as a symbolic act of breaking the chains of debt, until security forces intervened. Reverend Tony Robinson of Plymouth Congregational Church and 50 of his parishioners marched with several other clergy.

In one of the most remarkable coalitions forged from disparate groups, Christians, Jews, Buddhists, Muslims, the black community, environmentalists, civil rights leaders, students, and organized labor packed a sports stadium Tuesday morning for a rally. Late in the week Reverend Robinson and other church leaders met with the mayor to try to calm unrest. His church became a sanctuary for those felled by gas, while Seattle Advent Christian Church (Disciples of Christ) gave shelter to the homeless displaced by police action.

The pattern of division between liberal and conservative perspectives within the religious community was also evident in the reaction to the run-up to war with Iraq. In the aftermath of the September 11, 2001 attack on the World Trade Center and the Pentagon, mainline religious leaders in the Pacific Northwest provided opportunities for prayer and discussion; they also encouraged compassion and protection for Muslims who might be the target of discriminatory or violent acts.

By fall 2002 mainline religious leaders generally opposed the idea of war against Iraq. Both the Washington Association of Churches and the Ecumenical Ministries of Oregon issued statements expressing "grave and profound concerns" about the prospect of initiating military engagement. The WAC opposed the intent to launch a war as "morally indefensible." The Church Council of Greater Seattle called for a protest in October, and a crowd of between 12,000 and 30,000 marched through Seattle, one of the largest anti-war demonstrations in the country to that date.

Archbishop Alex Brunett of Seattle participated in the National Council of Catholic Bishops' decision to oppose instigation of military action by the president, finding that war with Iraq "would not meet the strict conditions in Catholic teaching for overriding the strong presumption against the use of military force."

In the wake of current revelations of sexual abuse, the Catholic Church is facing its most significant crisis since the Reformation. All dioceses in Oregon, Washington, and Alaska have been affected. It is too soon to predict the long-term impact the sexual abuse scandal will have on the church's public role, or whether the Seattle Archdiocese's policies serving for over a decade as a national model will make any difference in terms of institutional legitimacy. At the very least, it seems likely that leadership at all levels will be scrutinized as never before, and the credibility of clerical authority further undermined. Sexual abuse also is a concern across mainline Protestant denominations.

Nor is there any indication that the culture wars that have divided people and polarized discussion of public issues since the 1960s will abate. The religious dynamics of the region will continue to be affected by the now almost automatic severing of public and private, individual and communal that makes serious discussion of social and economic problems so difficult. Further, given the tendency of mainline churches to adopt strategies more associated with liberal than conservative perspectives, tension with more conservative subcultures of the Christian community will continue. Some church leaders accept and even welcome this. Believing that they are indeed "resident aliens" to use theologian Stanley Hauerwas's term, mainline religious leaders feel called to battle American cultural elements from consumerism and environmental exploitation, to free market capitalism and most American foreign policies.[21] At the same time, they feel equally called to battle what they believe are fundamentalist tendencies within the Christian community, particularly those that translate into intolerance of homosexuals, the homeless, female clergy, and a kind of broad American civic religion.

One possible sign within mainline Protestantism that the liberal/conservative split is moving in a slightly different direction is the Confessing Church movement. Since the mid- to late-1990s, virtually all mainline Protestant expressions in the Pacific Northwest, as in the nation, have seen increasing numbers of pastors and lay persons articulate principles that focus on a recovery of classical Christian orthodoxy. In part the movement seems directed specifically toward a critique of liberal theology and social policies insufficiently grounded in the gospel. In part the movement may be a strategy to stem the loss of membership that continues within mainline denominations. In October 2002 evangelical renewal groups from 12 denominations met in Indianapolis for the purpose of encouraging each other and upholding the historic faith of their denominations.

Participants in the Confessing movement consider it correct to view the movement also as another manifestation of the struggle within the mainline churches between conservative and liberal visions. All participants share a common focus on biblical authority, the divinity of Christ, and opposition to the ordination of gay pastors. At the same time, many participants are hopeful that this movement will reclaim something of the center that they believe has been lost over the last three decades.

Pastors interviewed for this essay are hopeful that by stressing more classically orthodox theological positions the mainline will be able to reach a new generation in the Pacific Northwest, people who are seeking a more complex theology than that available in most non-denominational churches. This movement is growing in the Pacific Northwest, and while its effects will vary across denominations, whatever transpires over the next several years likely will occur in more than one denomination.

Mainline religious organizations and individuals have played an important part in shaping the ethos of the Pacific Northwest. From colleges and universities to social service agencies, lobbying efforts and grassroots movements, mainline Protestants, Catholics, and Reform and Conservative Jews have placed their imprint on the region. Their history in the region suggests a pattern of adaptation grounded in a consistent commitment by these traditions to engage the culture at a number of levels on behalf of the good of the larger community. As long as succeeding generations are educated into the theological roots of that engagement, Catholics, Protestants, and Reform and Conservative Jews are likely to continue to influence the culture of the region.

Endnotes

1. Wade Clark Roof and William McKinney, *American Mainline Religion: Its Changing Shape and Future* (New Brunswick, NJ: Rutgers University Press): 236.

2. Ferenc Szasz proposes that the 1960s end in 1975 in his *Religion in the Modern American West* (Tucson, AZ: University of Arizona Press, 2000): 127.

3. Roof and McKinney, chapters 1 and 2.

4. Robert J. Lowenberg, *Jason Lee and the Methodist Mission, 1834-43* (Seattle: University of Washington Press, 1976); Robert J. Loewenberg, "'Not...by feeble means': Daniel Lee's Plan to Save Oregon," *Oregon Historical Quarterly* LXXIV (1973): 71-78.

5. Julie Roy Jeffrey, *Converting the West: A Biography of Narcissa Whitman* (Norman, OK: University of Oklahoma Press, 1991); Clifford Drury, *Marcus Whitman, M.D., Pioneer and Martyr* (Caldwell, Idaho: Caxton Printers, 1937); Deward Walker, *Conflict & Schism in Nez Percé Acculturation* (Moscow, ID: University of Idaho Press, 1985).

6. Francis Paul Prucha, "Two Roads to Conversion: Protestant and Catholic Missionaries in the Pacific Northwest," *Pacific Northwest Quarterly* 79 (1988): 130-137.

7. Robert L. Whitner, "Grant's Indian Peace Policy on the Yakima Reservation, 1870-82," *Pacific Northwest Quarterly* (October 1959): 135-142; Robert H. Keller, Jr., *American Protestantism and United States Indian Policy, 1869-82* (Lincoln, NE: University of Nebraska Press, 1983); Francis Paul Prucha, *American Indian Policy in Crisis: Christian Reformers and the Indian, 1865-1900* (Norman, OK: University of Oklahoma Press, 1976).

8. Gary Collins, "Oregon's Carlisle: A History of Chemawa Indian School," *Columbia: the Magazine of Northwest History* (Summer, 1998): 6-10; Alexandra Harmon, *Indians in the Making: Ethnic Relations and Indian Identities around Puget Sound* (Berkeley: University of California Press, 1998).

9. Egbert S. Oliver, "Obed Dickinson and the 'Negro Question' in Salem, *Oregon Historical Quarterly* (Spring, 1991): 5-40.

10. Richard White, *"It's Your Misfortune and None of My Own" A New History of the American West* (Norman, OK: University of Oklahoma Press, 1991); Carlos Schwantes, *The Pacific Northwest: An Interpretive History* (Lincoln, NJ: University of Nebraska Press, 1989): 112-206; Murray Morgan, *Skid Road: An Informal Portrait of Seattle* (New York: Viking Press, 1951); E. Kimbark MacColl, *The Shaping of a City: Business and Politics in Portland, Oregon 1885-1915* (Portland, OR: The Georgian Press Company, 1976): 185-260.

11. Ferenc Szasz, *Religion in the Modern American West* (Tuscon, AZ: University of Arizona Press, 2002); Charles LeWarne, *Utopias on Puget Sound 1885-1915* (Seattle: University of Washington Press, 1975).

12. Sandra Haasager, *Organized Womanhood: Cultural Politics in the Pacific Northwest 1840-1920* (Norman, OK: University of Oklahoma Press, 1997); Peggy Pascoe, *Relations of Rescue: The Search for Female Moral Authority in the American West, 1874-1939* (New York: Oxford University Press, 1990).

13. Alfred O. Gray, *Not By Might: The Story of Whitworth College 1890-1965* (Spokane, WA: Whitworth College Press, 1965): 11-22.

14. Schoenberg, *A History of the Catholic Church in the Pacific Northwest*: 239-40, 321; Christine M. Taylor and Patricia O'Connell Killen, *Abundance of Grace: The History of the Archdiocese of Seattle 1850-2000* (Strasbourg, France: Editions du Signe, 2000): 45-49.

15. Dale Soden, *The Reverend Mark Matthews: Activist in the Progressive Era* (Seattle: University of Washington Press, 2001).

16. Steven Lowenstein, *The Jews of Oregon 1850-1950* (Portland, OR: Jewish Historical Society of Portland, 1987): 84.

17. *Abundance of Grace: The History of the Archdiocese of Seattle 1850-2000*, 62.

18. Doug Dye, "For the Sake of Seattle's Soul: The Church Council of Churches, the Nikkei Community, and World War II," *Pacific Northwest Quarterly* (Summer 2002): 127-136.

19. David M. Buerge and Junius Rochester, *Roots and Branches: The Religious Heritage of Washington State* (Seattle: Church Council of Greater Seattle, 1988): 216.

20. Ann LaGrelius Siqueland, *Without a Court Order: The Desegregation of Seattle's Schools* (Seattle: Madrona Publishers, 1981): 62-73, 174, 189.

21. Stanley Hauerwas and William Willimon, *Resident Aliens: Life in a Christian Colony* (Nashville, TN: Abingdon Press, 1989).

CHAPTER THREE

THE CHURCHING OF THE PACIFIC NORTHWEST: THE RISE OF SECTARIAN ENTREPRENEURS

James K. Wellman, Jr.

The Pacific Northwest is known for its beauty, rain, planes, software, coffee and lack of church attendance. One does not expect to hear about crowds of 150,000 in Redmond, Washington enjoying Christian rock and roll and listening to Oregon evangelist Luis Palau. The August 2002 two-day event at Marymore Park was the largest in the park's history. In 1999 the Palau ministries had filled the Portland Waterfront Park with 93,000 people, and in 2000 143,000 attended a two-day festival.

This innovative Christian festival combined a dramatically youth-oriented style with an old-time gospel message and was larger than even the organizers expected. Kevin Palau, in an interview, said they expected around 100,000 for the festival. He said this new form of revival has increased the turnout for revivals substantially. Ordinarily, for a revival at the Rose Garden in Portland, attendance is around 10,000 in a facility that has the capacity for more than 15,000.

The combination of the Christian gospel, hard-core Christian rock music, and skateboard tracks, along with family-oriented entertainment, is a new way of doing Christian revivals that Palau ministries created in 1999. Kevin Palau, Luis Palau's 39-year-old son, who administers the programs, reported that over 700 churches supported the Seattle event, and raised $1.6 million to pay festival expenses. No offerings were taken; Palau attracted corporate sponsors that provided modest financial support and validation of the event as a public and "fun" experience for all.

Kevin Palau said his father wanted "to reach out beyond the normal revival venues to the unchurched and unaffiliated of the Pacific Northwest." Whether or not the event attracted non-Christians Palau could not say, but he did report that the response to the festivals has typically included 3,000 and 4,000 individuals seeking to speak to counselors about their faith and a new commitment to Christ.

This conversation with Palau was part of a larger set of 20 telephone and in-person interviews conducted in June and July 2002 for this chapter. Interviewees included 12 pastors, three associate pastors or lay ministers, and five specialists in theological education. Interviews were semi-directed and lasted an hour. They focused on interviewees' ministries, church demographics, their theological perspectives, and their views on the unique religious needs of the Pacific Northwest and the public voice of religion in the region.

Palau's Christian festivals in the Pacific Northwest illustrate the new churching of the region, the main agents of this movement, and the forms that are used to communicate the message. These forms, and the messages, are at once sectarian and entrepreneurial as well as deeply rooted in the American religious experience. These sectarian entrepreneurial churches are garnering a widening share of those who are affiliated with religious institutions in the Pacific Northwest. They are:

- predominately non-denominational
- skillful at using modern technology and the media
- run by entrepreneurs who use the logic of knowledge-based market economics
- promoters of a traditional and exclusivist evangelical theology.

This chapter explores the phenomenon by asking three interrelated sets of questions:

- One, who are these sectarian entrepreneurs? How do they relate to American Christianity and classical evangelicalism in particular?
- Two, what is the anatomy of these evangelical groups, their worship style, structures of authority, and organizational strategies? And, how do they address the political culture of the region?
- Three, why are they growing? What are the elements of their vitality in a region that is historically religiously heterogeneous and has challenged more mainline Christian denominations throughout the twentieth century?[1]

The religious market of the Pacific Northwest is changing. The mainline Protestant and Catholic churches that struggled to scratch out a place in the wilderness have seen a new breed of entrepreneurs come in who see the lack of church affiliation as an opportunity to expand their religious communities. No doubt this is a part of the upbeat and entrepreneurial ethos that permeates their rhetoric and their motivation. In an open religious field, new products have a greater chance of catching on. To be sure, trends show that evangelical entrepreneurs are making an impact and will become, if they aren't already, the dominant form of institutionally affiliated religion in the region. They can and do attract large numbers to their institutions; their message has appeal and sustains a commitment to their goals. This is not a group that will be satisfied with small congregations that barely survive. They want to expand and create larger circles of influence on the moral, cultural, and eventually the political life of the region. Their political forays in the region have been uneven, but the cultural seeds they are sowing create a much contested vision of the Pacific Northwest in the twenty-first century. In the coming years the Pacific Northwest's legions of unaffiliated but spiritually interested secularists will encounter another legion of entrepreneurial evangelicals. Such a clash suggests a future that will continue to be contested culturally, morally, and politically.

In a culture that has no dominant religious body and in a region in particular that is an open religious market, there is high potential for "subcultures" to expand their niche. Evangelicals have done precisely that not only in this region but also in many regions of the United States. They are an intense subculture that has maintained a tightly woven theological core, while being deeply engaged in reaching out to the unchurched and unaffiliated. Evangelicals are entrepreneurial, aggressive, and willing to adapt creatively in order to attract the unaffiliated. Their ability to exploit communications media is a major factor in their growth.

Indeed, if their theology were the key to growth, the older, classical evangelical churches would be growing, but we know from surveys that the Missouri Synod, Southern Baptists, and Seventh-day Adventists presently are at best maintaining levels of affiliation and in some cases declining. The independent evangelical and Christian Fellowships, on the other hand, are growing at rates much higher than the growth rate of the population in the Pacific Northwest.

This is not to say that theology is unimportant. The pattern of accommodation to the modern media and technology is combined with a distinct theological message that makes truth claims. This is precisely where there is tension with the wider culture of the Pacific Northwest. Their theology demands commitment, proclaims that the faith is absolute and ultimate, and that one must witness and show others the truth of its claims. This combination of sectarianism and the entrepreneurial spirit creates churches that are appealing to the lifestyle, aesthetics, and values of their market, all the while creating converts to a belief system that gives certainty, outlines a specific behavioral code of ethics, and demands reproduction (evangelism). This clarity is appealing in a culture that often lacks precise answers to moral and religious questions. There is no ambiguity in what is taught to sectarian young people. Children and youth are raised in a relatively demanding moral and religious atmosphere, combined with an engaging aesthetic that appeals to them in the form and formula of popular culture. It is a potent and persuasive mix.

The History of Sectarian Entrepreneurs

The term sectarian can be defined using a model of organized religion adapted from the work of William H. Swatos, Jr. and based on the distinction between church and sect. Religious organizations are plotted in a cultural field crisscrossed by two axes. The horizontal axis measures the space between acceptance and rejection of culture, while the vertical axis measures the space between a monopolistic and pluralistic concept of culture. For Christian denominations, the model presents the picture illustrated in Figure 3.1 (page 83).

Churches, particularly in America's pluralistic culture, are generally accepting of culture and more accommodated to, and tolerant of, the pluralistic nature of American religions. Sects, on the other hand, tend to reject what they call the "world" (i.e., secular culture), and are much less accommodated to, or tolerant of, American religious pluralism.

This model is dynamic and changes with the way sects and churches relate to the surrounding culture. Indeed, sectarian entrepreneurs are quite flexible in their use of cultural forms to communicate their message, even when their message is theologically exclusivist. What makes this group remarkable is precisely its ability to function in two worlds simultaneously, the sophisticated world of information technology, and a traditionalist theological world with a message that in the past was wedded to the rejection of modern culture and its many forms of media.[2]

It is this facility with modern media and a willingness to use it to communicate their message that completes the other term, entrepreneur.[3] These sects use technology to create campaigns to communicate the message and to grow their congregations. Thus, the aim of these groups is the churching of the region using the means of modern technology.

So where do these sectarian entrepreneurs come from? To some extent there is nothing new about these groups. They are members of a quintessential American form of religion that developed in the late eighteenth and throughout the nineteenth centuries. Early Baptists supported the disestablishment of religion in America precisely because they wanted the freedom to proclaim their message. The nineteenth century culture of Baptist and Methodist evangelists succeeded in persuading large numbers of Americans to convert and join their churches using the non-traditional means of outdoor preaching and revival meeting.[4]

Mark Noll, the American historian of evangelicalism, outlined a typology of four evangelical beliefs that, despite the diversity within these groups, aptly identifies their theological core:

- They believe in the need for a personal decision to follow Christ (conversion).
- They believe that Christ's death on the cross is the only way to forgiveness and salvation (crucicentrism).

Figure 3.1   Church-Sect Model

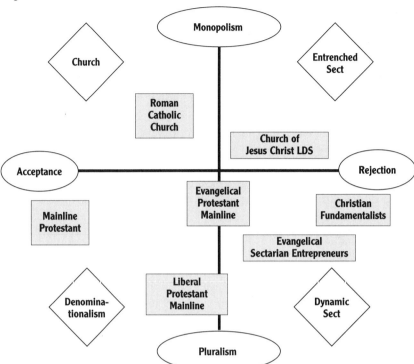

- They believe that the Bible is the unique, infallible, and often called the "inerrant" word of God. Inerrant often signals that scripture is interpreted as literally true (biblicism).
- They believe that the great commission to persuade others to come to Christ is the primary goal of Christian discipleship (evangelism).

This belief system distinguishes sectarian evangelical Christianity from what is called mainline Christianity, whether in its Protestant or Roman Catholic forms. That is, sectarians tend toward a rejection of secular pluralistic norms while mainline Christians possess less sharply articulated theological boundaries and are more tolerant of secular and religious pluralism. While identity for mainline Protestant churches often concerns what they do for the sake of others, evangelical congregations identify themselves more explicitly by their theological doctrines.

In the early twentieth century evangelicals were confronted by what is often called "modernity." Modernity is a social movement of educated elites that advocated an empirical and scientific view of all knowledge. Evangelicals felt the pressure of this movement, aptly illustrated by the Scopes Trial, which put evolutionary theory on trial and became a debate over both what Americans believed about the Bible and what students should be taught.

While fundamentalists won the battle of the trial, they ultimately lost the culture war. The media and public culture turned against conservative Christianity. Christian fundamentalists became more insular and defensive. The trial was the most publicized conflict in the modernist/fundamentalist controversy of the 1920s in the mainline Protestant churches. Fundamentalists rejected the Christian mainline and its accommodation to modern forms of culture.

The fissure between the fundamentalists and the Christian mainline lasted through much of the 1930s and 1940s, but at mid-century a new religious movement appeared called neo-evangelicalism. Billy Graham, its best known representative, grew up in fundamentalist and separatist churches, but in his ministry he accommodated himself to a larger spectrum of American religious culture. In the 1957 revival in New York City Graham partnered with mainline Protestant denominations and insisted that those who were converted at the revivals return to their mainline churches. This was the final straw for many fundamentalists who thought Graham had turned his back on his faith.

Nonetheless, this more accommodating mode of evangelical religion picked up momentum. It spread by way of new cultural institutions such as the Fuller Theological Seminary, which opened in 1947. Fuller Seminary, the dominant center of evangelical graduate education on the West Coast, has had a deep influence on moderate West Coast evangelicalism. This movement uses modern forms of technology and popular culture to attract the "unchurched" to their congregations while maintaining core evangelical beliefs. This form of evangelicalism permeates much of evangelical culture in the Pacific Northwest. But not all of these evangelical congregations are growing.

The older, or classical, forms of evangelicalism such as the Southern Baptists, Missouri-Synod Lutherans, and Seventh-day Adventists, have shown only marginal growth, as discussed in Chapter 1. The evangelical groups that are growing are a form of sectarian *and* entrepreneurial religion, willing to use modern methods to communicate a traditional message. Indeed, the vast majority—if not all—of these conservative evangelical congregations believe in the four principles of evangelicalism: conversion, crucicentrism, biblicism, and evangelism.

Thus, what distinguishes congregations that are growing tends to be skill at communicating their message, combined with a specific entrepreneurial style that appeals to a media-conscious region that expects a dynamic and entertaining presentation. Kevin Palau is emphatic that revivals in the Pacific Northwest are more successful relative to the rest of the nation, both numerically and in enthusiasm. "Revivals are new to this part of the nation. It is a difficult challenge to find churches to sponsor our meetings in the Northeast. In the Pacific

Northwest it was relatively easy."

The kind of congregations Palau refers to include Pentecostal forms of American religion such as the Assemblies of God and the Foursquare Gospel churches. Each of these more than kept pace with state population growth in the last ten years of the twentieth century (Washington, 21 percent, and Oregon, 20 percent). In Washington and Alaska, in particular, the big winners in numerical growth have been independent evangelical churches, increasing by nearly 200 percent, according to the Religious Congregations and Membership Survey 2000 (RCMS). The case of Alaska underlines this phenomenon, as the Southern Baptist denomination lost more than 20 percent of its membership during the last decade of the twentieth century; during this time the Alaskan independent evangelical churches grew by more than 10,000 members. These independent evangelicals include non-denominational churches that run the gamut from local Bible congregations to the new Christian Fellowship churches, Calvary Chapel, Hope Chapel, and Vineyard Christian Fellowship.

Identifying the actual population of entrepreneurial evangelicals is a speculative business. According to the American Religious Identification Survey 2001 (ARIS) approximate 25 percent of the U.S. population identifies with an evangelical group. For the Pacific Northwest ARIS puts the number at approximately 23 percent of the adult population. But identification is not affiliation.

Approximately 12 percent of the Pacific Northwest population are evangelical church members. This gap between identification and membership may be explained, in part, by the broader regional pattern noted in chapter one, namely that many adults in the Pacific Northwest identify with a religious tradition but do not belong to a congregation or religious group. However, especially with regard to newer evangelical groups, another problem arises—undercounting.

The NARA data depend primarily on denominational self-reporting, a methodology that by its nature often misses new and emerging religious groups, in particular Christian Fellowship groups. These are often large, sometimes charismatic, and relatively independent evangelical congregations marked by styles of creative worship that are designed to appeal to young people.[5] These market-savvy churches, common in the West, generally do not report membership numbers.

The Medford-Ashland, Oregon area illustrates the problem with undercounting by studies that rely on congregational or denominational reports. Table 3.1 (page 86) describes the Medford-Ashland area as captured by RCMS.[6] In a metropolitan-area population of 181,269, according to the 2000 United States Census, Catholics top the list in terms of members, according to denominational reporting, with just under 11,000 adherents; Mormons are second with about 6,000; Assemblies of God has about 2,300; and Presbyterian Church (USA) congregations

Table 3.1   Top 15 Religious Groups in Medford-Ashland Metropolitan Area,
             Rank-ordered by Number of Adherents

Rank	Religious Group	Number of Adherents in 2000	% Change from 1990
1.	Catholic Church	10,791	- 22.5
2.	Church of Jesus Christ, LDS	5,963	26.9
3.	Assemblies of God	2,732	-10.1
4.	Presbyterian Church (USA)	2,282	0.4
5.	Church of the Nazarene	1,737	-22.4
6.	Seventh-day Adventist Church	1,631	-11.9
7.	Southern Baptist Convention	1,375	-22.4
8.	United Methodist Church	1,347	-12.9
9.	Evangelical Lutheran Church in America	1,264	7.1
10.	Christian Churches and Churches of Christ	1,216	-17.7
11.	Episcopal Church	1,164	0.0
12.	Lutheran Church—Missouri Synod	1,112	6.4
13.	Conservative Baptist Association of America	1,106	NA
14.	Jewish Estimate	1,000	100.0
15.	Churches of Christ	681	-11.2

Source: "Top 15 Reporting Religious Bodies Medford-Ashland, OR,"Glenmary Research Center,
<http://ext.nazarene.org/rcms/189.html> (16 September 2002).

have about 2,300. No other group has more than 2,000 members in the metro area.

Yet there are at least five large and well known Christian Fellowship groups in the Medford-Ashland area. The largest of these, Applegate Christian Fellowship, draws several thousand attendees each Sunday. It was started by a protégé of Chuck Smith, founder of the Calvary Chapel movement. Since Calvary Chapel did not report nationwide membership data, it was not captured by RCMS. (The NARA data used for the Religion by Region project includes an estimate for Calvary Chapel.)

Taken together, according to the senior pastor at Applegate, the Christian Fellowship congregations in the area claim 10,000 to 20,000 adherents. Independent research suggests a better estimate is between 9,000 and 10,000 adherents.[7] Even with this more conservative estimate, Christian Fellowship groups should be near the top of the RCMS list of the largest religious bodies in the region, second only to Catholics; yet they are not on the list. This is more than likely a region-wide problem.

Even with Christian Fellowship groups undercounted, evangelical member-ship numbers have grown in the Pacific Northwest, as Table 3.2 (page 87), from RCMS 2000, shows.

Table 3.2	Religious Groups in Washington/Oregon/Alaska, Rank-ordered by Numbers of Adherents		
Rank	Religious Group	Number of Adherents in 2000	% Change from 1990
	Washington		
1.	Catholic Church	716,133	35
2.	Evangelicals	582,540	32
3.	Mainline Protestants	391,840	-5
4.	Church of Jesus Christ, LDS	178,000	18
	Oregon		
1.	Evangelicals	402,658	25
2.	Catholic Church	348,239	25
3.	Mainline Protestant	181,508	-9
4.	Church of Jesus Christ, LDS	104,312	16
	Alaska		
1.	Evangelicals	77,723	10
2.	Catholic Church	54,359	20
3.	Mainline Protestant	38,719	-2
4.	Church of Jesus Christ, LDS	19,019	21

Evangelical numbers have grown 32 percent in the last decade in Washington, and evangelicals now account for 38 percent of the church-affiliated population. They constitute the largest single block of religious adherents in Oregon and Alaska. Current evangelical growth rates exceed the general population growth in Washington and Oregon. Further, they are comparable to the levels of increase in the Catholic Church in all three states, increases accounted for primarily by Hispanic Catholic migration.

Conservatively estimated, entrepreneurial evangelicals constitute 5 percent of the adult populations in the Pacific Northwest and are gaining a larger portion of the market share among those affiliated with religious organizations. These are Christians who share the faith in aggressive ways that include modern technological innovations in their weekly worship and in how they interact with the broader public. Indeed, the trends show that of those affiliated with churches, evangelicals are, or will soon become, the largest institutional religious family in the Northwest.

As one evangelical leader, Ray Bakke, says, "Kirkland, Washington is the Bible belt of the Pacific Northwest, with more than ten mega-churches in this Eastside evangelical outpost." Indeed, most pastors of the larger evangelical churches in the Pacific Northwest question the "unchurched" tag given to the region and find it a poor description. While statistically they misread the demographics, what counts for these evangelical entrepreneurs is the growth of their own congregations, and that is certainly happening. Moreover, they tend to interpret the unchurched nature of the region as an opportunity for greater evangelism to the "unreached."

Rick Kingham, senior pastor of the 5,000-member Overlake Church, is particularly emphatic that, based on his experience, the Pacific Northwest is a region with enormous potential for evangelical growth precisely because of the strong interest in spirituality that is present. His experience includes extensive national travel as a top executive for the Promise Keepers before coming to the Overlake congregation in 1998.

The "success" of sectarian evangelical churches in the Pacific Northwest is borne out in my own study of liberal and mainline Protestant congregations on the West Coast. That investigation of urban congregations was unable to find any mainline churches in Oregon or Washington that had attendance of more than 1,000 on a Sunday. Mainline congregations may have a membership on the roles of over 1,000, but their actual attendance is most often a third of those numbers.

Evangelical congregational membership is expressed in the numbers that attend on Sunday morning more than by membership roles. In the 1,250 churches that supported the Palau festivals in Seattle and Portland, 50 congregations had weekly attendance of 1,000 or more, and 19 of those had weekly attendance of 2,000 or more.

For evangelicals, membership is an achieved identity, something that one must choose by one's desire to convert and become a Christian. This identity must be confirmed in a congregation, and discipleship within a small group of fellow Christians is often part of one's obligation as a member. In mainline denominations membership is more often something one may choose to hold more lightly, where personal conversion is either unexpressed or not considered an important part of one's religious identity.

The Anatomy of Sectarian Entrepreneurs

World-Affirming Worship Styles

Sectarian entrepreneurs show greater success at attracting and holding members. What are the social structures that make this possible?

As a family we take an annual summer vacations at a family resort in Eastern Washington. Manson, the town nearest the resort, has one gas station and one store. At the entrance of the resort is a growing Christian congregation, North Shore Bible Church—a quintessential example of a non-denominational and independent congregation, evangelical and entrepreneurial to its core.

In 2002 we attended the early Sunday church service where I expected midsummer attendance to be low. To my surprise, the church was nearly packed, with more than 300 people at the early service, and even more expected at the second. Moreover, the crowd included large numbers of young families—including fathers—an anomaly in most mainline Protestant congregations. The worship, largely a series of songs, was led by five female lay leaders at microphones. Lyrics were projected onto a screen. Featured songs were biblically based and intimate in their use of first person pronouns. Women led the singing with some accompaniment by guitar, drums, and piano. There was no offering, although a missionary came forth to witness to his families' ministry to a tribe in Latin America. He was translating the Christian scriptures into the tribe's language and recruiting indigenous leaders in the area to lead a local congregation. He was in his late 30s and had a wife and children. In his presentation and body language he reflected a sense of joy and expectancy about what he was doing.

The pastor then gave the "teaching" part of a series on "Life Style Breakthroughs." The bulletin contained an outline of the talk with three points on how modern life is stressful and causes individuals to want what they don't need. The pastor gave secular and religious examples of individuals who had overcome these temptations and achieved a more "balanced" lifestyle that would be "pleasing to the Lord."

This was not expository preaching that took a book of the Bible and interpreted it verse by verse, but a topical teaching that used scriptures to make its point. The pastor was lively in his delivery. At one point, for every suggestion from the congregation of their own healthy lifestyle change, he threw out health bars. He illustrated his points with personal examples of his own trials with stress. His preaching exemplified the evangelical tradition, if not always biblically based then at least biblically defended, pointing to personal transformation (the salvation prayer for conversion was printed in the bulletin) and aware of the need to address "the desires of the world" from which one must finally separate. This experience is not unlike what evangelical churches are like across the Northwest, indeed, across much of the country, as described by Mark Shibley and others.

Ron Mehl founded The Beaverton Foursquare Church just outside of Portland, Oregon in the mid-1970s. The church now has Sunday attendance of over 6,000. The Foursquare tradition takes its inspiration from the evangelist Aimee Semple McPherson, who started the fellowship with the dedication of her Angelus Temple in Los Angeles in 1923. In 1990 U.S. membership approached 200,000. There are nearly 1,000,000 worldwide and its growth continues.

Mehl, in his mid-50s, has remarkable energy and entrepreneurial drive considering he has lived half of his life with chronic lymphocytic leukemia, a debilitating disease for most. Mehl has published seven books and has given away nearly $500,000 to charities. He maintains a daily radio show, "Heart of the Word," and often is speaking and preaching up to 10 times in a given week. Mehl views his life-threatening disease as a reminder that life is short, that eternal life is near, and that much must be done while he is still on earth. "Heaven will be a better place, anyway," he said in an interview with Mark O'Keefe of the *Oregonian.* "So there's no anxiety or scheming to protect myself. That's His job."

The church service emphasizes all four aspects of evangelical belief: the need for conversion, belief that the cross of Christ is the only way to heaven, the focus on scripture, and the constant reminder to evangelize. There is a critique of the "world" but certainly not an outright rejection of contemporary forms of communication or the media, whose sophisticated technologies the congregation employs.

There is a specific worship style that has grown up in evangelical American culture that eschews pews, develops contemporary worship styles, and substitutes improvisational prayer for formal liturgy. The service is centered on a teaching pastor who is almost always male and distinguished from a pastor in mainline Protestant denomination in several ways.

While pastors in mainline denominations preside over worship, evangelical pastors are more like emcees hosting celebrations than leaders of a liturgy. Spouses, who are often either a co-minister or the head of the women's ministries, frequently accompany the male head. For instance, in the case of the Bible church I visited, the teaching pastor sat among the congregants until it was his time to teach—moreover, he wore no robe or other sign that would distinguish him outwardly from lay people.

This pattern is one that Brenda Brasher observed in the sectarian evangelical churches she studied in California, where a female "enclave" led by lay women empowers them even as it continues to reinforce female subordination and support male headship in the church as well as in the family.

The general messages from these evangelical churches tend to be centered on themes of empowerment, meant to help individuals and families deal with the stresses of everyday life in American culture. This is a conservative Christianity with a "happy face" that does not frequently advertise its theological exclusiveness. Its savvy marketing approach draws people in with dramatic styles of worship and life affirming messages often centered on successful methods of adjusting to stresses of contemporary American life. To be sure, there is a remarkable harmony between the entrepreneurial logic of this religion and the American corporate marketplace.

Evangelical methods include direct marketing and market segmentation that responds quickly to the needs of consumers based on age, interests, and defined preferences. What distinguishes the Christian entrepreneur is that he or she uses personal success to "witness" to good news that one is both blessed in this life and saved for the next. There is neither an outright rejection nor a critique of the instrumental logic of American marketplace culture. The message is that the Christian religion gives one remarkable rewards if one commits to its exclusivist theology.

The cost, of course, is taking on an ideology that proclaims an absolute truth, a claim that is in tension with the wider pluralistic culture. But it is a cost that many are willing to pay in part because of the promised rewards of eternal life and the epistemological certainty and moral clarity that it brings to the lives of individuals and families. To some extent this remarkable blend of eschatological certainty about the life to come that promises abundance in this world is a form of what many have called the "prosperity gospel."

In interviews with pastors there were few expressions of the over-the-top materialism that one sometimes sees in televangelists. Nonetheless, with the influence of Robert Schuller and his message of "possibility thinking," the idea of prosperity as a result of the gospel is certainly implied. Recently, the executive director of the Louisville Institute, an organization that sponsors a three-month sabbatical program for clergy, related surprise at receiving repetitive applications. Nearly every applicant wanted to attend the "Purpose Driven" church seminars held by Rick Warren, pastor of the Saddlebrook Church in Orange County, California, which regularly has weekly attendance of 15,000, or the Robert Schuller clergy seminars on possibility thinking.

In both cases, the ethos is entrepreneurial and numbers driven, a strategy and form that mimic knowledge-driven economic principles in corporate America. The bottom line is to "produce" successful ministries and "grow" more Christians. Recent scholarship has shown the tight link between the prosperity talk in the church and push to profit in the world.[8]

Changing Denominational Affiliations

Denominations are an American creation, most simply defined as voluntary organizations. Denominations have traditionally formed around groups of like-minded ministers and congregants to create structures of education for clergy, theological accountability, and support for church expansion. But since the middle of the twentieth century, with the dramatic decline of mainline Protestant denominations, America has come into what some have called a "post-denominational" era.

Congregations, particularly those in the sectarian evangelical mode, are independent and only loosely associated with wider organizational bodies, if at all. They tend to be more congregational in church polity than most mainline denominations. This is reinforced by their practice of educating pastors and other church leaders in local congregations. Some evangelicals do remain in traditional denominations such as the Southern Baptists; some in loose associations such as Pentecostal churches, comprising a dozen or more independent groups; and oth-

ers in independent or non-denominational churches that create informal associations. The latter is embodied in Bible-believing fellowships or in newer forms
called Christian Fellowships that include Calvary and Hope Chapel and the
Vineyard Christian Fellowship.

Within Pentecostal denominations, such as the Assemblies of God, denominational affiliations are often de-emphasized. Fulton Buntain, the senior pastor at
the Life Center in Tacoma, Washington since 1965, early in his ministry changed
the name of the church to Life Center. He took the denomination, Assemblies of
God, out of the title to appeal to a greater spectrum of the population. Buntain
explicitly compares this move to what Nordstrom's has done so well: "Listen to
your customers, understand their needs and fill those needs." Asked about the
mainline churches, Buntain says, "They have lost touch with the needs of their
customers."

Over and over these sectarian entrepreneurs unapologetically employ language and mimic strategies for success from the corporate world. Thus, the rejection of the "world" found in early American fundamentalists is missing from these
new evangelical entrepreneurs. Indeed, numerical success was emphasized in
almost every conversation I had with pastors. Buntain, with his 5,000-member
congregation, says his church is literally overflowing with ministries to every kind
of group, emphasizing young adults, youth, and children. The Friday night meeting for the "Junior High" attracts from 400 to 700. Buntain has a TV studio on the
church grounds from which he projects the morning service to more than 100,000
viewers. He runs a school for K-12th grade with more than 1,000 students. This is
a holistic ministry approach that attempts to provide for the needs of body, mind,
and spirit. Again, this approach is not dramatically different from evangelical congregations of the past that achieved a finely honed cultural style and ethos that
accommodated to the values of a middle- and upper-middle-class culture.

Interviews with leaders in Pentecostal, Assemblies of God, Foursquare, independent non-denominational, Vineyard, Baptist, and evangelical churches found
that many knew each other or were familiar with the others' ministries.
Distinctions and emphases among groups are maintained, though overwhelmingly the leaders focused on the core evangelical beliefs of conversion, the cross as
the saving event, the Bible as the authority, and evangelism as a necessary attrib-
ute of the Christian life. Several larger associations are mentioned repeatedly
when speaking with the leadership, including Robert Schuller's Crystal Cathedral
Ministries (the "possibility thinking" Christian pastor from California), World
Vision (a Seattle-based Christian global-service organization), the Willow Creek
Association (an umbrella organization for large evangelical churches across the
nation), and more locally Roy Bakke's Northwest Graduate School of Ministry,
an evangelical organization focusing on ministries to cities that split off from

Overlake Christian Church and moved to a downtown Seattle location.

These associations are loose confederations of like-minded pastors who share core evangelical beliefs and who organize to communicate better methods of translating the message to a wider audience. They are educational forums that in essence bypass mainline denominational offices and educational institutions that, these pastors believe, no longer serve them or support their core evangelical beliefs.

The best illustration of this shift is the case of evangelical ministers within mainline denominations such as the Presbyterian Church USA in the Pacific Northwest. The four largest mainline Presbyterian churches in the Northwest are led by evangelical pastors. All four have much more in common with post-denominational evangelical pastors than with their mainline colleagues. Each speaks directly to the four core beliefs of evangelicals, they attend evangelical associations, and they support the "revitalization" organizations within the Presbyterian denomination.

Ron Kincaid's Sunset Presbyterian Church in Portland is an example of a mainline church that is thoroughly evangelical. It is a fast-growing congregation with ambitions to build more buildings and an explicit mission to evangelize and reach out with the gospel of Jesus Christ. Evangelism is a "core value" of the church, and the first belief is that the Bible is "without error." The church's Web site contains a similar assertion about the cross of Christ as the only way to salvation, and conversion as the way one becomes a Christian.

Mark Toone, senior pastor of Chapel Hill Presbyterian Church in Gig Harbor, Washington, is another rising leader in Presbyterian evangelical renewal circles. In an interview he does not hesitate to suggest the possibility of a "gracious separation" from the Presbyterian Church USA, although he said that he is "committed to the denomination and felt called into it." But, as he says, "There is a growing syncretism in the mainline denominations, and leaders no longer take seriously the soul-saving work of Jesus." For Toone the theological attempts to "dialogue" with other religions in mainline denominations or mainline seminaries are markers of "syncretism," the suggestion that "salvation" can come from somewhere else than the "saving work" of Jesus on the cross. The church Web site and its information reflect all four of the evangelical core beliefs.

Denominational boundaries are exceptionally fluid for sectarian entrepreneurs, whether in newer evangelical denominations (Pentecostal or Holiness) or in mainline Protestant denominations. Theirs is a pragmatic philosophy asserting that what matters is the core message of evangelical belief; the methods for its expression depend on the creativity and ingenuity of those who use modern technology in whatever ways it takes to be persuasive and powerful.

Aggressive Entrepreneurial Styles in Mission

These evangelical churches are entrepreneurial and mission minded, with a strong emphasis on technology and media that serves to communicate the message. Joe Fuiten, Senior Pastor at Cedar Park Assembly of God Church, exemplifies the entrepreneurial spirit with ministries that span three campuses—one for the church, a second for a counseling center, and a third for a 1,200-student school.

A protégé of Buntain, Fuiten began his ministry with fewer than 100 congregants. He explains that, "The Assembly of God system is built for entrepreneurs and encourages local control and individuals who can build large ministries by the power of their leadership." The church polity is congregational; thus there is no direct bureaucratic or institutional control. Assemblies of God is the second largest Pentecostal association in the United States, numbering around three million.

Fuiten's hope is to create the "economics of the monastery," such that the school and counseling hubs would come to fund the church and its evangelical mission to the world. Presently, his school and counseling agency bring in $6 million and the church offering $3 million per year. Fuiten appears to relish the assumption of "risk" for his entrepreneurial enterprise, purchasing more land and expecting growth rather than cautiously waiting for support from a larger bureaucratic structure.

Fuiten's forceful and confrontational personality comes out in his drive to expand his ministries and in his disdain for mainline and liberal Protestant Christianity. He calls the latter a "Christian cult, a different kind of religion that is no longer in continuity with historical biblical faith. It is fundamentally apostate." As Fuiten says, "Every time the Methodists ordain a homosexual we gain more members."

To be sure, Fuiten's theological analysis of mainline Protestant denominations in the Pacific Northwest may not be accurate, but his estimation of their lack of numerical growth is. More to the point, the majority of evangelical leaders interviewed either pay no attention to the mainline or have some disdain for its lack of focus on the evangelical core. However, there is no evidence at this point to show that evangelicals are growing by picking up congregants directly from mainline churches. But clearly, differences in stances on social issues (the labeling of homosexuality and abortion as sin) do enable sectarian evangelicals to distinguish themselves from the mainline and to show how they "reject" the "world" as opposed to how the mainline has "accommodated" itself to the world. For growing numbers of people this stance is attractive.

These evangelical churches' independence allows them to be structured for action. They are intensively mission-minded and focused on enabling lay people to pursue their core interest in evangelizing and converting others to Christianity.

Lynn Ellis, the 36-year-old mission pastor at Overlake Christian Church, explained that the focus of her efforts is on "mobilizing people from the church looking to do short- and long-term mission trips locally and internationally."

Due to the restrictions on evangelism in many foreign countries, the new thinking in evangelical circles is to go to the country and do what they call "prayer walks" through the city streets. They wait for an opportunity to make contact with an indigenous person and evangelize him or her. The various mission teams adopt "unreached cities" with long-term relationships, sending prayer teams and supporting indigenous converts in the cities who go on to create their own ministries. As Ellis said, "We did this with one young man, and a year later we met him again and his five friends were converted and they had started a small, underground church."

As Rodney Stark's analysis in *The Rise of Christianity* has shown, the process of conversion happens precisely through these kinds of small, intimate circles and connections. Evangelicals are aware of the methods and they serve their overall evangelical goal. In interviews there is little explicit hesitation about restrictions on sharing the gospel in foreign lands. No one said that laws should be broken; nonetheless, the overwhelming emphasis is on evangelism, whether through implicit or explicit means.

Overlake Christian Church, like many of the churches studied, sent out more than 30 international and local missions in 2002. These missions featured evangelism as well as direct service through World Vision and Habitat for Humanity. Kingham, Overlake's pastor, strongly urges an international focus for families, encouraging them to vacation one year in a foreign country and do a mission trip the next year to that country. This international focus is integrated with local ministry, reflected in their 11 on-site international fellowships, including immigrant groups from Iran, China, Japan, Armenia, and Latin America.

Kingham wants these groups "enfolded" in the overall ministry of the church, nurtured by their own ministers. The Eastside of Seattle is becoming the "United Nations" of the Pacific Northwest, with the arrival of a diverse number of immigrant groups due to the growth of Microsoft and the availability of affordable housing. Evangelical churches have been aggressive and entrepreneurial in reaching out to the newcomers in these growing ethnic enclaves.

From my research evangelical entrepreneurs aggressively seek to create a congregation with real ethnic diversity. The long-term success of these efforts remains a question. Indeed, Michael Emerson and Christian Smith, in their analysis of race and evangelical culture, *Divided by Faith: Evangelical Religion and the Problem of Race in America,* assert that despite the strong rhetoric to reduce racial tensions in American culture and indeed internationally, "evangelicalism likely does more to perpetuate the racialized society than to reduce it." The chief problems are that evangelicals often overlook the complexity of social problems in their strong and passionate drive to evangelize others and so ignore the unintended consequences of actions that may exacerbate problems rather than solve them.

In particular, for Emerson and Smith, the unreflective way in which evangelicals take up the rhetoric of entrepreneurial capitalism and harness it for use in religious matters is a problem. They conclude that this has led to greater social inequality because the message is inherently conservative, tending to create social inequality and segregation rather than the reverse. It remains to be seen whether a similar pattern is occurring in the Pacific Northwest.

Education, Social Status, and the Postindustrial Culture

The Pentecostal tradition is known for attracting individuals from a lower socio-economic level. This tag is not welcome in the churches I studied. To be sure, in almost every interview pastors promoted their educational ministries again and again, particularly those from Pentecostal fellowships. Academic achievement and educational status are clear priorities for these ministries.

Fulton Buntain from Life Center told me about one of his graduates who had gone on to get his Ph. D. at Yale and several of his senior-high graduates who have been National Merit Scholar semi-finalists. Joe Fuiten, in his 20 years at Cedar Park Assembly of God, counts a handful of National Merit Scholar semi-finalist graduates from his academy. Education is integral to the mission and goals of many of these pastors who say explicitly, "The most important ministry we have is our school. To pass on the faith to our young people is the focus of our ministry."

As Peter Berger has noted, the conservative Protestant movement may be interpreted as a backlash against the postindustrial new class of knowledge workers. This new class is a product of higher education with strong tendencies toward secularity and materialism. From the perspective of this research, evangelicals want to beat the new class at their own game, seeking educational status to gain the cultural capital to compete with secular new-class liberals. Of course, their social agenda is a quite different agenda and, as we will see, faces an uphill battle in the liberal democratic political landscape of the Pacific Northwest.

This evangelical agenda is not the insular vision of traditional U.S. fundamentalism; indeed, when asked, one Pentecostal pastor responded of his own relation to the American fundamentalist movement with strong words: "When people go around asking for fundamentalists it is as if they were looking for niggers." He objects to the fundamentalist label and feels it is a pejorative and prejudicial way to dismiss conservative Christians. To him it is absurd to mention evangelicals and fundamentalists in the same breath. It appears that for many entrepreneurial evangelicals, their rhetoric is pitched to gain a mainline acceptance for their agenda. By distancing their movement from fundamentalism they "mainstream" the movement and create greater cultural plausibility for it against the backdrop of a relatively secular Pacific Northwest.

Donald Miller, in *Reinventing American Protestantism*, calls evangelical entrepreneurial congregations "new paradigm churches," in essence post-denominational congregations that use contemporary forms of worship and reflect a similar pattern of engagement with and in secular culture. The leaders of these congregations have common entrepreneurial capabilities, and Miller observes that on average the pastors he studied were around 40 years old and aggressively evangelical in their faith. They lacked academic credentials, with few having gone beyond a college education. But as Miller notes, this deficit may not be a hindrance but an advantage. Since leaders had not gone through the seminary bureaucratic structures, nothing had diminished their strong ambitions to construct and produce large evangelical ministries.

Nonetheless, in this obsession with growth and large ministries there is little critical analysis of the logic of market capitalism and its instrumentalism that these churches so closely mirror. The methods for evangelical growth were taken directly from corporate strategies, with Rick Warren's 1995 book entitled *The Purpose Driven Church* as a kind of "bible" for this entrepreneurial movement. Numerical growth becomes the overarching scheme, and converts can be seen as means to the end of having a large and "successful" ministry.

The pastors interviewed in the Pacific Northwest exhibited a similar kind of relentless entrepreneurial energy. However, they have better educational credentials. All of them have advanced degrees (generally from conservative Christian seminaries). Moreover, their knowledge of information technologies is extensive.

For example, Gary Gulbranson, senior pastor of Westminster Chapel in Bellevue, Washington, typifies the cultural and educational background of the pastors interviewed. He grew up in South Dakota, attended Moody Bible Institute, did further work at the Denver Conservative Baptist Seminary, and finished his academic work with a doctorate in educational guidance at Loyola University in Chicago. He is a trustee on the Denver Seminary Board, is involved in the Northwest Graduate School of Ministry, and is in a small prayer group with Philip Easton, president of Seattle Pacific University, a small private Seattle Christian university sponsored by the Free Methodist denomination.

This emphasis on educational achievement is mirrored in the educational background of many in the Pacific Northwest. More than half of Washington and Oregon residents have at least some college education. Every year Overlake Christian Church hires Percept, a survey data company for religious organizations, to give it up-to-date demographics on its market. Three preference factors on the Eastside skew higher than the national average: 10 percent higher on the need for recreation, 25 percent higher on the preference for contemporary worship, and 29 percent higher on the desire for intellectual enrichment. Once again, evangelicals are aware of the need to appeal to the intellects of parishioners and are doing well in markets where that need is expressed.

Karl Neils, a 33-year-old associate pastor at Seattle Vineyard, exemplifies the educational attainment of these Northwest clergy leaders. He is a Northwest native and a graduate of Stanford University in international development. He has traveled widely and lived in Southern Africa intermittently for several years. In the middle of his undergraduate education he underwent a crisis of faith, dropped out of school for a time, traveled, and went through a conversion process via a charismatic experience of Christian faith. He finished his degree and eventually became involved in the Vineyard movement.

The Vineyard movement is relatively new. The first Vineyard church was started by Kenn Gulliksen in 1974. John Wimber, a former musician and arranger for the Righteous Brothers, took over in 1982. Before his death in 1998 he nurtured the movement until it had more than 400 churches in the United States and another 200 overseas. Wimber often said the Vineyard emphasizes "the importance of being natural in the supernatural." The Vineyard movement is a variation of charismatic evangelical churches, with emphases on healing ministries, gifts of knowledge, and prophetic moments. This means that Vineyard leaders and lay people claim to attain supernatural gifts of knowledge about the healing of others or the gifts that others might have in ministry.

Like most of the other evangelical churches I saw and studied, contemporary music, improvisational prayer, and a Bible teacher shape the services. As in other evangelical churches, outreach is a priority. Associate pastors are "ordained" not so much to a church, but to a ministry that will eventually lead them to start their own congregations.

Theologically, the Vineyard's message appeals to a post-modern culture in which individuals experience a lack of absolutes and a need for meaning and truth. Vineyard's truth is aptly described by Donald Miller as "post-modern primitivism," a concrete theological epistemology that appeals to the search for meaning and roots within a culture that they think lacks both. Thus, theological clarity, visceral experiences of God, and precise moral imperatives provide the antidote to the epistemological and moral relativism of the culture.

Ambivalence over Gender

There is little of this same clarity when it comes to gender roles within the evangelical community. The majority of evangelical pastors interviewed were either against the ordination of women or ambivalent about the issue. In mainline evangelical congregations the story is more complex. Mainline evangelical

Protestants have ordained women to ministry for much of the last half century. Nonetheless, tensions over the issue percolate right below the surface.

Some of this ambivalence is seen in slow progress that women have made in attaining ordained positions even in churches that officially support their ordination. There has been only one female associate pastor out of a dozen or so associates at the nearly 5,000-member University Presbyterian Church—though the church recently called two more associate women pastors. There are no women associates at the Chapel Hill Presbyterian Church (there are women as directors of various ministries), and there are two women associates out of nine at the Sunset Presbyterian Church in Portland.

Kay Browleit, associate pastor of children's ministries at University Presbyterian Church in Seattle, was ordained in 1998. As she said, "The pastoral staff supports me 100 percent as a woman pastor and Earl Palmer is my number-one cheerleader." This may be the case, but there is resistance to women in ministry that often comes from lay people and from the general evangelical community. That resistance is sufficiently strong that Browleit reported organizing a meeting with a group of women to discuss the biblical evidence for women's ordination.

The tensions over women in ministry are more hotly debated in non-main-line evangelical congregations. It was the one issue for which interviewees asked not to be acknowledged. Many of the independent and non-denominational churches studied have women in ministry, primarily in areas of women's programs, counseling, and the assimilation of new members. Quite often, women in these congregations are "licensed" to minister but are not ordained, so unlike their male colleagues this licensure is not portable to other positions. Thus, with a change in church locations, licensing must be renewed for each new position. As one female minister said, "I am a holy irritation to the church. I believe God calls both females and males equally to ministries of preaching, teaching and healing. I have a very high view of Scripture and I believe that Scripture shows that God has gifted men and women in the same way."

Even when female ministers experience the "call" to preach, preaching on Sunday mornings is either not sought because of the theological axiom of male authority, or simply is not available because the church has determined that women should not have this kind of teaching authority over men. The teaching/preaching role on Sunday morning is the domain of male leadership.

One of the exceptional areas where women tend to have a greater role is in foreign missions, where women often find greater opportunities to take primary roles in church leadership. As one woman pastor said, "Foreign missions are a wonderful training ground for women in ministry that prove them as gifted ministers of the gospel." Even for women who serve in evangelical congregations, the importance of women in ministry is not about political equality or their rights as feminists—it is about a biblically sanctioned and felt vocation, expressed in the statement that women and men are called by God to proclaim the gospel.

The debate over women in ministry is most interesting in Pentecostal congregations, some of which have a tradition of women in leadership as evangelists and as leaders of the movement. One of Joe Fuiten's books, *Revenge of Ephesus*, is a self-published, comparative study of the parallels between Ephesus and Seattle. While it presents a harsh critique of the pagan culture of the Pacific Northwest region that includes a condemnation of goddess worship, it also forcefully defends women in ministry. For Fuiten, the early church clearly had women in leadership in every form of ministry and the "decline" of women in ministry, both in the Catholic tradition and in contemporary Pentecostalism, is a sign of corruption in the interpretation of the New Testament. While Fuiten condemns any form or influence of feminist ideology within the church, he expresses support for women in ministry—as senior pastors, evangelists, and missionaries with equal vehemence. Two of Fuiten's ten associate ministers are women. Nevertheless, Fuiten was the only evangelical pastor interviewed who declared himself so clearly in support of the ordination of women.

It is baffling to many outside these churches why women remain within these evangelical congregations. Brenda Brasher's study, *Godly Women*, asked this very question. She found four reasons why women remain:

- They find strength in a coherent worldview in the midst of a transitory culture.
- There is certainty and consistency that is not found elsewhere.
- There is accountability within these cultures that encourages men to stay with marriages and support families during years of some vulnerability for women as they raise their families.
- For those women who do have gifts of leadership there are spaces to exercise these gifts within female enclaves, which not only give them room to exercise their gifts but also provide real support and nurture for the women who participate in these tight knit groups.

Contesting Moral and Political Boundaries

The political activity of conservative Christians was intense in the last two decades of the twentieth century. As William Lunch has outlined, politics in Washington and Oregon are shaped by three positions on moralism, "the new moralists, the old moralists, and libertarians."

Old moralists represent a Republican party with a Christian base that is conservative economically and socially; they tend to be aligned with the older, natural resource-based economy (agriculture and lumber) that has traditionally dominated the region. The old moralists defend a traditional worldview, while new moralists (exemplifying the new knowledge economy of technology) advocate less social control while maintaining a moderately conservative economic approach to taxation and government. The libertarians represent the independent streak in Washington politics, with its generally liberal take on social control and advocacy to get government out of people's lives.

The National Surveys of Religion and Politics, conducted in 1992, 1996, and 200 by the Bliss Institute at the University of Akron, provide a sense of the ideological particularity of "high commitment evangelicals" in the Pacific Northwest. Small regional sample size makes these surveys more suggestive than representative of religious populations, but they do point to regional trends. In the Pacific Northwest high-commitment evangelicals (identified in polling as "a part of the Christian Right") express more extreme ideological loyalty than those in the nation in general and more even than those in the South, an area of the country known for its larger population of conservative evangelicals.

Highly committed Northwest evangelicals voted for George W. Bush (84 percent, nation 76 percent); they are pro-life (78 percent, nation 74); they advocate less welfare spending (41 percent, nation 38 percent); and they oppose help to minorities (60 percent, nation 47 percent). They are, however, not as high as national evangelicals in anti-gay rights (43 percent, nation 51 percent). While they are quite similar to the nation in their advocacy against environmental protections in general (35 percent, nation 34 percent), they are far less likely to support specific environmental protection than evangelicals nationally (28.6 percent, nation 42.9 percent). This suggests that, in general, Christians who identify as the "Christian Right" in the Pacific Northwest tend to be extreme in their ideological perspectives.

But does this translate into a generalization about entrepreneurial evangelicals in the region? The evangelical pastors interviewed did not reflect this ideological extremism. They seemed moderate in their politics, disinclined to political activism, and hesitant to take risks by advocating for specific moral and political agendas. Moreover, the Bliss data shows that "low-commitment evangelicals," those who do not attend church frequently, were similar to "highly committed Protestant mainline" types—reflecting a moderately conservative political and cultural agenda. Thus, this ideological extremism did not describe all evangelicals.

What I think the Bliss data tells us is that there is a base of political activism in that the Pacific Northwest, composed of highly committed evangelicals who identify with the Christian Right politically and culturally. This agenda supports limited governmental intervention (crime, military defense, and certain traditional moral values) but rejects welfare spending, affirmative action, and environmental protections. With the rise of entrepreneurial evangelicals one would expect a moderation of these political perspectives and a strengthening of the political advantage of these groups. With this moderation, one might also expect their forays into the political field to be episodic and motivated primarily by issues of personal morality.

While the conservative Christian community's lack of a central organizing denominational structure is a strength when it comes to local adaptation to the needs of particular communities, it hampers consensus building in efforts to organize for common goals. Kevin Palau said that his organization "takes no stands on political issues. Some may find this a problem, but it is only on the basis of proclaiming the gospel that we can gather this many diverse groups together in one place." The sheer diversity of this community enables it to appeal to multiple interest groups but undercuts its ability to frame common political agendas.

To be sure, as one would expect, in a region that has a history of political liberalism the political fate of conservative Christians in the region has been mixed. William Lunch summarizes the history in a book chapter he titles, "The Christian Right in the Northwest: Two Decades of Frustration in Oregon and Washington."

The Christian Right has attempted through elective politics to reverse the cultural, political and legal trends of the Pacific Northwest. It has challenged assisted suicide in Oregon, attempted to overthrow anti-discrimination ordinances on behalf of gays and lesbians, opposed affirmative action, pushed initiatives to make abortion illegal, and generally opposed protectionist environmental policies.

While Lunch recites the group's losses in the region's political landscape, he also outlines its gains. Christian conservatives have gained power within the Republican Party in the region and helped elect legislators like Linda Smith and Randy Tate. Other Christian Right candidates have made strong showings (gaining more than 40 percent of the votes in statewide elections), and initiatives often have lost by narrow margins, against assisted suicide (49 percent), against the teaching of homosexuality (48 percent). In Washington the state legislature passed a bill to ban gay and lesbian marriages over the veto of Governor Gary Locke. Conservative Christians have experienced frustration but they clearly are a growing presence and are having an effect on the political process.

To be sure, the old moralists are alive and well in many pastors. In more than half of the interviews the subject of political alliances was raised and affiliations were given, all Republican. Rich Kingham spoke about his position on the Republican Central Committee in Colorado before coming to the Overlake Christian Church. He said he continued to be active politically and was loyal to the Republican Party, though he said he "supported men of high moral and religious character in either political party." Nonetheless, sectarian entrepreneurs tend to be less hard edged in their politics than the ardent fundamentalist Christian Right, which Lunch outlines in his history. Entrepreneurial evangelicals are much more moderate and less apt to confront the political status quo.

Gary Gulbranson is a quintessential example of this moderation—clearly conservative on social issues but unwilling to advocate an explicit political agenda. He has led the Westminster Chapel since the mid-1990s. Twenty-seven hundred people attend Sunday services at the suburban congregation in Bellevue, Washington. Gulbranson is in his mid-50s. He embodies the evangelical entrepreneurial spirit in his commitment to theological education, foreign mission evangelism, and an aggressive focus on the moral boundaries of his community. In an interview, Gulbranson demurred from any political affiliation, saying he couldn't label himself. "The Christian faith is apolitical," he asserts. His task is to "challenge people to think and to vote their Christ-centered conscience." This moderation may be a function of the more liberal politics of the west side of the Cascades, though Gulbranson speaks of his own moral activism that certainly mirrors the moral agenda of the old moralists.

One Sunday morning in the late 1990s Gulbranson noticed that a strip club had just opened less than a mile from his sanctuary. "I brought this fact to the attention of my congregation, challenging them to stand up for their faith and their values in the community." The congregation responded at the next City Council meeting, turning out 300 members to complain; church members began to picket the club; and members of the congregation lobbied for ordinances that made it difficult for strip clubs to operate within the city limits. In slightly little less than four months the handful of strip clubs in Bellevue were out of business. When pushed for any further political advocacy Gulbranson spoke mostly about his ministry to business people in Bellevue and the strong emphasis on personal and professional morality, particularly in light of the recent corporate ethical lapses.

Sectarian entrepreneurs in the Pacific Northwest, particularly in the Western parts of Washington and Oregon, know that they are a long way from winning on a statewide basis. They have seen their churches grow dramatically and believe their political and cultural ability to shape policy will grow as well. Kingham, in fact, sees himself as a part of the Seattle political community and speaks of a close relationship with King County Executive Ron Sims.

The growing strength of sectarian entrepreneurs portends a continuing political battle over cultural, moral, and political boundaries, which are created symbolically as well as socially around questions of what is true and around issues of moral and cultural purity. Based on the present study, evangelical groups are positioned to continue to grow and with that growth affect the politics of the

Pacific Northwest. The new moralist and libertarian base of the Pacific Northwest will be met by a conservative Christian minority of old moralists advocating for stronger social controls and moral boundaries. This contestation certainly mirrors the recent history of West around religion and morality as outlined by Szasz in *Religion in the Modern American West*.

To be sure, evangelicals are not satisfied with creating religious enclaves, cut off from the mainstream culture. It is the nature of evangelical-entrepreneurial faith to be engaged and in tension with culture, striving to transform the culture in ways that are aligned with more conservative Christian values. This engagement is expressed in large part by evangelical-entrepreneurial ability to adapt and use the cultural tools of the contemporary scene to grow and flourish in a region not known for its strong church affiliations.

Endnotes

1. See Ferenc Morton Szasz, *Religion in the Modern American West* (Tucson, AZ: The University of Arizona Press, 2000).

2. See George M. Marsden, *Fundamentalism and American Culture: The Shaping of Twentieth-Century Evangelicalism* (New York: Oxford University Press, 1980).

3. See Donald E. Miller, *Reinventing American Protestantism: Christianity in the New Millennium* (Berkeley, CA: University of California Press, 1997).

4. For this background see Nathan O. Hatch, *The Democratization of American Christianity* (New Haven, CT: Yale University Press, 1989); Mark A. Noll, *The Old Religion in a New World: The History of North American Christianity* (Grand Rapids, MI: William B. Eerdmans Publishing Company, 2002).

5. See Mark A. Shibley, "The Californication of American Evangelicalism: Deviance and Cultural Accommodation in a Midwest Vineyard Congregation," *Religion and the Social Order* 5 (1995): 57-78; also Miller, 1997.

6. Religious Congregations and Membership 2000, "Top 15 Reporting Religious Bodies, Medford-Ashland, OR," October 2002 *http://ext.nazarene. org/rcms/189.html* 21 November 2002.

7. Students in Mark Shibley's sociology of religion seminar at Southern Oregon University have done fieldwork in a number of these congregations. Kellee Boyer contacted the eight largest Christian Fellowship groups in the Medford-Ashland metropolitan area. They report a total average weekly participation of between 10,225 and 10,600, though none of the congregations

keep ofifcial records. Applegate alone estimates weekly participation at about 6,000. ACF's main sanctuary seats 1,200 and they have four services every Sunday, but our fieldwork suggests that their worship attendance is typically only 70-80% of capacity. Including the many children in Sunday school programs, Applegate more likely draws about 4,500 people each weekend. Even so, we estimate that between 9,000 and 10,000 Medford-Ashland residents participate regularly in Christian Fellowship congregations. These numbers are from research conducted by Mark A. Shibley and Kellee Boyer, fieldwork and telephone interviews with congregational staff, Ashland, Oregon, November 2002.

8. Michael Budde and Robert Brimlow, *Christianity Incorporated: How Big Business is Buying the Church* (Grand Rapids, MI: Brazos Press, 2000).

ary, scholarly, artistic, and "ritual" activity, she argues, merely extends the "Pioneer Spirit" of stealing territory into the cultural and religious lives of native peoples. Similarly, Linda Barnes points out the sometimes problematic ways in which U.S. practitioners of "Traditional Chinese Medicine" exchange Chinese religious terms for Western psychological language, producing a complex synthesis of spirituality, psychotherapy, and medicine.[1]

Is this transformation of religious ideas, practices, and institutions in the Pacific Northwest a continuation of an expansive openness and ecumenism characteristic of the region? Or is it simply cultural imperialism from a pioneer heritage that sustains the "marketplace" for spiritual consumers? While these questions have no easy answers, they remain central for any description of Pacific Rim religions in the region.

Interest among members of the dominant culture in Pacific Rim religions raises the question of the presence of Native Americans and Asian Americans in the Pacific Northwest. In suburbs all around Puget Sound predominantly white mainline churches often display signs in Korean, Japanese, Chinese, Tagalog, Vietnamese, or other Asian languages, indicating a parallel congregation or shared space with Asian Christian congregations. Buddhist temples in old churches, as well as those built in various Asian architectural styles, are difficult to miss along major thoroughfares in Northwestern cities, and larger structures exist in the suburbs. These are the signs of Asian presence outside traditional ethnic enclaves like Seattle's International District. To live in the Northwest is to inhabit a space in which multiple traditions of the Pacific Rim spirituality coexist, not only in ethnic enclaves, but also among the "secular but spiritual" portion of the majority population.

The array of Pacific Rim religions in the region today arrived in the two ways traditions move across geographical boundaries: through migration or mission. The ancient in-migration of Native Americans established the basis for a variety of "indigenous" forms of spirituality in contemporary communities. Religious communities of Asian origin in the Pacific Northwest arose through both forms of movement.

Immigrants and refugees brought their religious traditions along with other elements of their culture and belongings. Missionaries brought new ideas and stimulated the growth of new identities in people who may have grown up with or without another religious affiliation. The combination of migrant and missionary traditions has produced a dynamic and complex religious environment in this region that often defies explanation. The authors of a new book on Asian American religion explain that:

> Asian and Pacific American individuals, families, and communities
> have been the loci of extraordinary cultural blending and transforma-

tion. They have been the agents through whom Asian religions such as Hinduism, Sikhism, Confucianism, and Buddhism have come to the United States, and in them those religious traditions have been altered to meet new challenges and circumstances. They have also, in large numbers, adopted Western religions such as Protestant and Catholic Christianity, and in them those religious traditions have taken on new forms and subtle new content. In addition, the spiritual world of APIs [Asian and Pacific Islanders] often exists beyond institutional bounds and includes a host of practices, personal beliefs, and worldviews that have yet to be fully recognized.[2]

This chapter outlines a few major facets of Pacific Rim religion found in the Pacific Northwest, as well as the demographic challenges to documenting Pacific Rim religious practice. The major issue is how one counts adherents in religious traditions where religious life is not organized like that of American Christians and Jews. It also reviews briefly the historical immigration patterns of various Asian-Pacific American communities and asks how the history of immigration (or seeking refuge and asylum) and settlement affects both religious identity and organization. Third, it describes some specific patterns of change in immigrant religious communities. How, for instance, do communities adapt religious practices to accommodate common U.S. notions of work-week, dress, and institutional organization?

Finally, the chapter suggests ways that Pacific Rim religious communities interact with the culture of the region to establish a presence in public life. In a region where being "unchurched" is normative, is it easier or harder for immigrant groups to establish and maintain religious identity and public presence? How do external social and political forces influence the decision to "go public" with a minority religious identity?

Demographic Challenges

Census data reveal the percentage of the entire regional population who trace their origins to the Pacific Rim. Native Americans constitute the largest single group of Pacific Rim people in the Northwest. According to the 2000 Census data American Indians and Alaska natives make up 15.6 percent of Alaska's population, 1.6 percent of Washington's population, and 1.3 percent of Oregon's population. These percentages are higher when including those who identify with more than one ethnic heritage.

Filipinos comprise the second largest Pacific Rim group in Alaska (2 percent), with Hawaiians and other Pacific Islanders (0.9 percent) and Koreans (0.7 percent) and small populations of other Asian American communities filling out the total picture of an Alaskan population that is approximately 21 percent of

Pacific Rim heritage.

In Oregon the Chinese and Vietnamese (both 0.6 percent) are the largest Asian groups, with Korean and Japanese (both 0.4 percent) and Filipino (0.3 percent) communities adding to a 4.5 percent of the population that is of Pacific Rim heritage.

In Washington Filipinos are the largest Asian-American group (1.1 percent), with Chinese (1 percent), Korean (0.8 percent), Vietnamese (0.8 percent), and Japanese (0.6 percent) the other major constituents in a Pacific Rim heritage group that makes up 7.5 percent of the total population. The Washington State Council on Asian Pacific American Affairs (CAPAA) reports that "Asian Pacific Americans (APAs) make up the fastest growing racial group in the state, with a gain of 78 percent since 1990." Only Hispanics have a higher rate of increase. CAPAA has published a number of detailed demographic essays in its quarterly journal, which have been used extensively in creating this demographic profile.

Both Native Americans and APAs have settled primarily in the populous western counties of Oregon and Washington. The rapidly growing APA presence and sometimes divergent interests of wealthier immigrants and poorer refugees present challenges to developing religious communities that serve the needs of these populations.

Population statistics, however, reveal little about the religious affiliation of these Asian Pacific Americans. Part of the difficulty in gauging the cultural significance of Asian religious traditions in the Pacific Northwest is that scholars are puzzled about how to count the people practicing them. The quantitative measures used by sociologists of American religion to track church membership often do not fit the patterns of practice and institution-building common in Asian traditions. As one scholar notes:

> Buddhists, Hindus, and Zoroastrians do not regularly attend communal worship services in their home countries; they do so for special festivals and they go as individuals and families to pray for personal needs and thanksgiving. In the {United States} as well as their home countries, virtually all practitioners of these three faiths have home altars at which many pray daily. They typically contain food, flowers, religious statutes, pictures, incense, candles, prayer beads, and/or other objects of worship. ... Families engage in special rituals at their shrines on the anniversary of a family member's death, as well as for births and on holidays. Among Hindus, regionally specific deity statues adorn their shrines and the rituals and holidays they celebrate there vary according to their ethnic/regional background.[3]

To add to the difficulty many Asian immigrants are Christians. Their emigration patterns to the West give them a presence significantly out of proportion to their numbers in their home country. Most national survey data, including the American Religious Identification Survey (ARIS) and the North American Religion Atlas (NARA), do not distinguish Asian American Christians from "other ethnic."

Though the profile of Native Americans in regional political discussions is relatively high, the strength and variety of indigenous religious practices is less well known. Part of the issue is that outside observers often have fairly narrow definitions of what constitutes the "religious" dimension of life, whereas many Native Americans (and other Pacific Rim peoples) insist on the continuity between ritual or spiritual activity and the rest of community life. Also significant is that, because of decades of repression, Native Americans often practice their traditions in "secret," avoiding the gaze of anthropologists, missionaries, reporters, and government officials.

Furthermore, many Native Americans in the Pacific Northwest practice forms of Christianity adapted to their indigenous beliefs. Perhaps the best known example is the Indian Shaker Church. Founded in the 1880s by John Slocum, a member of the Squaxin Island Tribe, his message of belief in Jesus and the practice of "shaking" for healing continue to draw members throughout the Pacific Northwest and beyond. Still others have chosen to reject these traditional beliefs entirely and practice more conventional forms of Christianity. Neither ARIS nor NARA data tell us of the presence of Native American religious traditions in the Pacific Northwest.

Even when numbers are available for various religions of Asian origin in the Pacific Northwest, they frequently vary widely. For instance, the ARIS 2001 study estimates the Muslim population of the Pacific Northwest as 5,418, while the NARA data estimate 15,553 Muslims in Washington alone, another 5,224 for Oregon, and 1,381 for Alaska. Similarly, while the NARA data list 18 mosques in Washington, the Pluralism Project at Harvard University lists 43 Islamic organizations, of which at least 30 hold regular Friday congregational prayers.

While Buddhists are difficult to count, the Pluralism Project and NARA agree on 33 Buddhist centers in Oregon, while the Northwest Dharma Association (NWDA) directory lists 100. And while the former two organizations identify 81 and 80 Buddhist congregations, respectively, in Washington, NWDA lists 171. None of these three organizations estimate the size of these communities, though ARIS estimates 56,323 Buddhists in the Pacific Northwest and 13,710 Hindus. In the course of this research I encountered Buddhist organizations that counted members on the basis of dues payment, by average attendance at festivals, and by the number of monks (not including laypeople who worship at the temple). Muslims may attend Friday congregational prayers at the mosque closest to their workplace and send their children to weekend school at another mosque or Islamic center more closely related to their ethnic identity or interpretation of the tradition.

Clearly, further refinement in methodology is required in order to get reliable numbers for gauging the presence of Asian and Native American religious communities in the United States. The point of this essay is not to establish a statistical case for the significance of Pacific Rim religion, but rather to suggest that its influence on regional culture may far outweigh the actual numbers of Pacific Rim peoples or the adherents of any given religious tradition.

Native Americans

While no statistical data on Native American religious practices in the Pacific Northwest is available for this project, some things are known about Native American religion in the region. Religious ideas and practices differ across the many different nations in the Pacific Northwest. For example, on the Yakima Reservation about 50 percent attend Christian services (Catholic, Presbyterian, Evangelical, Mormon), perhaps 25 percent attend Indian Shaker Churches, and 25 percent the traditional Longhouse meetings.

Only a small percentage of Native Americans, however, seem to be exclusive in their Christian identification and practice, generally those who are evangelical Christian or Mormon. Most will attend a service that meets particular needs, and may also attend Native American Church (peyote) ceremonies when the opportunity arises. On the Spokane reservation, for instance, most identify as Catholic, but many also participate in Native religious ceremonies when they are happening and available. By contrast, on some Western Washington reservations there is little participation in regular religious services. In Alaska indigenous people identify with a Christian denomination, generally the one that had access to their area and ran schools, and also continue indigenous practices. As in Oregon and Washington exclusive Christian practice is more often the case for persons belonging to newer evangelical or Mormon religious bodies.

The same variation occurs with Native American religious practices. On the coast traditional longhouse ceremonies occur, generally in the winter. Community members perform spirit-dances using traditional masks and regalia. These ceremonies generally are closed to outsiders. On the Plateau many Indians occasionally attend Washat, a different longhouse meeting that draws from the Washat or Seven Drums tradition and has its origin with the nineteenth century prophet Smohala. Services center around prayers to God and honoring of the natural world and the food resources it provides.

Indian Shaker churches exist on the Squaxin Island, Skokomish, Quinalt, Quileute, Makah, Clallam, Muckleshoot, Snohomish, Swinomish, Skagit, Songish, Sanetch, Cowichan, Chehalis, Yakima, Warm Springs, Kalamath,

Tillamook, Tolowa, Yurok, and Hupa reservations. These churches tend to have a small core of active participants with more tribal members participating during a particular life crisis or holiday.

Most Native Americans in the Northwest attend either one or a combination of several of the following:

- A Christian church (Catholic, Presbyterian, Methodist, Russian Orthodox are all strong among them);
- An Indian Shaker church (a tradition incorporating Christian and indigenous spiritual and healing traditions);
- Native American church ceremonies (a national, pan-tribal movement that incorporates all-night prayer meetings and the use of peyote as a holy sacrament).

Traditional indigenous religious practices in the Northwest were and are centered around relationship building: cultivating relationships with spiritual entities in the natural world, with one's ancestral spirits, and within one's community. Relationship building requires honoring them through vision quests and through dance, song, and ritual activity, usually within the Longhouse. One's success in life depends upon maintaining these healthy spiritual relationships.

Contemporary political issues, such as the resumption of whale hunting by the Makah; the fight to return human remains for re-burial (like Kennewick Man); or efforts to restore salmon runs have their basis in these traditional Native religious practices. They are, at their heart, efforts to restore spiritual relationships—with the natural world and with the ancestral world.

Traditional religious and cultural life in the Northwest underwent significant change in the early to late nineteenth century, primarily due to massively devastating epidemic diseases. Along the Columbia River, for example, it is estimated that 90 percent of the population was wiped out within 75 years. Missionaries and white settlers did nothing to stop the spread of disease among Native people, almost exclusively seeing it as God's will, clearing the land for white settlement.

Some traditional religious practices survive virtually unchanged. Traditional religious practices also survived by modifying themselves to fit new social conditions. The Washat tradition of the Plateau (north-eastern Oregon and eastern Washington) adapted by meeting on Sundays in a longhouse and structuring their gatherings to appear similar to prayer meetings. The Washat, or Seven Drums Religion, is widespread throughout the Plateau today. It originated with the Prophet Smohalla in the late nineteenth century and called for a return to traditional modes of subsistence, lifestyle, and spirituality. It integrated some Christian elements and concepts but remained a distinctly indigenous movement, drawing on traditional spirituality.

The Indian Shaker Church is another means by which traditional spirituality survived in modified form. Shakers venerate God, Jesus, and the Virgin Mary, but do so in a distinctly indigenous way, simultaneously incorporating indigenous healing traditions in their mode of worship.

Increasingly since the 1960s, rising political awareness has brought Native people from the Northwest into contact with broader pan-tribal movements. This was particularly the case with the fish-ins of the '60s and '70s, where people from other tribes all over the continent came to support regional tribes. Along with this, Native American Northwesterners have incorporated elements of pan-tribal spirituality, such as the Native American Church (and the use of peyote). Sweat lodges were a part of traditional spiritual practice in the Northwest, and they still are, though some are run in the Lakota fashion, a style popular throughout the United States.

Historical Immigration Patterns

"The Northwest," according to Thuy Vu, executive director of CAPAA as well as Refugee Services coordinator for Washington, "is different from other regions, because the Northwest accepts Asian Pacific Americans. The numbers make a difference." He contends that there may be larger populations of Asian Pacific Americans in California or New York, but the concentration is greater in Northwest cities; "it is relative, not absolute numbers that make the difference." While this statement may not hold up to statistical scrutiny, the heavy concentration and long historical presence of active APA communities in urban centers of the region have produced a significant number of APA public officials. Vu explains that the Northwest "is more exposed to Asia, through trade, tourism, and business" than other U.S. regions, thus making APAs a force of change.

With regard to religion, Vu says the community is large enough to support temples and grow institutions. "Diversity is more accepted here than in South Dakota or Michigan," he continues. "In many other states, diversity is just a black/white issue. But in the large metropolitan areas along the Puget Sound corridor, it means Asians."

The celebration of ethnic diversity and tolerance by APA leaders today provide a marked contrast to the historical experience of APA immigrants to the region. The history of discrimination, violent expulsion, labor exploitation, exclusionary laws, and internment camps has ingrained in many a suspicion that APAs remain "perpetual foreigners" despite high achievement.

Chinese

Chinese immigrants arrived in Washington and Oregon throughout the mid- to late-1800s, fleeing war, famine, and colonization, recruited for employment in the mining and railroad construction industries. Discrimination and harassment followed. Chinese women were excluded in the interest of worker mobility and control, weakening the development of Chinese communities. In the 1870s many moved to coastal cities to work in factories or salmon canneries, and the Chinese became the largest ethnic group in Portland.

The anti-Chinese movement built up steam in Washington after passage of the Chinese Exclusion Act of 1882, and Chinese were driven from labor camps and Chinatowns. The Chinese developed large businesses and family benevolent associations to provide social and economic assistance to other Chinese immigrants. The Exclusion Act was finally repealed at the outbreak of World War II, when Chinese men were drafted into the United States armed forces.

The second wave of Chinese immigrants, including urban professionals and students, began after the Immigration Act of 1965 phased out race-based immigration restrictions. Chinese Americans broke into the political life of the region when Wing Luke was elected to the Seattle City Council in 1963, and Gary Locke became the first Asian American governor in the lower 48 states in 1996.

Early Chinese immigrants brought with them various forms of Mahayana Buddhist traditions, as well as Confucian and Taoist practices. Many immigrants in the last 50 years of the twentieth century have come from mainland China, where most have no religious background and where Christian adherents have faced persecution. According to Ebaugh and Chafetz, "In general, the Chinese have long regarded Christianity as an aspect of western imperialism and converts were commonly chastised with the remark, 'One more Christian, one less Chinese.'" For many Chinese Christians in the United States, "a key issue is how to maintain their identity as cultural Chinese while adopting the despised religion of western imperialism; how to 'Sinocize' Christianity." Community institutions like Seattle's Chinese Baptist Church formed through American missionary work at the turn of the twentieth century.

Refugees from Tibet, many of whom were teaching lamas of the various Tibetan Vajrayana Buddhist lineages invited to teach at American universities, have likewise established centers in the Pacific Northwest. The Sakya Monastery in Seattle, under the direction of His Holiness Jigdal Dagchen Sakya and his wife, Her Eminence Jamyang D. Sakya, continues one of the Sakya lineages. Various Shambhala Centers offering "secular meditation" derive from the Kagyu lineage through the unique teachings of the late Chogyam Trungpa Rinpoche. The Nyingma lineage of Chagdud Tulku Rinpoche guides the several Chagdud Gompa communities in Oregon. Dechen Ling Buddhist Center in Seattle is one of the carriers of the Gelugpa lineage of the Dalai Lama. While Sakya and Gelugpa lineages emphasize the academic study of religion, the Kagyu and Nyingma are more focused on meditation, contemplation, and tantric practice.[4]

Filipino

The first Filipinos came to Seattle in 1883. Filipino Americans began arriving in the Pacific Northwest in larger numbers after the United States acquired the Philippines in the Spanish-American War and suppressed independence movements in 1899. By the 1920s Filipinos working for Alaska salmon canneries and Washington lumber companies became a major segment of the APA population. Filipinos faced anti-miscegenation laws, harassment in the Yakima Valley, and expulsion from Toppenish during the 1920s and 1930s. Washington State's Anti-Alien Land Law of 1937 prohibited Filipino citizens from owning or leasing land. The second wave of migration came after 1965, largely drawing Filipino professionals. Later waves included non-professionals as well, escaping the political, social, and economic problems in their homeland. Salmon industry segregation and discrimination sparked a major civil rights struggle in 1974.

Fred Cordova, in his *Filipinos: Forgotten Asian Americans*, characterizes Filipino religion as the ultimate flowering of "Indo-Malayan spirituality" in the "complexities of Catholicism." Despite forced conversion by the Spanish, Filipinos preserved an "innate sense of spirituality" that has made church life central to the Filipino American experience. While he charges that the Catholic Church's "commitment to Filipino Americans since their arrival in the U.S., including Hawaii and Alaska, was one of indifference—if not benign condescension," he notes two highlights. These include the formation of the parish of Our Lady Queen of Martyrs Church, staffed by Maryknoll Fathers in Seattle until 1954, specifically to minister to Pinoy (Filipino American) Catholics; and the late 1930s ministry of Monsignor Pedro Monleon, "one of the rare Catholic clerics of Filipino ancestry."

Cordova points out that despite denial of sacramental marriage, Christian burial, Catholic education, and Sunday masses, "Filipino American Catholics kept the faith even though many had not become regular church-goers." The family gatherings around christenings, rosary, wakes, and novenas, followed by an informal dinner for family and friends, became "not only a religious custom but also one that was culturally social." While most Filipino Americans remain Roman Catholic, Cordova praises Protestant churches for their consistent ministry to Filipino immigrants, from the Hawaiian plantations in 1912 to the university ministries of the YMCA in the 1920s. "Within fellowships, Pinoy university and college students found not only material assistance but also spiritual counsel and friendly advice. Some of these fellowships developed into organized student groups, which later served as core beginnings of existing Filipino American community organizations."[5]

Japanese

The Chinese Exclusion Act of 1882 led to active recruitment of young Japanese male workers for the railroads, farms, and oyster industry. Though Japanese immigration was restricted in the early twentieth century, the United States annexation of Hawaii and subsequent labor migration made the Japanese the fastest growing minority group in Washington from 1898-1907. The "Gentleman's Agreement" with Japan slowed immigration to the United States after 1907, though "Japanese picture-brides" and family members allowed the development of a permanent, thriving Japanese community. Many Japanese ran their own businesses, employing other Japanese, and many bought farms that produced nearly 75 percent of the vegetables sold in Portland in 1940.

Roosevelt's Executive Order 9066 in 1942 initiated the internment of 120,000 Japanese (two thirds of them U.S. citizens) in concentration camps in desert regions of the West. The internment tore apart the Japanese community, with some fleeing East or to Canada, some resisting induction into the armed forces, and others volunteering to prove their patriotism. This experience profoundly shaped Japanese American identity in the region. The redress movement since the war provided some measure of Japanese American unity and cohesion. The involvement of major Japanese churches and temples in this redress movement is a prime example of their public presence in the Pacific Northwest.

Japanese immigrants and missionaries have brought various forms of Pure Land and Zen Buddhism to the Pacific Northwest. The Seattle Betsuin Temple (formerly Seattle Buddhist Church) became in 1901 the first Jodo Shinshu or Shin Buddhist[6] temple in the Northwest, followed by a sister temple in Portland two years later. At roughly the same time, Seattle's Japanese Presbyterian and Japanese Baptist churches began to form as well. The various lineages of Japanese Soto and Rinzai Zen Buddhism[7] inform the practice of nearly every Zen center in the Pacific Northwest, attracting mainly European-American followers. The Dharma Rain Zen center in Portland, the Three Treasures Sangha in Seattle, and the Olympia, Washington Zen Center are significant examples of these, and the more ethnically diverse Nichiren Shoshu and Soka Gakkai International movements[8] have also established a regional presence in the last 40 years.

Korean

Koreans also began to come to Washington, Oregon, and Alaska in the early 1900s to work in railroad, mining, and service occupations. Between 1910 and 1924 many of the men sent to Korea for their "picture brides," and the community expanded significantly until the government disallowed the practice. Exclusion laws affected marriage, land ownership, and school attendance for Koreans.

During the second wave, between 1951 and 1964, many Koreans entered the region as wives or children of U.S. military personnel. The third wave, after 1965, saw continued economic development. The 1992 Los Angeles riots awakened Korean Americans to political action and caused a shift in leadership to the more acculturated "1.5 generation."

Korean Americans brought with them a number of different traditions, including Buddhism, Christianity, and shamanism. Buddhism had arrived in Korea from China in the fourth century C.E. and from there passed on to Japan in the sixth century. Christianity, however, came to Korea (also originally from China) in the seventeenth century. By the end of the twentieth century "Buddhism and Christianity had nearly equal shares in the population of South Korea (from which most immigrants come to the United States), Buddhists at 29 percent and Christians at 25 percent."[9]

Protestant missionaries have had more success establishing churches in Korea than in China from the mid-nineteenth century until now. United States immigration policy has favored Christian Koreans, who are predominantly urban and well educated; because of this nearly half of all Korean immigrants were Christian before leaving their homeland. In addition Ebaugh and Chafetz note that non-Christians have high conversion rates, resulting in a population of Korean immigrants in the United States that is about 70 percent Christian.

In the Puget Sound region prominent Korean Catholic and Protestant churches formed in the mid-1960s and early 1970s. By 1999 there were over 130 Korean churches in King and Snohomish counties, along with 70 community churches in Tacoma-Pierce County. Several of these churches had close to 1,000 members. Though concentrated in the Puget Sound area, there are approximately 30 additional Korean churches in other areas of Washington, including Spokane, Pasco, and Yakima. The *Seattle Times* estimated in 2000 "150 or more Korean-speaking Christian congregations between Federal Way and Olympia alone."

Korean Buddhism in the United States takes several forms. The Seu Mi Sah temple in Tacoma became the first Korean-American Buddhist institution in Washington in 1983, and the monks have since constructed a traditional Buddhist temple complex with help from the Tong Do temple in Korea. Approximately 500 people from Washington, Oregon, and California regularly visit the temple for services and classes on Buddhist teachings. Other Korean Buddhist temples and centers are located in Federal Way, Issaquah, Steilacoom, and Seattle.

Ethnic Korean temples often are related to the Chogye order lineage, which arose in response to Japanese colonial pressures to adopt Soto Zen doctrine and organization, the separate Korean celibate monastic traditions of S'on (Zen) and Kyo (Sutra and temple-centered) forming a united front.

The most familiar form of Korean Buddhism among European-Americans is a syncretic and socially engaged form brought by S'on (Zen) master Seung Sahn and his disciples in the 1970s and 1980s, now called the Kwan Um Zen School, with its national center in Providence, Rhode Island.[10] Branches of the Dharma Sound Zen Center in Seattle, Redmond, and Tacoma are linked to this Korean S'on lineage. The Korean form of Zen is much less common regionally than the more prominent Japanese Soto and Rinzai Zen schools.

South Asian

The first significant wave of immigrants from South Asia occurred between 1899-1913, the height of exclusion for other Asians, when mostly Sikh farmers from the Punjab came to California and the Pacific Northwest. Asian Exclusion movements swept the West Coast, and in 1907, Punjabi Sikhs (referred to as "Hindoos") were attacked and driven out of Bellingham and Everett, Washington. Federal law classified South Asians as "non-white" in 1923, denaturalizing or preventing citizenship for many. Many South Asians married Mexican-Americans and blended cultures.

After World War II the ban on South Asian immigration was lifted, and many students came to study in the United States. The third and largest wave, after 1965, included mostly educated elites. In the 1980s a fourth wave of mostly working class South Asians from Punjab, Pakistan, and Bengal fled political and religious turmoil. The most significant issues facing South Asians in the region include hate crimes, discrimination, and domestic violence.

South Asian Americans brought with them the wide variety of religious traditions from their homelands. Most immigrants from Pakistan and Bangladesh practice Islam, primarily in Sunni forms. Immigrants from India to the Pacific Northwest brought Sikh, Jain, Zoroastrian, and varieties of the majority Hindu tradition, while Indian Christians of Orthodox, Catholic, and Protestant traditions have come in large numbers as well.

Missionaries of the Vedanta Hindu tradition and actively proselytizing new forms of Sikhism (3HO), Hinduism (ISKCON, the International Society of Krishna Consciousness),[11] and Sufi orders with South Asian roots (e.g., Sufi Order International) have likewise cultivated followers in the Pacific Northwest, as have popular Indian gurus like the Bhagwan Shree Rajneesh, Ma Jaya, and Sai Baba. Followers of the latter gurus usually continue to practice their religious traditions of origin—often mainline Protestant Christianity, Catholicism, or Judaism—as well.

Southeast Asian

Southeast Asians arrived in the Pacific Northwest primarily as refugees fleeing war, poverty, and political instability in the 1970s. The Indo-China Migration and Refugee Assistance Act of 1975 allowed Vietnamese fleeing from the fall of

Saigon to settle in the United States. The first refugees tended to be from the educated class and military personnel, many of whom spoke English well. Waves of refugees—Vietnamese, Cambodian, Laotian, Thai, and indigenous peoples of Southeast Asia—came from 1975-1978, with Washington receiving 18,000 in 1975 alone. The subsequent era of "boat people" arriving in the United States brought a broader socio-economic range of refugees, and the Amerasian Homecoming Act of 1987 admitted nearly 100,000 children of American soldiers in Vietnam. Older war veterans and political prisoners have since arrived to take their place among Vietnamese Americans.

Southeast Asians and Pacific Islanders have also brought a wide variety of religious traditions with them. Early Vietnamese refugees tended to be or become Catholic as a result of the church's involvement in resettlement efforts. Later waves of Southeast Asians brought other Christians as well as a variety of Buddhist practitioners: Theravada Buddhists[12] from Thailand, Cambodia, and Laos, and diverse traditions of Vietnamese Buddhism, each shaped in its own cultural and political crucible, as well as the teachings of *vipassana* or Insight Meditation.[13]

Traditional shamanistic practices and ancestor veneration often coexist with Buddhist and Christian practice within families and even individuals, as Ryan Minato wrote in his essay "Vietnamese Americans" in the CAPAA journal.

> While many Vietnamese communities experience generational and regional differences in political commitment and involvement in the affairs of Vietnam, the common thread in much of Vietnamese culture is ancestor veneration. Commonly, families create a traditional altar in their homes, at which they may offer gifts of incense, fruit, and chants for the well-being of their ancestors. Many Vietnamese also join together for anniversaries and to celebrate the Vietnamese Lunar New Year, Tet.

According to Thuy Vu, many Southeast Asian refugees supported religious institutions as part of the reaction to and struggle against communism in their homelands. They actively formed local associations and community social groups, which in turn supported religious institutions, especially Buddhist temples. Because many of the highly trained religious leaders did not accompany the waves of refugees, the immigrants now face the task of training young people to become religious leaders, monks, or shamans. This task was never an issue in their native communities.

In many meetings the discussion leaders who help are learned in religion, but they are not monks. For Theravada Buddhists the establishment of a viable *sangha* of trained, ordained, celibate monks is essential to the survival of the tradition in America. The Washington Buddhavanaram in Auburn, Washington, founded by a Thai immigrant community in 1984, now serves a diverse population of Vietnamese, Laotian, and Cambodian Buddhists from a broad geographical area.

Cham Muslims represent an interesting Southeast Asian refugee story in the Puget Sound region. Miriam Adeney and Kathryn Demaster, in their essay "Muslims in Seattle," report that the first Cham Muslims fleeing from the Khmer Rouge in Cambodia and the Vietnamese Communist regime arrived in Seattle in 1978. Almost 80 percent of the Southeast Asian Cham population left between 1974 and 1977. Four hundred of the 1,000 Chams accepted by the United States settled in Seattle, with more arriving over the subsequent three years. Others, who were first resettled to different parts of the country, migrated to Seattle and Lacey, Washington, where they work in fishing, seafood processing, brush-cutting, auto mechanics, and construction industries. Over 50 percent of the Seattle Chams came from three villages in Indochina, where elders encouraged the young to escape persecution for Cham ethnic and religious difference and compulsory military conscription.

The Chams have maintained a strong sense of heritage, destiny, and community cohesion in their new home. In Seattle's Rainier Valley, many occupy adjacent units in government-subsidized apartment complexes, and in Lacey Chams have built their own neighborhood, a circle of houses with a mosque and imam's residence in the center. Though they do frequently participate in other mosques, the Cham Refugee Community purchased a couple of houses for use as a mosque, and educational and social service center.[14] The imam of both the Lacey and South Seattle Cham mosques is Mohammed Joban, an Indonesian who trained at al-Azhar University in Egypt. He also serves as a prison chaplain. Joban explained that he is "culturally closer" to the Chams than an Arab or Pakistani imam would be. At both mosques, Muslims of Arab, South Asian, African, African-American, and European-American heritage join in prayer and education sessions, but each maintains an emphasis on local Cham community support, including patronizing Cham-owned businesses. The Cham community in both locales is striving to create a close-knit Islamic community that preserves religious and cultural identity.

Patterns of Change in Immigrant Religious Traditions
The Expanding Role of the Religious Institution

Most studies of the religious life of immigrants to the United States note that "religious identity" has been an important, if not *the* most important, marker of identity for an immigrant group; the assumption is that to be American is to be affiliated with a particular religious community. Some argue that the alienation and confusion of becoming an immigrant or refugee causes people to turn to their religious traditions to make sense of the experience. The religious institution acts both to preserve ethnic identity and to aid assimilation to the new culture. For many immigrants religion becomes a more important part of their lives than it was in their homeland, where it may have been taken for granted.

In studies of Korean churches as well as Asian Indian and Pakistani groups religious institutions seem to play a central role in "settlement and incorporation" of immigrants by assuming socio-economic functions. As Ebaugh and Chafetz write:

> these religious centers serve as places where immigrants can worship in their own languages, enjoy the rituals, music, and festivals of their native lands, share stories from their homelands, and pass on their religious and cultural heritage to the next generation. Simultaneously, these religious centers help immigrants adapt to U.S. society by teaching them civic skills, providing economic and social services, providing the social space for networking and affording status opportunities by creating socially valued religious roles.

The Pacific Northwest offers numerous examples of such expansive roles in helping new immigrants adapt. Seattle's Chinese and Japanese Baptist churches, as well as the Buddhist Church (Betsuin) have supported scouting programs, sports and cultural programs, ESL classes, and social services aimed at particular ethnic communities for nearly a century. The Cham Refugee Community is a social service organization that owns and runs the Cham mosque in Seattle, providing not only service but leadership opportunities for refugees in a tightly knit ethnic enclave.

The Idriss Mosque in the Northgate neighborhood of Seattle, because of its prominent architecture and historical reputation in continuity with the earliest Muslim communities in Seattle, attracts many new immigrants as well, providing connections to basic services and support, as well as social opportunities. Similarly, parents and teachers at the Islamic School of Seattle often describe the school as a place where they can network with other Muslim immigrant parents who share particular values as well as challenges in a new environment. The school has at various times run programs for economic development for the Cham community and other services for immigrants, in addition to fulfilling its educational mission.

A leader of the Sikh gurudwara in Renton, Washington, Tarlochan Singh Khalsa, notes that in the Punjab, the gurudwara is almost exclusively reserved for the chanting of hymns and veneration of the Guru. Here, the gurudwara has become the setting of choice for funerals, marriage ceremonies, bridegroom dinners, and martial arts and theatrical performances. These religious institutions change in many ways to resemble churches and synagogues in the United States.

"Selective Assimilation"

The issue of "assimilation" is much more complex than in previous generations. The regional differences in American culture and the historical context created by changes in immigration law and civil rights after 1965 mean that many Asian immigrants and refugees in the last four decades of the twentieth century encountered a variety of pressures to assimilate, adapt, and yet preserve their ethnic and religious identities. The "diverse value systems" and "multiple subsocieties" immigrants encounter seem to explode the idea of a "core culture" or "American way of life" to which new residents must assimilate.

"Finding one's roots" and "remaining ethnic" represent positive values for many young second-generation immigrants, in contrast to their predecessors from earlier immigrant communities. Multiculturalism and diversity are institutionalized in legal and political terms, as well as in the practice of religious congregations. This shift in American culture and the prevalence of a "secular but spiritual" culture in the Pacific Northwest necessitate what some scholars call "segmental" or "selective" assimilation. Immigrants choose to assimilate into some sectors of American society while remaining in tight ethnic enclaves in other parts of their lives. These choices lead to a wider variety of religious institutions and patterns of practice among contemporary Asian Pacific Americans in the Pacific Northwest.

The two Sikh gurudwaras[15] in Kent and Renton, Washington might serve as examples of the generational differences in immigrant religious communities. The gurudwaras in Renton and Kent began as a small common house of worship in Burien, attracting Sikh immigrants of several generations. The tragic massacre of Sikhs at the Golden Temple in Amritsar in 1984 led to increased immigration to the United States by serious, orthodox young Sikhs escaping harassment in India. As in many Sikh gurudwaras around the country, conflicts began to arise between older immigrants, many of whom had abandoned the traditional markings of Sikh baptism, including the wearing of long beards and turbans by men, and newer immigrants, who insisted on purifying Sikhism of all Hindu and Muslim influences in Punjabi culture and compromises to Sikh identity. As Jasmit Singh put it in a speech to a youth conference in 2002, the "age old questions of who 'really' was a Sikh came to dominate political discussion" and to define leadership at the gurudwara level in many regions of the diaspora.

The two groups divided after Management Committee elections in 1986-7. The movement for an independent Khalistan or Sikh homeland, a demand for strict orthodoxy, and the memory of the martyrs of 1984 became an important part of community life for the group that founded the large Gurudwara Singh Sabha in Renton, with about 5,000 voting members. The huge langar, or dining hall, of the gurudwara is lined with pictures of martyrs, and the Management

Committee passed into the hands of only baptized Sikhs in 2001. The Renton gurudwara has an active program for youth, who study martial arts, kirtan (chanting scripture), Punjabi language and Sikh theology, and the gurudwara holds annual camps cooperatively with a gurudwara in Vancouver, British Columbia.

The older immigrants formed the smaller Gurudwara Sacha Marag Sahib in Kent, with a considerably smaller membership. The Renton and Kent gurudwaras do maintain cooperative relations when necessary, co-sponsoring the visits of important preachers from the Punjab, but otherwise the leadership remains separate. Many ordinary Sikhs at both gurudwaras, however, insist that they attend both with no distinction, and the leaders of both insist, "Anyone who comes is a member."

Korean churches provide further examples of this struggle to assimilate while preserving ethnic solidarity and tradition. The first Korean Catholic parish, Peace of Christ, was established in the Northgate area of Seattle in 1976, and it was rededicated as St. Andrew Kim Catholic Church in July 2002. An estimated 2,000 Korean Catholics travel from as far as Bellingham to attend services. A second parish, St. Anne's in Tacoma, began in the early 1980s, and an estimated 1,000 families worship regularly at this church. Another 80 families worship at Sacred Heart Church in Lacey, Washington, an English congregation with two Korean-speaking priests. Divisions in the Korean American Catholic community reportedly occur over issues of maintaining cultural identity and language or integrating into the larger Christian/Catholic community.

Similarly, the Korean Community Presbyterian Church in Seattle has four Sunday services (two in Korean, one English, one for young people). Organized by new immigrants in 1971 the church tends to disregard Presbyterian liturgy and to de-emphasize denominational ties. The pastor reportedly emphasizes the bicultural mission of the church: "We are also trying to keep a Korean-American identity, with the richness of both cultures."

The ambivalence of biculturalism also finds resonance in many of the region's Muslim communities. The largely middle-class, Western-educated Arab and South Asian immigrants who came after 1965 often had different experiences with the United States and different priorities from existing African-American and later economically disadvantaged refugee communities. While many wished to assimilate, others aimed to form a distinctive American Islamic identity.

Institutions like the Islamic School of Seattle have provided immigrant parents with a place to gather for solidarity and recognition of their difference. Their children attend school with people who share common Muslim names and religious practice. The school promotes a vision of Islamic unity that is distinct from both particular Arab or South Asian cultures and from mainstream American culture. Parents cite "protection" from drugs, crime, loose sexual mores, harassment, confusion, and prejudice as major reasons for sending their children to an Islamic school.

Despite unflagging commitment on the part of teachers and founders, conflict among Islamic institutions about the proper methods of teaching Islam, as well as fears on the part of parents who want their children to compete in the American educational system, have hindered the smooth operation of the school since its inception in 1980. Yvonne Haddad and Adair Lummis' study of attitudes toward parochial education in the United States found that Pakistani immigrants in particular were suspicious of any alternative schooling that might disadvantage their children for college or graduate school. Most Islamic centers in the region sponsor weekend or Sunday schools for children who attend public or non-Muslim private schools.

International Networks

Another factor that may distinguish contemporary immigrants from their predecessors is the rapid development of communication and transportation technologies. Many Asian Pacific Americans migrate back and forth between their host community in the United States and their homelands, while others maintain communication through telephone, video, and electronic media. Several Pacific Northwest religious institutions, such as the Vietnamese Buddhist Tinh Xia Quan Am in Lynnwood, Washington, receive significant funding from Taiwan. The True Buddha School of Taiwan-born Grand Master Lu (Living Buddha Lien Shang), headquartered in Ling Shen Ching Tze Redmond, Washington, claims chapters in 21 different countries. These represent what Yang calls "transnational families and global communities and religious institutions." The recent completion of a Hindu Temple in Bothell, Washington likewise represents a continuation of a temple-building movement in the Indian diaspora that has begun to flourish in the past 30 years.

Diaspora communities face a constant struggle to define their relationship to the homeland. As the World War II Japanese internment and the contemporary mass registration of Middle Eastern and South Asian Muslims illustrate, such associations often are forced upon immigrants by domestic politics and U.S. foreign policy.

One of the young monks at Quan Am, Jason Tong, emphasized the monastery's policy of eschewing political involvement in the United States and in Vietnam. He said, "We don't salute the Vietnamese flag or the American flag." Other Vietnamese temples in Seattle and Portland are involved in the Unified Vietnamese Congress of America, and they actively campaign for human rights in Vietnam. The politics of the Vietnam War remain both a unifying and divisive force within Vietnamese Buddhist communities in the region, and the voluntary associations the temples join often reflect their political position.

Despite the differences in the historical and cultural context to which recent Asian immigrants to the region come, many scholars expect certain adaptations to occur. For instance, particularly for those immigrants whose religious group is a majority in their homeland but a minority faith in the United States, "ascriptive membership" or taken-for-granted religious identity is weaker. This often means a change from assumed membership to voluntary participation in a religious organization. It may also mean that the role of religious practice in one's life changes, for example, from public to private, or from perfunctory ritual to central, essential framework for one's life.

A video made by the Muslim Students Association of the University of Washington illustrates this point. Jamil Abdul Razzak, a retired Boeing engineer, articulates the theme of the "golden years" in the 1960s and 1970s, when everyone had one common goal: "the cultivation of Islam." In the spirit of Islam, Muslims from different countries worked together.

Sr. Irene Junejo agrees, recalling how people were happy, working together without regard to ethnic differences. Her late husband, Mushtaque Junejo, a Boeing colleague of Abdul Razzak, wrote in his reflections, "I think the 1970's were the golden years of Muslim activities in Seattle ... Those were the days of close knit families where fun, food and camaraderie were emphasized."

Ann and Mohammed El-Moslimany, whose family joined the Junejos and Abdul Razzaks in the 1960s, also recall fondly these years, when Sunnis and Shiis, even Nation of Islam members, worked together, and ethnic divisions were unimportant. Mohammed El-Moslimany headily recounts his vision, inspired by his experience in the Muslim Brotherhood movement in Egypt, saying that "in the US, we are rediscovering our Islam; here, we have a better chance than anyplace else." The mosque could recover its original sense as a community center, beyond its function as a place for "ritualistic purposes," they say.

Such testimonies of rediscovering one's faith are fairly common among immigrant religious communities in the United States, and such sentiments receive support from religious movements abroad as well as social developments in the host society.

Also in this new situation mosques and Islamic centers, Buddhist and Hindu temples, and Sikh gurudwaras tend to adopt Sunday school and religious education patterns that resemble Christian churches. Religious officials such as monks assume a teaching and translating role not common in the homeland, to explain doctrine and practice to laypeople who do not absorb it through public education or social conditioning.

Thai monks at the Washington Buddhavanaram run education classes, an open library, and summer camps for children. At Chua Lien Hoa, a Vietnamese

Buddhist temple in Olympia, Washington, a Sri Lankan monk holds several classes for the congregation, and the youth program is the most active group in the community. At Quan Am, however, the young Vietnamese monks eschew public teaching and restrict themselves to answering questions and giving advice to those attending services.

In traditional Muslim majority countries the imam or prayer leader is hired and trained by the government to deliver the Friday sermon, while religious education of youth takes place at school and home. Several national Islamic organizations in the United States now publish religious education curricula and run training sessions for weekend lay teachers.

In addition, many Asian religious institutions develop governance structures that include laypeople and operate more democratically than is customary for similar institutions in the homeland. The Vietnamese Buddhist Temple (Chua Viet Nam) in Seattle's Central District, according to a senior member, Khan Nguyen, is financially independent, supported only by its members, and governed by an elected board. The temple is registered under the name of the organization rather than the monk. In Vietnam, he says, a village decides to build a temple, and they then invite a monk to serve. In America, monks can establish their own temple and recruit followers. Examples in Seattle include Tinh Xia Quan Am and Chua Van Hanh, the latter founded by a nun as a women's temple.

Similarly, the Cham Refugee Community has a board of directors, as does the Northgate Idriss Mosque. While the former has hired a trained imam as teacher, preacher, and spiritual adviser, the latter has consistently refused to do so, relying solely on lay leadership, as do most Islamic centers in the region. A primarily European-American Tibetan Buddhist organization like Seattle's Sakya Monastery may provide a more complex combination. The Tibetan lama is the sole authority for decision-making, yet members serve on a variety of committees organized like most Protestant churches.

The Challenge of Multi-ethnic Congregations

Some groups have formed multi-ethnic congregations that include Asian Pacific and non-Asian Americans, while other groups maintain "parallel congregations" divided not only by language and custom, but by religious style. Madeline Duntley, in her essay, "Heritage, Ritual, and Translation: Seattle's Japanese-Presbyterian Church," argues that the Japanese Presbyterian Church, though it began as a Japanese mission, defies easy categories of "ethnic club," urban, suburban, neighborhood, or immigrant church. The current community, while still committed to ministry in the city and to immigrants and still maintaining a Japanese-language service for new Japanese immigrants, has become multiethnic, multigenerational, and multilingual.

Duntley argues that in its rituals of commemoration on anniversaries, the church translates its ethnic heritage and Christian identity in ways that are relevant to the multicultural present congregation, which includes Chinese, Mien, and Caucasian members. But she warns against using a political label like "pan-Asian" lightly, as the impetus behind pan-Asian activity at the church is its evangelical Christian mandate.[16]

Many options for Japanese and other Asian ethnic churches exist, and members choose Japanese Presbyterian on other grounds, such as "religious practice and preference, aesthetics, and the desire for a community that will encourage and support one's distinct spiritual orientation." While maintaining important cooperative ties with other Japanese churches, the congregation "translates" its historical Japanese identity in ways relevant to a multicultural present.

A similar process has occurred at the Chinese Baptist Church, which conducts one Chinese-language service, a traditional English language service, and a contemporary service each Sunday. The latter two have become much more multi-ethnic, including non-Chinese Asian-Americans as well as non-Asians through a pattern of intermarriage and outreach into wider social circles in recent generations. The sermon on the church's 106th anniversary in August 2002 wove together the ethnically specific history of the church with its continued evangelical mission to a more diverse society.

Inviting or Incorporating non-Asians

The generational shifts in the Japanese-American community in the Northwest are quite significant for established Japanese-American religious institutions. More than half of third- and fourth-generation Japanese Americans marry partners of another race. Few new immigrants have arrived from Japan in recent years, and Japanese Americans make up a smaller percentage of the Asian-American population.

Assimilation and suburban migration may be threatening the cultural unity of Japanese Americans, but racism and "Japan bashing" have provided occasions for political cooperation, as in the redress movement. The Seattle Betsuin Temple has felt the shift as well. As Alex Tizon of the *Seattle Times* noted in 1999, "At its peak, in the 1950s and '60s, the temple had an estimated membership of 1,500, including 250 to 300 kids in Dharma school..." But in 1999 membership was about 600, with an anticipated loss of 60-70 percent of the membership to death in the next 10 years.

Rev. Don Castro, the first European-American head minister, holds out hope that the temple will survive through outreach to non-Japanese Americans. Tapping into the growing interest in Zen and Tibetan Buddhism in temple classes, he has also been attempting in recent years to organize a "Buddhism *as*

Ecology" or "Earth Household Sangha" movement. From the Buddhist doctrines of interdependence and non-duality, Castro argues that "Buddhists are naturally ecologists," offering both wisdom and compassion to the conservation movement. Though he has had some difficulty convincing traditional Japanese Buddhists of the link, he is encouraging other temples to incorporate the Buddha's "ecological posture" into shrines. He also hopes this aspect of the Buddhist message will appeal to young people in the broader environmental movement in the region.

To that end, he has begun developing a Web site and postcards, one of which displays the ecology symbol superimposed on a Buddhist flag, with the words in a pseudo-Sanskrit Roman font, "Earth Household Sangha." Another depicts a statue of the seated Buddha, his right hand touching the ground (the "earth-touching posture"), with the quote, "...the earth will bear witness." Such creative appeals to the dominant culture of the Pacific Northwest may provide a new avenue for integrating Japanese heritage with an environment this heritage has helped to shape for over a century.

Some scholars of Asian American religion suggest that a high level of devotionalism, elaborate imagery, and ritual activity characterizes Asian American religiosity. More assimilated Asian-Americans and Western observers tend to see such devotional activity as "folk," "cultural," or "popular" tradition.

Madeline Duntley provides an analysis of Our Lady Queen of Martyrs parish, which became a mixed Filipino and Japanese church prior to World War II. She points out that interethnic APA relationships were shaped both by the history of Roman Catholic mission work in their respective countries of origin and by decisions of the archdiocese of Seattle regarding ethnic parishes. The relics of the "Japanese Martyrs" and a concomitant emphasis on a devotional religious style sustained the symbolic unity of the parish for several years. Duntley argues that this unity was lost when the mission shifted from devotion to social service, and as World War II tensions increased hostility between the communities. Accounts of daily church attendance at St. Andrew Kim parish attest to such a devotional emphasis among Korean Catholics as well.

Western adherents of Asian religions, on the other hand, tend to emphasize the philosophical and meditative elements, to the exclusion of devotional ritual and elaborate festival. In her master's thesis study of four European-American Buddhist groups sharing the Bellingham, Washington, Dharma Hall, Caroline Kingsbury concluded:

> The questions of why people are practicing Buddhism, and what they like about it can be summarized with an affinity for the meditation practice and cognitive resonance with the ideas. Neither pro-

found changes in ethical behavior nor transformed belief systems figure largely into the process. Also, practitioners are not interested in creating or participating in exclusive, tightly drawn social groups, nor did they express interest in converting others to the practice or belief systems. ... They find themselves practicing Buddhism as a result of, first and foremost, their personally qualified spiritual searches... The attraction as described by these interviewees is primarily intellectual, as opposed to affective, religious, or social....

My own interviews with European-American Buddhists practicing in the Tibetan tradition indicate that such intellectual affinity and freedom from doctrinal conformity (in the Christian or Jewish sense) played a major role in attracting them to the practice. Kingsbury further notes that the four groups (two Zen, one Tibetan, and one Vipassana) in Bellingham are nearly indistinguishable on the basis of practice and belief.

Kingsbury finds that "no significant differences in beliefs, practices, and backgrounds are discernible between the members of the Hall, except for a more youthful average age in the Zen and Shambhala groups." Such uniformity may indicate a process of acculturation to the "secular but spiritual" norms of the Pacific Northwest atmosphere in which these Buddhist teachings have found a home.

Rick Fields, author of several articles and books on European-American Buddhism, including "Confessions of a White Buddhist" in the journal *Tricycle,* comments on the differences between "ethnic" and "American" Buddhism. As a participant-observer, he notes that "it seems that American Buddhism as defined by white Buddhists is based on a strenuous, if not athletic, practice of meditation and is becoming increasingly democratized, psychologized, and socially engaged..." The different "styles of practice," he says, "may be not so much racial as . . . a continuation of an ongoing sectarian dialectic about how best to realize liberation, with the white Buddhists tending toward the 'self-power' of Zen and the Asian-American Buddhists tending toward the 'other-power' of Pure Land, though even that distinction hardly holds in the Chinese and Tibetan traditions."

Zen is the path to enlightenment through individual physical and mental discipline. "Pure Land" traditions emphasize that enlightenment is the free gift of compassionate bodhisattvas who have taken a vow to help all sentient beings reach liberation. Victor Sogen Hori, in his essay "Sweet and Sour Buddhism" in the journal *Tricycle,* similarly comments on the differences of Asian-American Ch'an and European-American Zen practitioners:

> For those who see the person as fundamentally autonomous and individual, Buddhist practice is conceived as freeing the self from inces-

sant social conditioning and releasing its own pure nature; meditation is social deconditioning designed ultimately to affirm and realize the self. But for those who assume that personal identity is created out of social relationship, Buddhist practice is conceived as breaking habits of selfishness in order to become open, responsible, and compassionate with others; meditation is personal reconditioning designed ultimately to dissolve attachment and de-realize the self.

While such contrasts may be too broad and generalized, they point out much of the tension within the larger American Buddhist scene. This becomes particularly significant when it comes to choosing journalistic sources to "represent" a tradition.

The task is, of course, further complicated by the fact that Asian missionaries and contemporary spokespeople of Buddhist, Hindu, Sikh, and Muslim traditions in particular have often significantly adapted the message of their faith to fit into a Western cultural and scientific context. From the first emissaries to the Parliament of the World's Religions in 1893 to the writings of D.T. Suzuki, continuing to contemporary monks who teach throughout the Pacific Northwest, all participate in a process of cultural absorption to establish the rational, scientific appeal of their traditions to "modern" society. Swami Bhaskarananda of the Vedanta Society, in an interview, explains it this way:

> In the West, there is a love of science thanks to the Industrial Revolution. Today it is very respectable. True science, though, is based on pure reasoning. Everything is reasonable, and explainable step by step. I don't say, "have faith." Through reasoning we can know certain things beyond sensory experience. ... Science operates in the field of sense perception, and this leads it to certain truths. I present all these things, and ask if it makes sense. There is no faith or reward elsewhere. The way has to help the person here and now. Vivekananda said, if it can't help me now, it is worthless.

The celebration of the Vu Lan or Ullambana festival in Buddhist temples in the Puget Sound region provides an example of the variety of perspectives that emerge within Buddhist groups in the Pacific Northwest. For a layperson at the Vu Lan festival in Lynnwood, the festival was explicitly meant as an opportunity to venerate and petition Buddhas and bodhisattvas for their direct intervention in the path of relatives living and dead to assure a better rebirth in a Pure Land.

The monk Jason Tong, however, remarked, "we teach that we create our own karmas. In Chinese culture, they believe they can pray their way out of things. We don't pray literally; we look at Buddhas as examples. I guess we believe [in intervention] but we don't count on it. The bodhisattvas might play a role in pushing us toward the right way."

A pamphlet at the Seattle Betsuin Temple describes the origins of Obon, the Japanese version of the same festival, and how the dancing of Bon Odori and the Chinese Taoist lantern lighting for ancestral spirits were added to it. The conclusion notes that, in contrast to traditional notions of the services and rituals being done for the benefit of dead relatives, whose spirits return at this time, Jodo Shinshu Buddhists observe Obon as "a time to remember and honor all those who has (sic) passed before us. It is to appreciate all they have done for us to continue the Buddhist path." The Bon Odori is described by a Seattle Betsuin Temple brochure as a dance for "the joy of being shown the path of liberation and enlightenment." This spectrum from mystery to rationality speaks to shifts within the traditions that occur in the homeland and in the new environment.

Finally, the question of how Pacific Northwest regional culture affects Asian Pacific American religions needs to be addressed. In his assessment of religion in the American West D. Michael Quinn suggests, "the lapse of religiosity in Asian immigrants and their children is worthy of exploration in respect to the larger phenomenon ... of the 'unchurched' in the American West."[17] Given the assumption in most studies of immigrant religion that religious identity is central to both ethnic preservation and assimilation in the United States, does the fact that religion is not a dominant identity marker in the Pacific Northwest suggest that immigrants to the region are less religiously engaged (or more "lapsed," in Quinn's terms) than in other regions?

In fact, these Pacific Rim religious groups interact with the hegemonic "secular but spiritual" culture in a variety of ways. One important way is by learning the "game" of religious voluntarism, tolerance, and ecumenism characteristic of the region.

The Vedanta Society of Western Washington provides a good example. Vedanta is perhaps ideally suited to the regional environment, as the legacy from its founder, Sri Ramakrishna, and chief exponent in the United States in the early twentieth century, Vivekananda, is one of universal embrace of other religious traditions. Headquartered in Calcutta, the mission sends monks to staff over 20 Vedanta Societies in the United States as teachers and organizers. The monks or swamis do not actively proselytize but welcome "broad-minded people" who are "hungry" for the truth.

As Swami Bhaskarananda explains, "In the US, we have a spiritual ministry. We emphasize the importance of experiencing God here and now. We study different scriptures of different religions in order to learn, not to find fault with them." The teachings emphasize divine oneness, the divinity of humanity, and many paths to self-realization. The altar in the chapel includes portraits of Ramakrishna and Vivekananda, images of Buddha and Christ, and symbols of several other world religions. The swami wears Western suits, leads services on Sunday morning, and holds study sessions on weekday evenings. Though the appeal is primarily to Westerners, other Vedanta Societies are beginning to attract new Indian immigrants to a form of Hinduism already adapted to the U.S. environment.

The Northwest Dharma Association is another attempt to organize ecumenically a group of ethnically diverse voluntary associations. Its mission is to support Buddhist teachings and to "foster a network of friendship among Buddhist groups from all traditions." Through its Web site (*www.nwdharma.org*) and regular publication of the *Northwest Dharma News*, the society tries to promote "communication among Buddhist groups and the larger community." Board members are active sponsors and initiators of "activities of interest and benefit to Northwest Buddhists," including annual "Change Your Mind Days." The society's work is still done primarily by and for non-ethnic Buddhists, despite many efforts to encourage greater cross-cultural communication. Language, socio-economic, educational, and style differences, not to mention sectarian issues, may yet present obstacles to such intra-Buddhist ecumenical organization. Nevertheless, Northwest Dharma Association staff make easy partners for mainline Protestants and Catholics interested in "interfaith" dialogue and cooperation in public life.

Presence In "Public Life"

The participation of Pacific Rim religious groups in the "public life" of the Pacific Northwest arises under certain conditions. The history of European displacement and suppression of indigenous cultures and traditions is an important part of the underlying fabric of Pacific Northwest life. The public presence of Native Americans in major debates over environmental issues, treaty rights, gambling, and education is a staple of Northwest politics.

Religious freedom issues also arise. Two members of the Native American church were fired for ingesting peyote and denied unemployment compensation by the state of Oregon. The Supreme Court's Smith decision in 1990 ruled against the two and in favor of the state, and reversed the precedent of "balancing" religious freedoms of minority groups against the "compelling state interest" necessary to infringe upon them. It is often the case that external forces impel minority religious groups into "public life." The case of Japanese American internment and the redress movement of recent decades is an important case in point.

Respond to Larger Forces

After the attacks on the World Trade Center and Pentagon on September 11, 2001, both Muslim and Sikh communities in the Pacific Northwest began to mobilize. Muslims have recently found themselves the subject of Justice Department investigations that threaten to violate their freedom of religious association and freedom from discrimination on the basis of religion. Several high-profile arrests in Oregon and Washington and the detention of long-time Muslim residents by the Immigration and Naturalization Service (INS), now part of the Department of Homeland Security, have raised the alarm. The formation of a Seattle chapter of the Council on American-Islamic relations and the active engagement of many local Muslim leaders in interfaith dialogue and political coalitions are signs of a new public voice.

After the terrorist attacks of September 11, 2001, Sikhs in the Puget Sound area experienced hate crimes in the form of beatings and harassment. They were mistakenly branded as Muslims and as terrorist supporters of Osama bin Laden. Such mistreatment has led many Sikhs in the area to take a more public role in interfaith efforts to combat racism against all groups in the area and to educate the public about Sikhism's traditions of tolerance for other religions and strong moral values. Sikh spokespersons have taken a much greater role in conferences and meetings of public school teachers and interfaith groups around the region.

Interestingly enough, groups traditionally less visible held public memorials after the September 11 attacks. For instance, the Khmer Community of Tacoma, together with Buddhist temples and community organizations held a Buddhist memorial service for the terror victims. Church Councils and interfaith groups throughout the region found renewed interest in public interfaith dialogue and solidarity work after the tragedy. While the religious communities with roots on the Pacific Rim vary markedly in their immigration and settlement patterns, their approaches to engaging in public life, their shared heritage as objects of racist policies, and romanticization in the dominant culture locate them both on the periphery and at the center of Pacific Northwest religious life.

Many of the Pacific Rim religious communities discussed in this essay remain isolated or invisible to the majority population, except in "ethnic festival" mode. Yet their presence is often cited as evidence for the openness and tolerance of Pacific Northwest culture. The work of the Muslim community for "justice and freedom" to create a truly "American Muslim" identity that informs the moral fiber of the region, and the clever teaching of meditation and yoga techniques as "secular" methods of stress relief and successful living, may be "Islamizing" or "Buddhizing" or "Hinduizing" Pacific Northwest culture in subtle yet significant ways.

It remains to be seen whether more intimate, regular, or public interaction between Native American and Asian-American religious communities and the larger "secular but spiritual" population will produce challenges to the easy appropriation of the "other's" spiritual heritage as well as new forms of Native American and Asian-American, not to mention Western, religious traditions.

Endnotes

1. Wendy Rose, "The Great Pretenders: Further Reflections on Whiteshamanism," in *The State of Native America: genocide, colonization, and resistance,* ed. M. Annette Jaimes (Boston: South End Press, 1992).

2. Linda Barnes, "The Psychologizing of Chinese Medicine in the United States," *Journal of Culture, Medicine, and Psychiatry* (1998).

3. Jane Naomi Iwamura and Paul Spickard, eds. "Book Prospectus" for *Revealing the Sacred in Asian and Pacific America* (forthcoming).

4. Helen Rose Ebaugh and Janet Salzman Chafetz, eds., *Religion and the New Immigrants: Continuities and Adaptations in Immigrant Congregations* (Walnut Creek, CA: AltaMira Press, 2000): 391.

5. Amy Lavine, "Tibetan Buddhism in America: The Development of American Vajrayana," in Charles S. Prebish and Kenneth K. Tanaka, eds., *The Faces of Buddhism in America* (Berkeley, CA: University of California Press, 1998): 99-115.

6. Fred Cordova, *Filipinos: Forgotten Asian Americans* (Seattle: Demonstration Project for Asian Americans, 1983): 167-172.

7. Jodo Shinshu means "True Sect of the Pure Land." It began with the teachings of Shinran in 12th c. Japan, who reinterpreted earlier forms of Chinese and Japanese Pure Land Buddhism. He taught that rebirth in the Pure Land (from which ultimate liberation or enlightenment is easily attainable) is available to all who recite the name of Amida Buddha (*Namu-amida-butsu*). Shinran also broke with the tradition of celibate monastic styles of Buddhism, so that married laypeople might serve in priestly roles (Alfred Bloom, "Shin Buddhism in America: a Social Perspective," in Prebish and Tanaka,1998: 32-47).

8. Rinzai Zen, introduced to Japan from China by Eisai in the 12th c., emphasizes the use of *koans*, enigmatic questions that may lead to a flash of insight. Soto Zen, introduced in the 13th c. from China by Dogen, taught that enlightenment comes through seated meditation (*zazen*) alone.

9. Both of these twentieth century Buddhist imports from Japan have their roots in the teachings of thirteenth-century reformer Nichiren Daishonin, who taught that "anyone who chants the *Lotus Sutra*, and *Nam-myoho-renge-kyo* ['devotion to the Mystic Law of the *Lotus Sutra*] to the Gohonzon [enshrined copy of this text] can become one with Universal Law of cause and effect and change his or her own karma." The intentionally anti-intellectual emphasis on personal faith and chanting contrasts with the meditative and contemplative emphases of other Mahayana traditions. Soka Gakkai began in 1930

and revived after WWII as an active lay organization spreading the teachings of Nichiren Daishonin, considered the only true Buddhist teachings, in the midst of Japanese social crisis. Missionaries proselytized actively in the United States in the 1960s and 1970s, establishing a number of communal houses with an ethos of "individual power, change, and the mission for world peace." The Nichiren Shoshu and Soka Gakkai movements split in 1991 over a number of issues. The former continues in priest-centered Hokkeko temples, while the latter continues as a lay organization with significant financial support from Japan. The high proportion of African-American membership relative to other American Buddhist organizations distinguishes both (Jane Hurst, "Nichiren Shoshu and Soka Gakkai in America: the Pioneer Spirit," in Prebish and Tanaka, 1998: 79-97).

10. Ho-Youn Kwon, Kwang Chung Kim, and R. Stephen Warner, eds., *Korean Americans and Their Religions: Pilgrims and Missionaries From a Different Shore* (University Park, PA: Pennsylvania State University, 2001): 5-6.

11. Seung Sahn Sunim brought his unique combination of Buddhist forms to the United States in 1972. Mu Soeng, a longtime monk, describes the Kwan Um School as a unique amalgam of elements of Pure Land, Ch'an (Chinese predecessor of Korean S'on and Japanese Zen), chanting of the name of the bodhisattva of compassion, and vigorous prostrations that are characteristic of Korean folk Buddhist practice. The Kwan Um school emphasizes socially engaged "together action" by groups of followers living in a common house, *koan* or mantra practice tools, and a pastor-parishioner relationship between monks and lay members characteristic of the Chogye order in Korea. The Chogye order, incidentally, was formed in response to Japanese colonial pressures to adopt Soto Zen doctrine and organization, the separate Korean S'on (a celibate monastic tradition emphasizing individual effort and meditation), and Kyo (celibate monastic tradition emphasizing chanting of scripture and temple ritual) forming a united front (Soeng 1998).

12. An excellent introductory source for all of these South Asian traditions is Raymond Brady Williams, *Religions of Immigrants from India and Pakistan: New Threads in the American Tapestry* (New York: Cambridge University Press, 1988).

13. Theravada Buddhism, or "the way of the elders," typically centers around the *sangha* or assembly of ordained, celibate monks, who embody the ideals of renunciation of the world by following the *vinaya* or disciplinary code, and who preserve and convey the teaching (*dharma*). Laypeople gain merit by serving the *sangha* through acts of charity and devotion, in anticipation that such acts will gain them a favorable rebirth. The monastic life represents the

greatest opportunity for achieving full liberation or buddhahood.

14. Vipassana, or "insight meditation," is a form of traditional Theravada Buddhist meditation. As the loosely organized "movement" has attracted followers in the United States, Vipassana teachers have incorporated many aspects of Western transpersonal psychology in offering a "secular" but "spiritual" technique for personal transformation and individual experience. See Gil Fronsdal, "Insight Meditation in the United States: Life, Liberty, and the Pursuit of Happiness" in Prebish and Tanaka, 1998: 163-180.

15. Miriam Adeney and Kathryn Demaster, "Muslims of Seattle," in Yvonne Y. Haddad and Jane I. Smith, eds., *Muslim Communities in America* (Albany, NY: State University of New York Press, 1994): 202-203.

16. In the Sikh tradition, Guru Nanak (fifteenth century) was the first in a line of 10 charismatic leaders who collected teachings, hymns, and poetry. Upon the death of the 10th Guru, Gobind Singh, he passed the spiritual leadership of the community to the *Adi Granth*, the collection of these scriptures now honored as the *Guru Granth Sahib*, a book venerated and recited in Sikh worship, housed in a *gurudwara* ("house of the Guru") or temple. Personal leadership is invested in the Khalsa, the group of Sikhs who undergo initiation rites, assume the name "Singh" for men and "Kaur" for women, and preserve the five symbols of a baptized Sikh: uncut hair and beard; a special comb; special underwear; a short sword; and a steel bracelet.

17. Madeline Duntley, "Heritage, Ritual, and Translation: Seattle's Japanese Presbyterian Church," in Robert Orsi, ed., *Gods of the City: Religion and the American Urban Landscape* (Bloomington, IN: Indiana University Press, 1999): 295-6.

18. D. Michael Quinn, "Religion in the American West," in William Cronon, ed., George Miles, and Jay Gitlinin, *Under an Open Sky: Rethinking America's Western Past* (New York: W.W. Norton and Co., 1992): 150.

CHAPTER FIVE

SECULAR BUT SPIRITUAL IN THE PACIFIC NORTHWEST

Mark A. Shibley

The Pacific Northwest is the region of the United States with the lowest population of people affiliated with a religious institution, part of an unchurched belt
running up the Pacific coast from Mexico to Canada. Data, including that used for
the Religion by Region project, consistently show Northwesterners to be less likely
than other Americans to claim a religious preference (i.e., they decline to identify as
Protestants, Catholics, Jews, etc.) or to belong to a religious congregation.

But can it be assumed that people in the Pacific Northwest are *less* religious
than other Americans? Maybe not. Perhaps religious matters are simply experienced
and expressed differently in this region. Perhaps a new interpretive framework will
better illuminate the core values, ritual practices, types of transcendent experience,
and forms of community that engage non-church-going Northwesterners.

Since the 1990s scholars have argued persuasively that American society has
become a "spiritual marketplace" where individuals, in their quest for self-fulfillment, actively construct religious identities that are malleable and multifaceted,
often blurring the boundaries that separate one faith tradition from another. For
seekers in this marketplace, "spirituality" (direct, personal experience with the
sacred) is more important than "religion" (mediated, institutionalized experience
with the sacred).[1] In many cases, this leads seekers away from organized religion.

In *Religion and Personal Autonomy* Phillip Hammond argued that the institutional power of religion is weakest in the West because there is no history of a
dominant religious tradition, only pluralism created by successive waves of
immigration and cultural diffusion. Because mobility has loosened them from
ascriptive social ties, individuals in the West are freer than elsewhere to choose
their religion, or whether to be religious at all. Moreover, the cultural geography
of the Pacific Northwest is very different from southern California.

In his groundbreaking study the geographer Wilbur Zelinsky found the Northwest (Oregon, Washington, northern California, Western Nevada, and parts of Idaho and Montana) to have the least recognizable religious personality of all the nation's regions. As "the recipient of steady streams of migrants from all other sections of the nation," he argued, "this region has substantial numbers of members in almost all the denominational groups, but is not the major center for any."[2] Later, James Shortridge identified a pattern of western pluralism, and he found the "Pacific Coast" states, especially Oregon and Washington, to be the country's most religiously diverse region. Where Zelinsky saw a lack of personality in the West's religious makeup, Shortridge regarded religious diversity as precisely the quality that gives the Northwest its unique character.

Religious affiliation data from the North American Religion Atlas (NARA) show this pattern to be unchanged. As illustrated in Table 5.1 (page 141), most Northwesterners (62.8 percent) do not affiliate with established religious traditions. This unaffiliation rate is higher than in any other region. In fact, among all states Oregon, Washington, and Alaska rank first, third, and fifth in the percentage of the population that is unaffiliated.

Table 5.2 (page 141) presents complementary data on religious identification. The American Religious Identification Survey (ARIS) estimates that one-quarter of the population in the Pacific Northwest has no religious identity (i.e., are "Nones").[3] By comparison, there are twice as many Nones in the Northwest as there are in the Bible Belt.

Moreover, no religious tradition in the Northwest has nearly as big a share of the spiritual marketplace; Nones are the largest 'religious' group in the region. In New England there are more than twice as many Catholics as there are Nones, and in the South there are more than four times as many conservative Protestants as there are Nones. Even in California, where 19 percent of the population claims no religious identity, there are almost twice as many Catholics as Nones.

In short, many people in the Pacific Northwest are unattached to religious congregations, and the consequence of this relatively open religious market is clear: New religious movements (from Rajneesh to Ramtha), entrepreneurial Protestants (e.g., from old-line Pentecostals to the Christian Fellowship movement) and Mormons have flourished in the region in recent decades. Because Northwesterners are less tied to traditional religion, they are freer to explore alternative spirituality and more available for recruitment by new religions. Proselytizing churches and counter-cultural spirituality movements have always found this region attractive.

While many Northwesterners are institutionally unencumbered, there is no reason to believe they are a-spiritual. Most people in the region who claim no religious preference (one-quarter of the region's residents) and who do not appear on

Table 5.1   Religiously Unaffiliated as a Percentage of the Total Population, Rank-ordered by Region

Rank	Region	Unaffiliated as % of Population
1.	Pacific Northwest	62.8
2.	Rocky Mountain West	48.3
3.	Pacific Southwest	47.3
4.	Midwest	41.0
5.	South	40.5
6.	New England	38.5
7.	Mid-Atlantic	34.2
8.	Southern Crossroads	32.6
	Nationwide	40.6

Table 5.2   Percentage of the Population Claiming No Religious Identity, Rank Ordered by Region

Rank	Region	% of Population
1.	Pacific Northwest	25
2.	Pacific Southwest	19
3.	Rocky Mountain West	18
4.	New England	15
5.	Midwest	14
6.	Mid-Atlantic	13
7.	Southern Crossroads	12
8.	South	11
	Nationwide	14

church rolls (a majority of the population) are, it can be argued, *secular but spiritual*. They encounter the sacred and cultivate spiritual lives outside mainstream religious institutions.

ARIS data show, for instance, that most Nones have spiritual inclinations, as illustrated in Table 5.3 (page 143). While only one third of Pacific Northwest Nones regard their outlook as "somewhat religious" or "religious," more than two-thirds agree that "God exists" and that "God performs miracles." About half of all Nones believe that God helps them. Furthermore, there is very little difference between the spiritual orientation of Northwest Nones and Nones nationwide. In other words, a majority of Nones everywhere are spiritually open. This suggests that what is distinctive about religion in the Pacific Northwest is not the psychological orientation of individuals so much as social structural facts noted above—religious heterogeneity and low-affiliation rates.

This chapter explores what is sacred to Northwesterners who claim no religious preference, where and how they experience the sacred, and the difference their spiritual convictions and practices make in the public life of the region. It uses the term "spirituality" in the sense defined by Robert Wuthnow, to mean an individual's personal experience with sacred things (e.g., God, a divine being, a transcendent reality) and the beliefs and practices that express that experience.[4] Certain "religious" convictions held by these secular but spiritual Northwesterners drive conflict over how to use and care for natural resources on public land in the region. Belief that nature is sacred, rituals that connect people to place, and movements seeking to protect the environment together constitute a widely held and vibrant civil religion in the Pacific Northwest, though it is and always has been contested terrain.

Three clusters of alternative spirituality are prevalent in the Pacific Northwest. One is a constellation of New Age spiritualities including neo-paganism, metaphysics, and the "new spirituality" literature (e.g., *The Celestine Prophecy, Conversations with God, The Power of Now*). A second is the apocalyptic millennialism of a loose set of anti-government groups, such as Patriots, white supremacists, the Militia, and various kinds of survivalists. The third is earth-centered spirituality, which is expressed in a variety of ways in the secular environmental movement (particularly the campaign to protect old-growth forests), in Native American religion, and even in official religious organizations. Taken together these movements represent the bulk of alternative spirituality, at least the kind with consequences for public life. While none of these movements is unique to this region, many of them are expressed here in their purest form, and their high profile in regional culture is unmatched elsewhere in the United States.

In Search of the Self

In the first years of the twenty-first century, Powell's Books in Portland reorganized its "religion" titles. Most world religions (e.g., Buddhism, Christianity, Judaism, and Islam) now have their own aisle, and there are large, distinct sections on metaphysics, holistic health ("Mind, Body and Spirit"), and earth-based religion, among other spiritual themes. The "Spirit Team" manages all this material. According to BookWeb, an online source of book sales information, the "religious" category more than doubled in market share of consumer purchases of adult books in the United States between 1991 and 1998, growing far faster than any other single category. And according to *Book Industry Trends*, "non-bible" religion books largely account for this growth. Mirroring national trends, non-Christian religion and spirituality books are popular in Northwest bookstores.

Table 5.3   Percentage of Nones with Spiritual Inclinations, Pacific Northwest Compared to the Nation

Secularism Item	Pacific Northwest	Nation
"When it comes to your outlook, do you regard yourself as....?"		
Percent answering *somewhat religious* or *religious*	34 %	36 %
"Do you agree or disagree that God exists?"		
Percent answering *agree somewhat* or *agree strongly*	67 %	66 %
"Do you agree or disagree that God performs miracles?"		
Percent answering *agree somewhat* or *agree strongly*	69 %	76 %
"Do you agree or disagree that God helps me?"		
Percent answering *agree somewhat* or *agree strongly*	52 %	53 %

In individual interviews, staff at several prominent independent bookstores in the Northwest attested to the popularity of a new spirituality literature. Best sellers in late 2002 included *The Power of Now: A Guide to Spiritual Enlightenment,* by Eckhart Tolle, *The Four Agreements: A Practical Guide to Personal Freedom*, by Don Miguel Ruiz, *When Things Fall Apart: Heart Advice for Difficult Times*, by Pema Chodron, and *Mystical Dogs: Animals as Guide to Our Inner Life,* by Jean Huston. In the 1990s, the *Conversations with God* series, by Neal Donald Walsch and *The Seat of the Soul,* by Gary Zukav, were hot sellers throughout the country, including the Northwest. Prior to that, people across the United States read the *Celestine Prophecy,* by James Redfield, and *A Course in Miracles*. Not only are books like these popular in the Northwest, several of these authors reside in the region. Tolle, for example, lives in Vancouver, British Columbia; Walsch, Zukav, and Huston all live in Ashland, Oregon; and all four are immigrants to the region.

Collectively this literature is central to what Walsch calls the "new spirituality movement." Many of these prominent authors, like Walsch, have foundations or institutes that organize retreats and workshops featuring their work; they travel widely giving public lectures and interviews; and they maintain Web sites that serve as information conduits and associational hubs for spiritual seekers. These Web sites convey "new spirituality" ideas but also work to connect individuals of like mind in study and support groups. As Robert Wuthnow has shown, "small groups" are the grass-roots structure of spirituality today. This is as true for evangelical mega-churches that operate with a "house group" substructure as it is for quasi-underground expressions of neo-paganism in the Pacific Northwest. Wiccans, for example, typically find community in a small local coven. The Conversations With God (CWG) Web site calls its community structure "Wisdom Groups." Dozens of *The Power of Now* study groups, listed by city, state, and local leader, appear as hot-links on Tolle's Web site; more than half of these groups are in the Northwest. Followers of Nordic gods congregate in "kindreds," which are surprisingly plentiful across the United States, including the Pacific Northwest.

Closely related to this new spiritual literature are metaphysical practices like the use of crystals for healing, psychic consultations, shamanism, and spirit channeling; all are prevalent in the region. Perhaps the most prominent metaphysical happening in the last quarter of the twentieth century in the Northwest was the emergence of Ramtha, a 35,000 year-old warrior who in 1977 "made himself known" to J.Z. Knight, then a housewife in Tacoma, Washington. He speaks through her, delivering the message that "the Kingdom of Heaven is within you." Knight and Ramtha became an icon of the 1980's personal development movement. In 1988, after achieving international stature, Knight established Ramtha's School of Enlightenment in Yelm, Washington. A decade later, the school sponsored an international conference called *In Search of the Self*, designed to "prove the existence of a consciousness vastly different from that of Knight when she [channels] Ramtha." According to Michael Brown's ethnographic study of spirit channeling "the willingness to suspend disbelief and open the self to messages from other places, other times, is the defining feature of the channeling zone."[5]

Another prominent metaphysical happening in the Northwest was the "Harmonic Convergence," an astrological event in 1987 that coalesced the attention of New Age practitioners around sacred sites like Mt. Shasta, just south of the Oregon boarder. One New Age Web site described it as "a trigger for an incredible spiritual re-birth on our planet, involving the whole planet, bonding to mother Earth for a major spiritual surge." Whatever its astrological significance, the Harmonic Convergence became a major social event as thousands of people made the pilgrimage to Mt. Shasta and other sacred sites worldwide.

Along with "new spirituality" and various metaphysical practices, paganism and other earth-based religions flourish in the Northwest today. Estimating the size and scope of these religious practices, however, is difficult. Recent news coverage of neo-pagan beliefs (animism) and practices (seasonal rites) nicely captures the spiritual texture, grassroots nature, and growing public presence of the movement in the Northwest. It is increasingly easy to find open pagan communities and interview witches willing to have their name published. Nine Houses of Gaia, a non-profit organization promoting the interests of earth-based religions, publishes a monthly online newsletter, annually hosts The Northwest Fall Equinox Festival (in a forest near Portland), and keeps a Web site that posts a Pagan Community Directory for the region. The directory lists 87 separate organizations, about half of which are located in the greater Portland area. Finding pagan communities is not difficult.

Three organizations in this directory illustrate the growing breadth and depth of neo-paganism in the region. First, the Ásatrú Council of Washington (ACW), headquartered in Renton, is the networking hub for Nordic spiritual traditions in the United States. Its Web site lists dozens of kindreds (local congregations) in suburban areas throughout the Northwest.

Second, one of the oldest (established in 1979) and most institutionalized neo-pagan congregations in the country is Aquarian Tabernacle Church (ATC) in Everett, Washington. It is an accredited Wiccan congregation that holds regular monthly worship. ATC owns property and church facilities, offers pastoral counseling, performs weddings, sponsors festivals, teaches public classes about their tradition, offers seminary training with ministerial degrees, and sponsors SpiralScouts (the Pagan equivalent of Boy/Girl Scouts). The congregation founder, Pete Pathfinder Davis, has served as President of the Interfaith Council of Washington.

Third, neo-pagan organizations, like Women in Conscious Creative Action (WICCA) based in Eugene, nurture women's spirituality in particular. WICCA was founded in 1983 and incorporated with the state of Oregon in 1984 because "we felt it was important for Women's Spirituality to be recognized as a bona fide religion," according to the organization's official "herstory." In function, WICCA is much like any religious congregation. It fosters shared belief and ritual about sacred things (the individual, the earth) that bind adherents together in community. WICCA is state sanctioned (the Rev. Norma Joyce can perform weddings), and it is openly pagan. WICCA, ATC, ACW, and a growing number of similar organizations in the region suggest that neo-paganism is increasingly mainstream. It has a growing presence in suburbia, and organizations like Cauldron of Changes in Eugene and Portland Pagan Pride are devoted explicitly to creating and maintaining a *public* pagan tradition through community outreach.

While neo-paganism, metaphysics, and the new spirituality literature, as expressed in the Northwest, are directed toward nurturing religious experience, and thus privilege practice (ritual) over doctrine (belief), there are clear ideological dimensions to this diffuse movement. Paul Heelas' benchmark study of the New Age movement shows that underlying the hodge-podge of spiritual practices associated with it throughout the twentieth century is a striking consensus about the human condition and how it can be transformed.[6] He argues that the centerpiece of the New Age worldview is a belief that the self is sacred: "Everyone is

God. Everyone." Many New Age practitioners, particularly neo-pagans, also emphasize the sacredness of the natural order as a whole, but the initial task in New Age spirituality has been to connect with an authentic self.

In this worldview, the self as an outcome of socialization must be overcome for an authentic self to emerge. The journey toward self-discovery is clearly at the core of the new spirituality literature, but in the Pacific Northwest, more often than not, this impulse is connected to earth-spirituality and a desire for social as well as personal transformation. WICCA's statement of purpose, for example, proclaims:

> We are women …[d]edicated to the concept of healing ourselves and Mother Earth, we have an effect on our culture and the political scene. We believe in the sanctity of Mother Earth…. We consciously learn to work with the power of the Universe, empowering ourselves and one another. We know that in learning to tap into that power we will be able to help the Mother.[7]

Here the self and the earth are objects of spiritual work, which then become the basis for cultural change. In this way, the personal growth is understood to be political.

According to Heelas, there are essentially three dimensions to the worldview of self-spirituality in New Age movements.

- It is explanatory: "Your lives do not work" because you are living in a belief system provided by the dominant culture rather than living based on experience.
- It is normative: "You are God and Goddess in exile"; this is the truth about who you are and what you must strive for.
- It is prescriptive: "Let go"; salvation comes through exorcizing the tyrannical hold of the socialized mode of the being.

In short, the world is a mess because individuals are not in touch with their true self, which is obscured by culture. In principle, therefore, the primary work in New Age spirituality is a process of empowering individuals over dominant cultural institutions and ideologies.

Neale Donald Walsch's new spirituality is congruent with these general features of the New Age movements. As Walsch stated in an interview, "Our world is in very deep trouble right now." The CWG Web site culls from news headlines the evidence of a world gone awry—stories about violent crime, neglect, disease, famine, war, and impending war. Humanity, Walsch says, is facing a spiritual crisis (i.e., separation from one another), and if we want to see real change in our world, we have to alter the belief systems advanced by "Exclusivist Organized Religion." Walsch says he honors the wisdom at the core of all historic religious traditions but believes that religious institutions need reform. They propagate inflexible ideologies, which are the source of most social conflict. Thus, Walsch's latest conversations with God led to the publication of *The New Revelations,* a direct challenge to ecclessial authority. He urges people to "become modern-day Martin Luthers, nailing [the Five Steps to Peace] to [their] chosen house of worship—church-house door, and the door of every mosque."

Notwithstanding this reformation impulse, the broader movement exemplified by New Spirituality literature, particularly Walsch's early books, is about personal transformation, about healing one's self. The hope, indeed the expectation, is that social transformation will follow (i.e., the birth of a "new age"), but it will come only if individuals are spiritually reborn.

Why has self and earth-based spirituality grown over the last quarter of the twentieth century? Simply put, the dominant institutions, including churches, lost legitimacy in the 1960s for a relatively affluent and well-educated generation of young Americans disillusioned by the moral and spiritual contradictions of middle-class life (e.g., crass materialism and ecological crisis; persistent inequality based in race, class, and gender) and U.S. foreign policy (e.g., a pointless war in Vietnam; neo-colonial "development" in Latin America). A crisis of meaning and purpose, and breaking free from cultural institution, became defining characteristics of the baby-boom generation.

Ultimately, anti-establishment rebellion in the 1960s led to spiritual exploration and alternative religious movements in the 1970s. Walsch's current critique of organized religion echoes the anti-establishment voice of his generation: "We are seeking ways to reform tradition.... Not only are the institutional forms of religion limiting, they are dangerous. Fundamentalists are inspired to fly planes into buildings and kill people." ·

Places like Eugene and Bellingham were at the center of counter-cultural rebellion, so spiritual exploration and new religious movements prospered in the Northwest. Ken Kesey, guru of the psychedelic movement, made his home just outside Eugene, and in 1972, the Unification Church ("Moonies") began its effort to recruit North Americans at the University of Oregon. While self-development spirituality was not invented in the Northwest, it has drifted steadily up the coast with equity refugees fleeing the material culture of southern California in search of a simpler, more fulfilling lifestyle. Self- and earth-based spirituality find ample space and fertile ground in the cultural geography of the region, particularly urban centers like the Puget Sound area and the Willamette Valley.

According to Walsch, affluence is a prerequisite for New Spirituality because people with relatively high socio-economic status (wealth and education) are more open to spiritual exploration. Scholars too have observed a correlation between socio-economic status and spiritual exploration, but it is as much a function of generation as of class. Walsch believes that more education leads to a broader range of experience and an openness to new ways of seeing the world. Such people are "more willing to embrace the challenge of looking beyond tradition," he says. "University towns, places with little or no industry, are places where people are 'socially sensitive,' open to diversity." Walsch sees his movement as "trickle-down spirituality"; the first to be spiritually enlightened are well educated, urban, and affluent. Others will follow, he believes, as new modes of thinking and living spread through the culture. Walsch settled in Ashland, Oregon because it is an affluent university town where people are receptive to his spiritual work.

Whether reading *The Power of Now*, channeling spirits, or celebrating seasonal rituals in community with neo-pagans, New Spirituality clearly represents a turn away from the hyper-rationality of modern institutions (the bureaucracy and dogma of churches and secular organizations alike), but it also fulfills a core value of modern Western culture, the elevation of the individual above community—what Emil Durkheim called the "cult of the individual." Michael Brown put it this way: "Channels and their clients have elevated the protean impulse to a sacred principle." Or in Shirley MacLaine's own words, "I am God. I am God. I am God."

But what difference does radically individualized religion make in the public life of the region? While spiritual quests are often private journeys in search of self-fulfillment, they draw from available culture and contribute to it. In the case of channeling, what started as a novel spiritual exploration in the western United States now permeates American culture. This practice, which uses "altered states of consciousness to connect to wisdom emanating from the collective unconscious or even from other planets, dimensions, or historical eras," writes Michael Brown in *The Channeling Zone*, has become "a well-established form of religious exploration that is likely to be with us for a while." So just as Nancy Reagan regularly consulted an astrologer during her White House years, Hillary Rodham Clinton was guided through imaginary conversations with Eleanor Roosevelt and Mahatma Gandhi by the New Age psychotherapist Jean Huston. Presumably, insights from spiritual explorations like these influence subsequence action, but how so?

One way New Spirituality contributes to cultural change is by facilitating innovation. Shifting authority in spiritual matters from institutions to individuals promotes creativity. Brown expects that "channeling and related techniques of self-expansion will continue to offer a lively arena for the free play of the religious imagination. Committed rationalists will never find the channeling zone an attractive destination, [but for others] it is likely to remain a site of emotional and spiritual renewal."

This propensity for spiritual exploration and growth, according to the sociologist Paul Ray and the psychologist Sherry Anderson, is a characteristic feature of an emerging group of people they call "Cultural Creatives." In contrast with "Traditionalists" (cultural conservatives) and "Modernists" (those content with the status quo), Creatives care a lot about the environment, women's rights, and the disenfranchised, as well as spiritual growth. "These people are practical," Anderson says. "They love the Earth, and they want to live their values." Ray and Anderson claim that among Cultural Creatives spirituality (i.e., the capacity to examine one's conscience, to sit in silence, to listen deeply) is essential to social movements. Creative political action flows from creative reflection. Perhaps many Northwesterners involved in personal growth movements and earth-based spirituality are among the estimated 50 million Cultural Creatives in the United States, and perhaps the political significance of new spirituality is that it provides a spiritual foundation to the environmental movement, the women's movement, and the like.

One of the most internationally prominent Cultural Creative voices is *YES! A Journal of Positive Futures,* published on Bainbridge Island by the Positive Futures Network (PFN). PFN is an independent, nonprofit organization dedicated to supporting people's active engagement in creating a just, sustainable, and compassionate world. Author David Korten and the other founders were acting on their belief that humanity has reached a turning point where only creative change can meet the "unprecedented threats to the Earth's ecosystems and our social fabric." In their Web site manifesto, they continue:

> In the years since PFN was founded, our communications and networking activities have helped deepen the commitment of hundreds of thousands of people to contribute to transformational change in their personal lives, their communities, their nation, and the world.

People like David Korten are crafting new ideas, new ways of living, new forms of community in the hope of transforming what they see as an unjust and unsustainable world. A new spirituality is central to this cultural enterprise. However, not all Northwesterners welcome the exploration of non-Christian religion. Young, college-educated urbanites may see it as a tool for self-enrichment and as a vehicle for social change, but older, more conservative rural Northwesterners often lament New Spirituality as evidence of cultural decline, movement away from America's Christian roots.

Ironically, both groups share the view that government and big business (through international trade agreements, to name one example) are in no small measure responsible for many of the region's economic convulsions and social ills. For cultural conservatives, however, a world gone to hell invites not the birth of a New Age but rather retrenchment, a reactionary survivalism. As a result, one of the most significant and least understood spiritual impulses in the Northwest is apocalyptic, anti-government millennialism, a nationwide phenomenon with particularly strong resonance in the Northwest.

Apocalyptic, Anti-Government Millennialism

The Aryan Nations, Christian Patriots, the Militia, assorted survivalists, and other like groups have flourished in the Pacific Northwest. Taken together, they represent a loose network of anti-government millennialists united by a strong conviction that the U.S. government is cooperating in a "New World Order" conspiracy designed to restrict the God-given liberties of American citizens (e.g., property rights, the right to bear arms, free speech). After the terrorist attacks of September 11, 2001 their Web sites and newsletters expressed indignation at the Bush administration's pronouncements that American citizens must be prepared to accept some limitations on their individual freedom in the fight against terrorism. Suspicion of government runs deep.

Participants in these organizations believe they are American patriots (i.e., defenders of the U.S. Constitution) and authentic Christians (i.e., most are theologically and culturally conservative). They expect societal collapse and are preparing largely in defensive but often creative ways to survive it. While these groups are not unique to this region, in the last quarter of the twentieth century the Northwest became the cradle for much of the movement's core leadership, and it provided fertile ground for the movement's growth.

Viewed over time and from a distance, anti-government millennialism in the Northwest is fluid organizationally and even ideologically; leaders come and go (some are indigenous to the Northwest, some not), and new martyrs are made. Several excellent studies have reliably documented the evolution of this diffuse movement, its key players, and its driving concerns.[8] This brief review draws heavily from this literature, as well as personal correspondence with current Militia participants in the Pacific Northwest and a careful reading of dozens of linked Militia Web sites.

According to the Southern Poverty Law Center's (SPLC) Klanwatch Project, there were dozens of anti-government groups active in the United States in the mid-1990s. Some observers call this assortment of overlapping organizations the "Patriot Movement," but the term "movement" exaggerates their organizational and ideological coherence. According to the SPLC and the Anti-Defamation League of B'Nai Brith (ADL), these "extremist" groups are all essentially the same. They are racist; they are armed; they are engaged in illegal actively; and thus they are dangerous. Some proved to be so, particularly in the 1980s and early 1990s, as the following example illustrates.

In the mid-1980s the Aryan Nations and related groups, such as The Order, centered in northern Idaho, were planning acts of domestic terrorism designed to destabilize the social order and act as a precursor to establishing an all-white "Aryan Homeland." Participants in this movement, chiefly Robert Mathews, were responsible for a number of dramatic robberies throughout the West and the murder of the Jewish talk-show host Alan Berg in Denver. Following Berg's assassination, federal agencies (the Treasury Department's Bureau of Alcohol, Tobacco, and Firearms [ATF], the Federal Bureau of Investigation [FBI] and the Internal Revenue Service [IRS]) stepped up their aggressive pursuit of racist, anti-government activists, thwarting several conspiracies to commit further violence. When federal agents finally caught up with Mathews he refused to surrender and died in a dramatic, western-style shootout on Whidbey Island in the Puget Sound, securing his martyrdom in the eyes of some fellow activists.

Groups like the Order, the Order II, the Phineas Priesthood, and Posse Comitatus were among the most explicitly racist and militant arms of anti-government activism. And while many key actors and organizations in the Patriot movement did (some still do) have racist intentions and were convicted of tax-evasion, counterfeiting, or conspiracy to commit murder, among other things, most anti-government millennialists are not actively engaged in destabilizing the social order. Rather, most are actively preparing to survive what they perceive to be an extant lack of order.

What is anti-government millennialism? The worldview of participants in the Patriot movement is fundamentally dualistic and apocalyptic, though it ranges from the quasi-Christian racist ideology of Christian Identity[9] to a secular millennialism that thrives on conspiracy theories, or a combination of both. Whether religious or secular, these are perilous times, movement propaganda suggests, a secret regime seeks to disarm American citizens and subjugate them to a totalitarian world government. For some, the Battle of Armageddon is thus at hand.

Said Gordon Kahl, an infamous member of the Posse Comitatus, "We are engaged in a struggle to the death between the people of the Kingdom of God and the Kingdom of Satan." When Kahl was killed in a shootout with U.S. marshals he became a martyr for the posse and other anti-government groups. Many movement leaders (e.g., Louis Beam, Richard Butler, Bo Gritz, Larry Pratt, William Pierce, among others) have drawn inspiration and direction from Christian Identity, but others have worked to distance themselves from such racist ideology.

Carl Worden, the liaison officer of the Southern Oregon Militia, said in an interview for this essay that most militia members are "mainstream conservative Christians, not racist CI (Christian Identify) freaks. The true constitutional Militia groups do not fraternize with the various racist and anti Semitic groups festering here and there, and we in fact oppose them." Because of increased scrutiny of anti-government groups by SPLC and ADL, some Northwest militia groups do seem to have distanced themselves from Christian Identity and overt racism.

Nevertheless, these groups share a distrust of government institutions and expect a bleak future. To some in the movement, if America is to be saved, government must be destroyed. A member of the of Unorganized Militia of Stevens County, Washington, quoted by Klanwatch, said after the tragedy in Waco, "the reason the Second Amendment was put into the United States Constitution...[was] so that when officials of the federal and state and local government get out of hand, you can shoot them.... eventually people like Janet Reno will be...summarily executed."

The conspiracy theories that dominate Patriot propaganda all suggest that the U.S. government, in collusion with an international syndicate, is intent on disarming Americans and creating one-world government. New levels of international cooperation (e.g., the Gulf War alliance, which President G. H. Bush referred to as "The New World Order"); free trade agreements (the North American Free Trade Agreement {NAFTA} and the General Agreement of Tariffs and Trade {GATT}); domestic gun control (the Brady Bill was signed by President Clinton in 1994); and two federal law enforcement disasters (Ruby Ridge and Waco) are all taken to be evidence that the government is intent on undermining national sovereignty and destroying constitutional rights. These developments, together with the federal government's aggressive efforts to disarm, prosecute, and bankrupt the most dangerous and corrupt elements of the movement, have worked to solidify perception that the U.S. government is illegitimate and a threat to its own people.

Conspiratorial perspectives have a remarkable capacity to absorb even contradictory information in a way that reinforces rather than challenges an existing worldview. Patriot discussions on the Internet still suggest that the federal government itself orchestrated the bombing of the Murrah Building in Oklahoma City and that inept government agencies (CIA and FBI) are largely responsible for the terrorist attacks of September 11, 2001.

"Patriots," whether religious or secular, also share an apocalyptic vision. Social, economic, and political collapse is imminent. Patriots expect the future to be explosive. One of the most forceful and widely read expressions of this apocalyptic vision is *The Turner Diaries*. First published in 1978 by William Pierce, a former physics professor at Oregon State University, it is a fictional account of rebellion against the New World Order in defense of an exclusively white and Christian nation, but for some anti-government millennialists, such as the convicted Oklahoma City bomber Timothy McVeigh, it is a prophetic call to arms.

Christian Identity has provided ideological coherence and theological justification for some branches of the Patriot movement, but non-religious magazines and newsletters too play a role in the formation and maintenance of a millennial worldview (e.g., *Soldier of Fortune*; *The Seditionist*; *The American Bulletin*; *National Vanguard*). Together with powerful new media for information dissemination (e.g., linked Web sites, talk radio), these ideas have blended into a populist form of apocalyptic millennialism. Like any comprehensive religious meaning system, the movement's ideology explains experience and proscribes action in ultimate terms for those operating within communities (temporal or virtual) that support a Patriot worldview.

Many of the cultural themes advanced by anti-government millennialists intersect with mainstream—albeit right-of-center—political debate in the Northwest. Some of these issues (e.g., taxation, property rights, and resisting gun control) are secular; other issues dovetail with the cultural agenda of the Christian Right (e.g., anti-homosexuality, prayer in public school, and restoring America as a Christian nation).[10] According to Worden, many in the movement situate their anti-government millennialism in a particular fundamentalist Christian reading of Scripture that identifies the United States with the new Babylon, and that makes clear that "God is not a pacifist. Jesus is not a pacifist."

From outside the subculture, this worldview seems strange, implausible, and dangerous. From the Patriot perspective, it is sensible, practical, and empowering. It explains disruptive social change; it assigns blame; it gives purpose and direction to groups and individuals; and it sanctifies action. Christian Patriots believe their anti-government cause is just. The movement has grown in recent decades because it provides meaning and belonging for people whose lives are upset by social change.

Political and religious movements are always forming in response to social change. The civil rights movement of the 1950s and '60s, the Vietnam War, and the emergence of a counter culture, for instance, were the tumultuous backdrop for the establishment of Aryan Nations in 1978. Richard Butler moved his church away from the cultural diversity and turmoil of southern California to northern Idaho to establish an Aryan homeland, a haven for white supremacist organizing and Christian Identity teaching. The Posse Comitatus (meaning "power of the county") successfully recruited rural folk in the upper-Midwest and Pacific Northwest during the farm crisis of the late 1970s and early 1980s by refusing to recognize law enforcement or government authority higher than the county sheriff.

As Joel Dyer put it in *Harvest of Rage*, "[i]f the federal government won't help rural America, then rural America will simply govern itself by ignoring federal authority." Populist movements like these thrive on real social unrest, and they sometimes create more of it, for example when the efforts of the FBI, the ATF, and the IRS to crack down on the illegal activities of anti-government groups centered in the Pacific Northwest in the 1980s led directly to the confrontation with the Weaver family at Ruby Ridge in 1992. In that confrontation, an FBI agent and two members of the Weaver family died.

Millennialism is in many ways a self-fulfilling prophecy; in defying government authority, it invites confrontation and violence. Yet real economic and cultural conditions fuel anti-government movements. A Montana rancher "who counts Freemen as neighbors and has incurred their wrath by standing up to them," recounted to David Neiwart the growing internal colonization of farming in the United States and the rage it engenders in people caught in an economic system "where more money leaves the farm to pay interest than ever stays; a system where any disaster, a sick child, a blizzard, a flood, or a hailstorm can tip the balance towards foreclosure." "Political opportunists of the radical right" recognized the fertile ground of discontent.

The Northwest is still seen by outsiders and natives alike as a larger-than-life frontier province, a mythic place where industrious individuals and visionary communities can prosper close to the land and unencumbered by government. This perception has attracted utopian movements on the left (back-to-the-land communes and Rajneeshees) and neo-fascist movements on the right (Aryan Nations and Christian Patriots).

In reality, the tentacles of a global capitalism have thoroughly infused the region, and in the 1980s, turbulence from the farm crisis was exacerbated by dramatic changes in the resource-extraction-based economy of the Pacific Northwest. Jobs in the woods and the fishing industry disappeared almost overnight, and these changes affect more than opportunities for income; they undermine a way of life. The shift to a new Northwest economy—urban-based high tech and outdoor recreation-based tourism—has upset rural culture.

Beyond this structural change, the Patriot movement has flourished here for several specific reasons:

- First, there is geographic and cultural space for alternative religious (or quasi-religious) movements.
- Second, federal entities (e.g., the Environmental Protection Agency [EPA], the U.S. Forest Service and Fish and Wildlife Service of the Department of the Interior, and federal courts) have enacted new environmental policies and enforced laws that have radically altered how people may live on the land, an affront to Northwesterners' fierce independence.
- Third, to the extent that rural Northwesterners are conventionally religious, they adhere to conservative Protestant traditions where apocalyptic and millennial themes are readily available.
- Finally, the emergence of a survivalist industry centered in the Pacific Northwest has successfully exploited the millennial hopes and fears of people disoriented by economic and cultural change.

This largely unexplored theme—the commodification of survivalism—has been critical to the growth of the Patriot movement. Market processes connect like individuals and are efficient vehicles for the production of a survival culture and the distribution of its goods and services. Richard Mitchell's *Dancing at Armageddon* examines this industry and uncovers a more benign dimension to anti-government millennialism.

A sociologist at Oregon State University and an avid outdoorsman, Mitchell spent more than a decade exploring the subculture of survivalism in the Pacific Northwest from the inside. The common premise of all survivalism, he suggests, is this: "There are troubles ahead but ways to cope. It is a matter of being in the right place at the right time with the right stuff.... Protection can be bought. Survival is for sale." This is good news for worried millennialists, news spread through the Preparedness Expo, a survivalist trade show that moves around the west (Denver, Portland, Phoenix, Seattle and Salt Lake City) like a mixture of gun show and traveling revival. The Expo provides networking opportunities that connect individuals to local support groups, not unlike the "house group" model used so successfully by mega-churches. That is, individuals find community and become imbedded in the subculture through the formation of small groups of like-minded neighbors.

According to Mitchell, "It is the imaginative work of *culture crafting,* not the artifacts of culture, to which survivalists are attracted." This characterization of anti-government millennialism is far less menacing than most portraits of the Patriot movement. Whatever else they may be, they are "culture crafters." They are struggling to define the culture and make meaningful lives. According to Mitchell, a spiritual impulse runs through all these anti-government groups. He calls it "creative transcendence of calamitous cultural change."

This spiritual form finds a home in the Northwest because the calamitous consequences of social and economic change are everywhere, particularly in rural communities, and because there is geographic and cultural space for religious innovation. Ultimately, however, Christian Patriots, survivalists, and the like are less influential culture crafters than the Culture Creatives of the Pacific Northwest. Along with a non-Christian spirituality of self-transformation, nature religion has emerged as the dominant vehicle in this region for encounters with the sacred.

Northwest Nature Religion

The ideas, activities, and organizations comprising the third cluster of alternative spirituality are the most central to the cultural ethos of the Pacific Northwest. This is "nature religion," which according to Catherine L. Albanese, in her book *Nature Religion in America,* is an elusive pattern of thought and action in American history, difficult to follow in part because of its grass-roots origin and plural character. "Unorganized and unacknowledged as religion," she writes, "it is—given the right places to look—everywhere apparent. But it is also a form of religion that slips between the cracks of the usual interpretive grids." In the Northwest, where official religion does not pervade the cultural landscape, nature religion is ubiquitous—in regional literature, in the rituals of leisure, in environmental movement ethics, in Native American culture, and even in official religious institutions.

Because great literature ultimately explores the meaning of human life, it unavoidably raises religious questions: What do people hold sacred in this place? Like literature of the American West more generally, Northwest writers grapple with epic frontier themes (e.g., provincialism; rugged individualism; the landscape as beautiful but inhospitable; the folly of industrial farming and resource extraction). In the fiction of Ken Kesey, for instance, nature is a powerful and irrepressible character in human tragedy (e.g., *Sometimes a Great Notion*). In the poetry of William Stafford, this most western province is a secret treasure, worth dying for to preserve (e.g., *An Oregon Message*). In the non-fiction of Barry Lopez, the Alaskan tundra is a crucible for learning to see fundamental relationships between human and non-human nature, connections that are understood to be spiritual as well as ecological (e.g., *Arctic Dreams*).

Along with frontier themes, the conviction that nature is sacred is particularly resonant in the canonical texts of Northwest literature. Many of America's most prominent "nature writers" write about and/or reside in the Pacific Northwest. They publish regularly in *Orion: People and Nature,* and virtually all explore significant spiritual themes.

In "The Naturalist," Barry Lopez argues that to be truthful and useful, those who observe and write about nature must recognize "that a politics with no biology, or a politics without field biology, or a political platform in which human biological requirements form but one plank, is a vision of the gates of Hell." In "Patriots for American Land," Richard Nelson suggests that the perseverance of Native American spirituality in Alaska is responsible for the presence of healthy ecosystems where nearly "every species of animal and plant known to have existed before Europeans arrived is still present, and almost all are not significantly diminished in numbers." He continues:

> In Alaska we have the privilege of bearing witness to the world exactly as God (of the Great Raven of Native Alaskan creation stories) intended it to be, the world complete and intact, *making Alaska the rarest of all American treasures and a brilliant source of hope for our future.*

He argues further that Native Alaskans, like the Koyukon Indians, still follow ancient customs of reverence for the natural world. A Koyukon elder, Lavine
Williams, told him, "The country knows. If you do wrong things to it the whole
country knows. It feels what's happening to it. I guess everything is connected
together somehow, under the ground." These Northwest writers, drawing on various religious and philosophical traditions, all worship in the same outdoor temple. Time spent mindfully in the wild places of the Northwest is a religious experience.

No writer more aptly illustrates Northwest nature religion than David James
Duncan, whose "confessions, Druidic rants, and reflections" have become gospel
to nature lovers in the Northwest. His latest book, *My Story as told by Water*, is
an autobiographical collection of essays wrestling with the moral and spiritual
implications of environmental degradation. For Duncan, the natural world is
sacred, and so its degradation is a spiritual as well as ecological catastrophe, and
healing nature requires a spiritual antidote.

Even if books like these are widely read, shared ideas alone do not constitute
religion. "To be religion," according to Albanese, "the symbol of nature
must...get out on the street....[It must] become the property of everybody's people....The homespun quality of what they produced, the do-it-yourself edge to
their ideas and practice, should not deter us from acknowledging the seriousness
of the religious mentality among nonspecialists."

How do people in the region live with respect to nature? The ethics and
actions of environmental groups (e.g., wilderness preservation and grassroots
activism) are a popular organizational form of nature religion in the region, as are
common leisure pursuits like hiking and gardening. "Tree-hugging Dirt
Worshiper," reads a bumper sticker in Ashland, Oregon.

"We joined Grace Memorial Episcopal Church," writes a friend, "but we're
your perfect Oregonians. If it's nice out we...take a hike instead...of going to
church." This everyday form of recreation in nature has of course become institutionalized in weekend hikes sponsored by local chapters of the Sierra Club and
like groups. On a recent public education tour through sections of the Squires
Peak Fire in southern Oregon (the site President Bush visited in August 2002), a
prominent local environmental activist was sporting a T-shirt that read, "May the
Forest be with You." Indeed, the "ancient forest" has become an archetype that
inspires environmental activism in the region.

Much contemporary environmentalism in the Northwest is a religious system, not simply because it is sometimes dogmatic and moralistic but rather
because its rituals and core beliefs distinguish between things sacred (wilderness)
and things profane (all else, often including people). Nature religion is visible in
the mission statements and policy goals of mainstream and radical environmen-

tal movement organizations, in conflicted public discourse over resource management (i.e., the fate of ancient forests), and in how people organize their daily lives. Northwesterners think of themselves as nature lovers and stewards of the environment, people living close to nature, and this identity has spiritual meaning. Linda Duffy, The U.S. Forest Service Ashland District Ranger, said in a public speech, "stewardship is the spiritual stream I stand in."

In the 1980s the tone of environmentalism in the Northwest became more strident and invoked religious metaphors. No issue symbolized this more than the crusade to preserve old-growth forests on public land. Oregon Natural Resource Council (ONRC), based in Portland, and its outspoken conservation director, Andy Kerr, played a key role in transforming the issue into a battle for the last great forests of the Pacific Northwest. ONRC in fact coined the term "ancient forest" to replace scientific jargon like "late-successional" and "old-growth." It was chosen to invoke awe. It quickly caught on, and it was effective in galvanizing broad public support for the cause.

Local groups like the ONRC and the Native Forest Council (NFC) took the lead in the campaign to preserve ancient forests on public land and were soon joined by national groups like The Wilderness Society and Sierra Club. Together they formed powerful new coalitions such as Ancient Forest Alliance that proved adept at using federal law to halt the harvest of old-growth forests. By the early 1990s their collective efforts had won broad public support, and by 2001 the timber harvested on federal land in Oregon was about 4 percent of the historically high volume of 1986.

The ancient forest campaign has a moral dimension (i.e., human exploitation of forest resources in the Northwest violate the rights of non-human species), but it has a clear spiritual dimension as well. Both dimensions are illustrated by an NFC pamphlet, entitled "Stop the Chainsaw Massacre." One page reads,

> The Indictment:
> - America's forests are priceless. They give us cold, clear water to drink. They regulate global and regional climates. They provide habitat for wildlife. And perhaps most important, in their beauty and tranquility we find spiritual enrichment and renewal.
> - Yet in the time it takes to read this brochure, several acres of irreplaceable virgin forest will be clearcut. And there isn't much left, as shown at the left. Called ancient, native, virgin, primeval, or old growth, these are the original, untouched forests that existed when the first-settlers arrived in North America. And only five percent is left.

Something "priceless" is understood to be sacred, and "perhaps the most important" feature of ancient forests is that they are a source for "spiritual enrichment and renewal." Nature may have intrinsic value, but part of the campaign's appeal is that people will find spiritual nourishment in ancient forests.

Several years after the ancient forest campaign began, U.S. Congressman Peter DeFazio (D-OR) observed, "This controversy has begun to resemble a religious war: those who deviate from the true faith—whichever true faith—are condemned as sinners, heretics, or worse. There is no compromise for the true believer...." [11]

As with any religious or quasi-religious movement, there are prophets and zealots. Radical forest activism in the Northwest has played a key role in drawing public attention to the ecological consequences of industrial forestry and in framing the management of public forests as an urgent problem. Earth First! activism, for instance, grew during the late 1980s in the Northwest, alongside more conventional elements of the movement. Cascadia Forest Alliance (Eugene-based) and Earth Liberation Front (underground) engage in direct action to liberate forests from human exploitation.

Radical environmentalists tend to be young, idealistic, and alienated from mainstream religious, economic, and political institutions that they find morally bankrupt. In grassroots activism, they find an alternative meaning system (neo-Marxism and some variant of "deep ecology"), symbolic rituals (forest camps and tree-sits), a compelling purpose (earth liberation; "no compromise in defense of Mother Earth!"), community (the movement), and indeed religious experience (a mindful awareness of and reverence for the beauty, power, and fragility of forest ecosystems). Forests, and forest activism, are clearly sources of religious experience for many in the environmental movement, but political action is not the only context for spiritual environmentalism in the Northwest.

Two recent PBS productions, *Affluenza* and *Escape from Affluenza*, document a growing interest in "simple living" among Northwesterners, particularly in the major metropolitan areas. They explore the history of simple living movements, interview influential leaders, and examine how families, businesses, and communities arc working to implement ecologically sustainable patterns of living in the region. The movement is guided by the spiritual principle that in a society with abundant material wealth, less consumption brings greater fulfillment.

A striking feature of the simple living movement in the region is the way participants enact this principle in their daily lives. Effectively resisting the dominant culture requires more than conviction; it requires ritual—sustained patterns of symbolic action (e.g., always buying and preparing locally grown whole foods; habits that reduce, recycle, and reuse material goods; regularly supporting businesses that align with these principles; etc.). To the extent that people reorganize their lives to reflect these values, the simple living movement is the ritualization of everyday life. It is impossible to successfully challenge the dominant culture without being thoughtful, careful, and habitual. In this sense, simple living propo-nents are not merely protesting against consumer culture, they are remaking cul-ture through prayerful living.

While the simple living movement has deep roots in American cultural histo-ry, from Anabaptist communities (Shakers, Quakers, and Amish) and the Transcendentalists to mid-western Mennonites, by the 1990s Seattle—The Emerald City—became a vibrant center for the movement. "Simple Living: The Newsletter of Voluntary Simplicity" is published there. The authors of *Your Money or Your Life* and *Simpler Living, Compassionate Life: A Christian Perspective,* two influential new books in the movement, also reside there. Participants in the movement draw inspiration from a variety of religious traditions. This burgeoning form of Northwest environmentalism is lived as an everyday spiritual practice; it is contemplative environmentalism.

In recent years even traditional religious organizations developed theological justifications for environmental activism. The National Religious Partnership for the Environment (NRPE), founded in 1994, has coordinated church-based envi-ronmental activism nationwide, but local church-based environmentalism in the Northwest pre-dates the NRPE initiative, though now they often work in concert. Seattle-based Earth Ministry (EM), for example, is one of the largest and oldest grass-roots religious environmental organizations in the country. Interfaith Network for Earth Concerns (INEC), an affiliate of Ecumenical Ministries of Oregon, is a similar coalition of liberal-to-moderate Protestants, Catholics, Jews, and others working to bring faith perspectives to bear on local and national envi-ronmental issues.

NRPE is top-down religious environmentalism. In the Pacific Northwest, EM and INEC represent bottom-up, church-based activism. As well, the pastoral letter on the Columbia River from the region's Roman Catholic bishops is serving as a model for bishops elsewhere to reflect on the environment theologically.

Even some religious conservatives are becoming "green," and the Northwest landscape is a source for that transformation. The work of Peter Illyn, a former Foursquare Gospel preacher from southwestern Washington, exemplifies theolog-ically conservative Christian environmentalism. He is an itinerant, Jesus-loving tree-hugger. At Tomfest 2000, an annual Christian rock festival on the banks of the Columbia River, Illyn gave his environmental witness:

> We're out here talking to people about the environment and how God's word calls for stewardship of his domain. I work with a group called Target Earth—we're all about serving the earth and serving the poor. You've heard of Earth First? We're like Earth Third: We were made to love God, love people, and love creation. Environmental stewardship is part of our calling as Christians, but the church has

remained silent for so many years that we've defaulted to New Age pagans and industrialists.[12]

Since falling in love with wild places through a wilderness epiphany at Big Crow Basin in the North Cascades, Illyn has led hikers deep into God's mountain cathedrals, sojourns he calls "keggers for Christ." His llama packs Northwest microbrew so he and his fellow pilgrims can sip a cold one while contemplating God's creation under the starry night sky. Illyn hopes that religious experience in the wilderness will inspire evangelicals to be better earth stewards.

Alongside growing neo-paganism and emerging religious environmentalism, there is a renewed interest in Native American myth and ritual, which includes earth-based spirituality. Native-Americans themselves have labored to preserve the remnants of religious traditions that are a basis for cultural identity, and many non-natives disaffected from Western religion have shown a keen interest in those aspects of native spirituality that speak to how humans ought to live in relation to nature. While the Indian/environment relationship has been romanticized (i.e., the myth of the noble savage and nature as undisturbed), there is no doubt that animism and rituals of reverence structured human-environment relations in the Pacific Northwest prior to European settlement, and that those cultural practices are fundamentally different from the utilitarian view of nature brought by settlement and industrialization. Therefore, many New Age practitioners and environmentalists today look to Native American traditions for spiritual guidance.

One eloquent example of Native American nature religion is found in the comments of Ted Strong, former Executive Director of the Columbia River Inter-Tribal Fish Commission, who addressed President Clinton with these words to close The Forest Conference in 1993: "American Indians—natives to this land—hope and pray that the pen that you wield will be guided by the sacred beings who created and authored the perfect laws of nature by which all mankind has existed since the beginning of time...." Elsewhere, Strong has said:

> The sacred salmon runs are in decline. It is the moral duty, therefore, of the Indian people of the Columbia to see them restored. We have to take care of them so that they can take care of us. Entwined together inextricably, no less now that ever before, are the fates of both the salmon and the Indian people. The quest for salmon recovery is about restoring what is sacred to its sacred place.[13]

Whether found in the metaphors of Northwest nature writers, the symbols and ideology of ancient forest campaigns, the rituals of simple living, or the hopes and prayers of indigenous people, nature religion pervades this region.

Undergirding this variegated form of alternative spirituality is a worldview characterized by two general principles: "deep ecology" and wilderness preservation. Deep ecology is a mindful exploration of human connection to natural processes; it is the basis for ritual practice that transforms an individual's relationship with nature and thereby reforms human/environment relations generally. As a guidepost for the cultivation of alternatives to consumer culture and the growth economy, it has been influential in the simple living movement, and has blended with a wilderness ethic in the campaign to save ancient forests. But nothing is more central to Northwest nature religion than the idea of wilderness.

To be so influential, the concept of wilderness had to become loaded with some of the deepest core values of the culture. According to William Cronon, it had to become sacred. The doctrine of the sublime and the myth of the American frontier did just that: "Wilderness as a landscape where the supernatural lay just beneath the surface was expressed in the doctrine of the sublime," Cronon writes in his essay "The Trouble With Wilderness." "[S]ublime landscapes were those rare places on earth where one had more chance than elsewhere to glimpse the face of God." In the romantic movement of the nineteenth century, God was in the chasm, in the waterfall, in the sunset. Mountains and valleys became cathedrals.

The Sierra Club, founded by the patron saint of the twentieth century environmental movement, John Muir, is now working in coalition with most major environmental groups in the United States to stop all commercial logging on public land, arguing that since wilderness is divine, the forests cannot be commodified. Wilderness preservation, more than conservation, has become the environmental movement's core value. In the myth of the vanishing frontier, argues Cronon, lay the seeds of wilderness preservation: "If wild land was so crucial in the making of the nation, then surely its last remnants must be saved as a monument to the American past and as an insurance policy to protect the future. To protect wilderness is to protect the nation's most sacred myth of origin."

For environmental groups, wilderness preservation is precisely what is at stake in the debate over oil drilling in the Arctic National Wildlife Refuge in Alaska. *The Last Wilderness: Arctic National Wildlife Refuge,* a photo essay, was designed to win public support for what The Wilderness Society calls "America's Serengeti." Robert Redford, a long-time member of the Natural Resources Defense Council, circulated this plea in defense of ANWR:

> To me, the Arctic Refuge represents everything spectacular and everything endangered about America's natural heritage: a million years of ecological serenity…vast expanses of untouched wilderness…an irreplaceable sanctuary for polar bears, white wolves and 130,000 caribou that return here each year to give birth and rear their young. For 20,000 years—literally hundreds of generations—the native Gwich'in people have inhabited this sacred place, following

the caribou herd and leaving the awe-inspiring landscape just as they found it.

Drilling in ANWR has even become a religious issue for mainstream churches: "The National Council of Churches contends that the solution is to consume less and leave the ANWR as God made it, clean, frozen and populated by wild animals, not pipelines, jetports, scrap metal and contaminated waste sites," that organization said in an official statement at the time the legislation was being considered in Congress in 2002. Religious metaphors abound even in scientific publications. A *National Geographic* cover story on ANWR was titled "Oil Field or Sanctuary?" Few American's will ever see the Alaskan landscape, but in the imagination of many, ANWR has become a sacred place.

Northwest nature religion has geographic and socio-economic as well as cultural sources. The Pacific Northwest is a vibrant and dramatic landscape; it is geologically imposing, biologically rich, and geographically vast. It contains the world's most diverse temperate rain forests. Knowledge that forest ecosystems were being dramatically altered by industrial timber production was a disturbing revelation, one that required a moral and spiritual response. Yet this revelation did not strike uniformly across the population.

Like Walsch's new spirituality movement, the nature religion expressed in contemporary environmentalism appeals largely to the middle and upper-middle class. Conservation biologists "discovered" that the loss of old-growth habitat was jeopardizing vulnerable species; lawyers pressed the issue in public policy arenas; environmental organizations recruited young, well-educated urbanites to lead the ancient forest campaign; and the movement targeted people most interested in recreational and aesthetic forests values—the professional middle class. But because the livelihood of many rural Northwesterners depended on resource extraction, the environmental movement appeared not to be in their near-term class interest.

Thus one of the consequences of this form of alternative spirituality is tension between rural Northwesterners (remnants of the pioneer culture) and urban/suburbanites. Nature religion did not "cause" this culture clash, but it has played a key role in legitimizing environmental movement politics and thus distinguishing urban (secular but spiritual) from rural (church-based) culture. Because space and resources are vast in Alaska, the frontier ethic still reigns in that state, and hence a politics favoring resource extraction. In Washington, with a strong tech-based economy and a developed cosmopolitanism in the Puget Sound area, politics lean more to the left on resource issues. In Oregon state politics break along city/country lines. Rural communities have been devastated by the economic and cultural changes of the last quarter of the twentieth century, but these communities no longer dominate the state demographically. As a result, the debate over management of public land in Oregon, heavily influenced by national environmental groups, has been shifting toward the environmental sentiments of urban America.

Another consequence of Northwest nature religion is the rapid emergence of new land use practices: the restoration of forests and fisheries, a reluctance to commercially harvest timber from public land, the ongoing drive to preserve more wilderness, and the increasing recreational and spiritual use of national forests. These new practices simply reflect new cultural understandings.

As Mary M. Berlik, David B. Kittredge, and David R. Fostor state in their Harvard Forest Paper No. 26, "The Illusion of Preservation: A Global Environmental Argument for the Local Production of Natural Resources," non-anthropocentric views of nature are now commonplace, but sacralizing forests does not necessarily lead to reduced consumption of forest products. In the case of this region, it simply means importing wood fiber harvested from forests around the globe (e.g., Canada's portion of the temperate Northwest rain forest, the pine forests of the American southeast, and topical forests in South America and Southeast Asia). While Northwest nature religion gives individual lives spiritual depth and gives the preservation movement moral authority, it tends toward romanticism and ideological rigidity, particularly when we fail to recognize that the desire for wilderness preservation is a religious impulse.

One environmental movement veteran, William Ashworth, notes in *The Left Hand of Eden: Meditations on Nature and Human Nature,* the "environmental community has a full set of gods and ghosts and demons," generally unrecognized as its members go after "the evil spirits of developers and industrialists." He continues, "in a world increasingly in need of solutions rather than rhetoric, this lack of recognition becomes more and more dangerous."

For example, since there has been no corresponding decline in United States' consumption of wood products, forest preservation in the Northwest simply means resource depletion elsewhere. We are "saving" ancient forests but the most difficult problem remains, how to achieve ecological *and* social sustainability. The Whidbey Institute and the Positive Futures Network, both based in the Puget Sound, are two leading examples of the effort to craft ecologically and socially sustainable culture.

In God's Country

To understand religious life in the Pacific Northwest requires thinking outside institutional boxes. In this relatively unchurched region, alternative spiritualities flourish. Today's lead generation made a point of spiritual questing outside the parameters of organized religion. Now we are witnessing what the scholar of

American religion Phillip E. Hammond described as the "extravazation of the sacred," a medical metaphor suggesting that the sacred has escaped the vessels that once contained it. Just as matter cannot be destroyed, only transformed, the sacred is seeping into surrounding cultural tissue. Things outside church-based religion have become holy in the Northwest, and significantly, secular spirituality in this region is not simply a private matter. As public debate over the use, abuse, and preservation of natural resources makes clear, reverence for nature is an important feature of civil religion in the Pacific Northwest.

The secular but spiritual alternatives have striking similarities as well as obvious differences. All are provincial: The Northwest is a remote paradise, an Aryan homeland, or the garden of Eden. They share apocalyptic and millennial themes: The world has gone awry; outsiders, particularly government, cannot be trusted; this is the last chance for redemption. And they are similarly dualistic: The world is neatly divided into the forces of good and the forces of evil. The government is always evil, either because it thoughtlessly facilitates resource extraction or because it does nothing but limit individual freedom.

Meredith McGuire argues that such sentiments in social movements generally are understood to be responses to problems of meaning and order produced by social change. Anti-government millennialists and environmentalists are struggling to defend or redefine what it means to live in the Northwest. One nature-loving environmentalist, Ana Maria Spagna, makes this observation in her essay "Doing Without": "There's an apocalyptic desperation that makes us believe, along with the survivalists and the New Agers, that it's all gonna be gone soon."

Culture in the Northwest is shifting toward an earth-based spirituality, which is significant in at least two ways.

First, nature religion, from John Muir to the present, fulfills the romantic project of secularizing a Judeo-Christian vision. God is to be found in nature, and salvation thus depends on experiencing the wild. Unlike Native American spirituality, however, preserving wilderness gives little direction for the sustainable *use* of resources. Therefore, wilderness preservation in the Northwest has mainly transferred resource extraction to other global regions while local wood consumption per capita remains high. Managing for ecosystem health is the goal of public land management today, quite different from the goal of the 1980s and earlier. Land ethics and changing public sentiment do have consequences for behavior.

Second, while hardly perceptible in the region's prosperous metropolitan areas, rural life in the Northwest was remade in the space of a generation, and the process has been wrenching. President Clinton's Northwest Forest Plan was supposed to retrain unemployed timber workers, but it now seems clear that many rural communities were simply left behind. The nation-wide recession that began in 2001 hit the Northwest hard. At the end of 2002 Oregon had the nation's highest unemployment rate, followed closely by Washington and Alaska. All this breeds resentment in the countryside. While civil religion in the Northwest is tilting toward reverence for nature, anti-government Patriots are sure to exploit the newly disenfranchised.

Though not an exhaustive survey, this chapter has tried to show that understanding religion and religious change in this unchurched region requires examining what is holy in peoples' ordinary lives. In periods of rapid social change, looking for the sacred in old organizational structures is not illuminating. While the sacred has escaped the vessels that once contained it, there is no reason to suspect that people are less likely to seek or find transcendence. Nor should it be surprising that in this region, the most profound experience comes from encounters with nature and that the deepest meanings are drawn from and forged in mythical narratives about wilderness and the last frontier. Whatever else the Northwest is to Northwesterners, it is an expansive and awesome place that looms large in their imagination.

Endnotes

1. Wade Clark Roof, *Spiritual Marketplace: Baby Boomers and the Remaking of American Religion* (Princeton, NJ: Princeton University Press, 1999): 33-35.

2. Wilbur Zelinsky, "An Approach to the Religious Geography of the United States: Patterns of Church Membership in 1952," *Annals of the Association of American Geographers* 51 (1961): 164.

3. A *census* attempts to measure attributes for all elements of a population, and *sample* is a representative subset of the population. NARA is based on census data and ARIS is based on sample data.

4. Robert Wuthnow, *After Heaven: Spirituality in America Since the 1950s* (Berkeley, CA: University of California Press, 1998): 23.

5. Michael F. Brown, *The Channeling Zone: American Spirituality in an Anxious Age* (Cambridge, MA: Harvard University Press, 1997): 14.

6. Paul Heelas. *The New Age Movement: The Celebration of the Self and the Sacralization of Modernity* (Cambridge, MA: Blackwell Publishers, 1996): 2.

7. Women In Conscious Creative Action, <*http://www.wiccawomen.com/herstory.html*> (27 November 2002).

8. James A. Aho, *The Politics of Righteousness: Idaho Christian Patriotism* (Seattle: University of Washington Press, 1990). James Coates, *Armed and Dangerous: The Rise of the Survivalist Right* (New York: Hill and Wang, 1995). Joel Dyer, *Harvest of Rage: Why Oklahoma City Is Only the Beginning* (Boulder, CO: Westview Press, 1998). Philip Lamy, *Millennium Rage: Survivalists, White Supremacists, and the Doomsday Prophecy* (New York: Plenum Press, 1996). Richard G. Mitchell, Jr., *Dancing at Armageddon: Survivalism and Chaos in Modern Times* (Chicago: The University of Chicago Press, 2002). David A. Neiwert, *In God's Country: The Patriot Movement and the Pacific Northwest* (Pullman, WA: Washington State University Press, 1999).

9. According to Coates, Christian Identity imagines history thusly: "For two thousand years the world has mistaken the true identity of the Jews. The true Jews, the actual descendants of Moses, Abraham and Jesus whom God called his Chosen People, are the people of the British Isles. The people known today as Jews are actually a race of Mongolian-Turkish 'Khazars'—read Ashkenazim—who are descended from the seed that Satan planted in Eve's belly right along with the seed planted there by Adam. Nine months after eating the apple, Eve bore two sons. Adam's son was Abel. Satan's was Cain. Cain killed Abel. Cain's descendants killed Jesus. Now, under the banner of world Jewry, they're trying to kill all white Christians."

10. This impression is based on a systematic content analysis of more than one hundred pieces of e-mail correspondence with the Liaison Officer for the Southern Oregon Militia between August 2002 and March 2003. The analysis was conducted in March 2003 by the author and his undergraduate qualitative research methods class.

11. Peter DeFazio, "Forests: It's Time to End this 'Religious War'," *Eugene Oregon Register-Guard* (29 April 1992): A 11, quoted in Samuel C. Porter, "The Pacific Northwest Forest Debate: Bringing Religion Back In?" *Worldviews: Environment, Culture, Religion* 3 (1999): 3.

12. Bruce Barcott, "For God So Loved the World," *Outside Magazine* (March 2001): 86.

13. Ted Strong, "What is CRITFC?" *<http://www.Critfc.org/text/ WHATIS.HTM>* (28 December 1998), quoted in Samuel C. Porter, "The Pacific Northwest Forest Debate: Bringing Religion Back In?" *Worldviews: Environment, Culture, Religion* 3 (1999): 11.

Conclusion

Religious Futures In the None Zone

Patricia O'Connell Killen

In the Pacific Northwest most people do not participate in a church, synagogue, temple, or mosque, and never have. This central fact shapes everything else about religion here. For two centuries the region has forced successive waves of immigrants to rethink their religiousness for this setting, where currently the single largest denomination claims barely 11 percent of the population and no other denomination or religious family claims even 5 percent. Religions become a force in public life here only through alliances that appeal successfully to the unchurched population. These alliances coalesce, experience stress, and are reconfigured as part of a larger process of political, social, economic, environmental, and cultural change. In today's context of significant and disruptive change that is remaking the region, late-twentieth-century religious trends are converging with the Pacific Northwest's distinctive culture to reshape religion's public presence.

The Pacific Northwest is now the site of a visible, on-going cultural conflict in which an evangelical cluster and a spiritual environmental cluster constitute centers of religious gravity. Neither has the power to govern public policy on any issue without attracting allies from among the unaffiliated and other clusters of religious communities. Yet, the chasm between their worldviews and sensibilities feeds a highly polarized public discourse that complicates alliance building. The contest between evangelicals and spiritual environmentalists is testing the durability of the region's social fabric.

The ascension of these two clusters in public life during the last 20 years of the twentieth century is driving realignment in the relative power, visibility, and coherence of all four clusters described in this volume. That realignment is repositioning the mainline Protestant, Catholic, and Reform and Conservative Jewish

169

cluster and creating challenges for ethnic religious communities. Yet, in the midst of this realignment, long-standing patterns in the region's religious environment continue to shape religion's public presence and point toward future developments. Important for understanding current conflicts are a pattern of testing the limits of individual freedom and social control as well as a pattern of alternating impulses between cooperation across boundaries of religious communities and a sharpening and hardening of boundaries to clarify identity and protect membership. Particularly significant for the future is the region's pattern of innovation in forms of religious organization. All three are endemic to an open religious environment.

Theologically Based, Civic-minded Mainline

Mainline Protestant, Roman Catholic, and Reform and Conservative Jewish communities continue to be important in the region's public life even as they negotiate internal stresses and social trends that have affected their public visibility and influence. A significant recent demonstration of the mainline cluster's ongoing vitality occurred from November 30 through December 3, 1999 in Seattle, when a World Trade Organization (WTO) meeting, intended to celebrate the spread of global commerce, was effectively shut down by the largest rally of its kind in modern history. Mainline religious communities, in partnership with Buddhists, Muslims, followers of indigenous religions, and "Nones," joined organized labor, students, and non-governmental organizations to stage a protest that changed the protocols for all future WTO meetings and made Seattle synonymous with anti-globalization sentiment.

Most of the news coverage overlooked religion's role in the protest. In the months leading up to the WTO meeting, Seattle churches and ecumenical and inter-faith groups prepared by sponsoring educational forums on global justice, arranging housing for the homeless who would be displaced, and recruiting members to march. During the demonstrations churches provided food, shelter, and other services to protesters; opened their buildings as venues for non-governmental organization (NGO) presentations; hosted inter-faith prayer vigils; and negotiated with police over treatment of demonstrators. In all of this, the region's religiously civic-minded communities welcomed protesters who would never darken the door of a church, synagogue, temple, or mosque as companions who shared with them a purpose that transcended individual lives and narrow self-interest.

This cluster also demonstrates on-going vitality in its continuing work providing social services to the broader community and influencing social policy. Out of fidelity to their theological visions, these communities address public policy issues, especially housing, poverty, health care, immigration, and environmental protection. State associations of Protestant churches, Catholic Conferences, Jewish Federations, and ecumenical organizations are well-established entities with long histories of political involvement aimed at providing for the vulnerable in society.

Today, however, there is less appreciation for these communities' contribution and less understanding of their theological grounding than existed in the 1950s and early 1960s when this cluster functioned nominally as the religious voice of the region. A 30-year process of massive disaffection from civic institutions, erosion of long-term civic commitments, and a growing acceptance of unfettered market mechanisms in the private sector have altered the terms of public discussion. Now leaders of the mainline Protestant, Catholic, and Reform and Conservative Jewish communities have a more difficult time making their vision of the common good intelligible to members and to the wider population.

In the current context of polarized public religious discourse the theological and spiritual heritages that inspire these communities' commitment to the shared public good are not well understood. Their theological visions have long histories, demand intellectual effort to grasp, and are integrally connected to a concern for the common good. In the current world of religious seekers who pursue personal healing, energy replenishment, and a safe haven from the pressures of work and relationships, prophetic connections between salvation and social justice are not easily comprehended.[1] Further, making this connection intelligible and compelling is aggravated by a climate in which issues that explicitly relate to economics and politics are perceived as part of a secular "liberal" agenda and issues of personal morality part of the "conservative," "Judeo-Christian" agenda. A regional religious environment that minimizes concern about theology and promotes individual autonomy reinforces this dichotomy.

The greatest challenge these communities face is showing members and the larger public how their positions on social policy issues are, in fact, rooted in rich faith traditions and not political ideology. But that task is hampered by internal tensions within the communities. Mainline Protestant denominations are torn by conflict over sexuality, biblical interpretation, and theological identity. The Roman Catholic Church is wracked by a clergy sexual abuse scandal that is accelerating a process of declining credibility that began in 1967 with *Humanae Vitae*, the papal letter proscribing artificial birth control. The Reform and Conservative Jewish communities are dealing with on-going tension over the ethnic and religious meanings of Jewish identity and affiliation, and debate over how to respond to what appears to be a growing anti-Semitism in the region. This is aggravated by the nation's role in the Israeli-Palestinian conflict.

The alliance also experienced strain among member communities during the 1980s and 1990s. The Roman Catholic Church aligned with conservative evan-

gelicals on abortion and assisted suicide, though it maintained its historic relationship with mainline Protestants and Jews on protection of civil rights for sexual minorities and the need for state-funded social services to the poor. Some
evangelical elements within mainline Protestant denominations began promoting
evangelization of Jews, creating more tension, as have positions taken by some
Protestant denominations on the Israeli-Palestinian situation.

Evangelical Entrepreneurs

The same factors that have stressed mainline Protestant, Catholic, and
Reform and Conservative Jewish communities have contributed to growing visibility for evangelicals. Conservative Christians, both explicitly fundamentalist
and neo-evangelical, have long been present in the region. Their numbers, educational and economic status, and presence in suburban population centers have
increased since 1970, over the same period that mainline Protestant denominations have been losing members.[2] The evangelical cluster became publicly
active during initiative campaigns in the 1980s and 1990s, when their successes
and close losses on issues of sexual politics, physician-assisted suicide, and
affirmative action made clear their strength and emphasized the shifts in the public religious landscape of the region.

In 1994 Oregon voters narrowly rejected (52 percent to 48 percent) the
Oregon Citizens Alliance's (OCA) initiative Measure 13 that would have eliminated "civil rights protection for homosexuals in public employment." That
defeat was another round in an on-going battle between religious and political
conservatives represented by the Oregon Citizen's Alliance, and religious and
political moderates, liberals, and libertarians that stretched back to 1988. In that
year OCA-sponsored Measure 8, seeking to overturn rights for "homosexuals in
public employment" that Governor Neil Goldschmidt had extended by an executive order, won with 53 percent of the vote, though the Oregon Supreme Court
later overturned it. The OCA tried again in 1992 with Measure 9, which described
homosexuality as "abnormal, wrong, unnatural and perverse." That measure was
defeated 56 percent to 44 percent, a relatively close loss, given that the coalition
organized against it included the state's political and business establishment,
mainline and liberal Protestant clergy, Jewish leaders, the Archdiocese of
Portland, and secular activists. During the campaign St. Matthews' Catholic
Church in Hillsboro, Oregon was vandalized, and the slogan "God hates
Catholics, Jews, and fags" spray-painted on walls inside the church. The OCA
failed to qualify a new anti-gay initiative for the 1998 state ballot.[3]

In Washington in 1998 Governor Gary Locke vetoed a bill that banned gay
and lesbian marriages, but his veto was overturned by the state legislature. That
year Washington voters also easily passed Initiative 200, banning state affirma-

tive action programs, an initiative promoted by an alliance of Christian conservatives, libertarians, and business conservatives. It is unclear the extent to which this measure was linked to protection of sexual minorities in the minds of voters.

Conservative evangelicals attracted significant support for starkly defined positions on sexual politics from 1980 to 2000. Their ability to continue to attract allies in the future and so extend their power in public life is not certain. This will be conditioned by several factors: the social niche that sectarian entrepreneurial churches, which are the largest evangelical congregations, occupy; evangelicals' preferred style of organization; their theological worldview; and the alignment between evangelical theology and Republican-party economic policies.

Sectarian entrepreneurial congregations often attract people who have experienced the dislocation of educational, economic, social, and geographic mobility, which helps to explain their attractiveness in Portland, Seattle, Anchorage, and other regional population centers. Members volunteer for activities that involve their children and participate in groups for their own development. They do not consider long-term civic involvement valuable. They volunteer for community projects on a task- and time-circumscribed basis. Members tend to be concerned about their families and themselves. They expect the church to help their lives work more smoothly.[4] These congregations serve today's in-migrants' needs for community and support, just as extended family or ethnic networks, neighborhoods, and neighborhood congregations have done for others. Members' focus on personal and family needs likely contributes to a tendency toward moderation of belief among evangelicals as they move away from the South, as Mark Shibley and others have noted.

Evangelical entrepreneurial churches, then, tend not to be oriented toward long-term, sustained involvement in the political process. Their style is more episodic, focused on discrete local issues, and carried out through temporary networks, a style congruent with the new knowledge economy in which large numbers of their members participate. Evangelical entrepreneurs constitute a potential pool of voters that can be galvanized around particular issues, especially those perceived to threaten "family values." Thus far sexual politics, constraints on business, and environmental conservation have been their major focus, all issues that involve limits on personal freedom and social control.

Data on religious identification and voting patterns provided by the Bliss Institute at the University of Akron support this picture. Though the Bliss data do not separate evangelical entrepreneurs from other evangelicals and their sample size for the Pacific Northwest is too small to draw statistically significant conclusions, they are suggestive. On abortion, high-commitment evangelicals are less likely regionally than nationally to be pro-choice, while low-commitment evangelicals are more likely to be pro-choice regionally than nationally. Both high-commitment and low-commitment evangelicals are less likely to favor gay rights regionally than nationally.

Sexual politics likely will continue to be a definer of individual and group identity that evangelicals in the Pacific Northwest emphasize for the foreseeable future. The issue readily symbolizes personal righteousness, status as believer, and self-definition as a member of the Christian community against the unchurched and ungodly. Further, sexual identity is a high stakes issue for adolescents, made visible in recent conflicts over authorizing and allotting resources to sexual minority student clubs in Washington's Puyallup and Federal Way school districts.

The affinity between evangelicals and conservative Republicans and Libertarians on economic policy also will affect this cluster's future influence. Many evangelicals believe loosening constraints on business and the free market is a divine imperative. They consider unobstructed capitalism to be biblically based. As long as Republican Party economic policies support this belief, evangelicals regionally will continue to support that party (today 54 percent of evangelicals are registered as Republicans, compared to 27 percent as Independents and 15 percent as Democrats). Currently, evangelicals control or wield significant power in the Republican party organizations in all three states.

Another significant factor for evangelical politics and economics is the correlation that some evangelicals, especially in Pentecostal and non-denominational congregations, make between godliness and economic prosperity. Some evangelicals see a cause-and-effect relationship between personal righteousness and material plenty. Making that connection is a source of conflict within the wider evangelical community. Though there is no scholarly assessment of how widely a prosperity gospel permeates the regional evangelical community, it appears with regularity in advertisements for new congregations and in members' comments to the media.

Several questions regarding the future of the evangelical cluster remain open. For instance:

- At what rate do these congregations gain and lose members?
- Is there an impact on local evangelicals of the waning of evangelical political activism nationally since the late 1990s, as noted by political scientists?
- Is sustained involvement in public life on the part of large numbers of people generated by a theological vision in which the supernatural is a direct force in personal life, including one's economic life?
- Do those who construct life primarily in terms of face-to-face relationships and a focus on personal and family development create effective political modes for on-going public involvement?

- Will there be an expansion of cooperation with Roman Catholics that thus far has been grounded largely in a shared anti-abortion stance?
- To what degree are the region's active para-church organizations that focus on adolescents, such as Young Life, successful at channeling members into evangelical churches?
- To what degree will sectarian entrepreneurial evangelicals make common cause with older forms of evangelicalism, some ethnically and racially grounded, and other more sectarian denominations such as Seventh-day Adventists, whom some evangelicals do not consider Christian?
- Will some accommodation be made between evangelicals and Mormons who, while they share many values with evangelicals, are considered opponents in the contest for souls?
- Will preference for loose organizations developed on the model of temporary networks that are drawn from the new information economy contribute to or detract from evangelicals' public presence?

Emerging Centers of Religious Gravity— Evangelicals and Spiritual Environmentalits

Sexual politics captured energy, attention, and money in the region during the 1980s and 1990s when the economies of Oregon, Washington, and Alaska were being remade. Regional, national, and global economic change disrupted life in the region. Those whose livelihoods depended on timber, agriculture, fishing, and mining saw their economy erode and with it their way of life. Manufacturing also declined. Those whose livelihoods were tied to the rise of Microsoft and Intel, many of them in-migrants to the region, benefited from the emergence of the new information and service-based economy. Today income disparity between the richest and poorest in the region reflects the vagaries of this economic shift. In 2000 Oregon, Washington, and Alaska led the nation in levels of childhood hunger. By 2003 the vulnerability of the knowledge economy became clear, and in that year Oregon, Washington, and Alaska led the nation in unemployment.

Economic disruption paralleled growing confrontation with the finite character of the region's natural resources. In the summer of 2002 farmers in the Klamath Basin clashed with state and federal officials over water. In 2003 Senator Ted Stevens of Alaska made clear that he took personally the Senate's defeat of the measure that would have opened the Arctic National Wildlife Refuge (ANWR) to oil drilling. Whether it be protecting temperate rain forests in the Tongass National Forest on Alaska's southeastern peninsula or in

Washington's Olympic National Forest, saving salmon runs, or keeping ANWR pristine, environmental protection now is pitted against the need for jobs and national security.

Posing the conflict as jobs versus environment obscures a deeper cultural crisis in regional self-understanding. As the Oregon writer William Kittredge put it in his book *Owning It All*, the story that motivated his family to turn a wild country into a parable of pastoralism, has proven rather to be "a rationale for violence—against other people and against nature."[5] Children and grandchildren of those who viewed uncut timber as a waste now face the consequences of their inherited guiding myths. The growing conflict between evangelicals and spiritual environmentalists is joined squarely over the issue of the continuing adequacy of a regional myth of abundant natural resources and economic opportunity.

In the Pacific Northwest conflict over the land and its resources is mirrored in conflict over the boundaries of human bodies. Both this mirroring and a growing public religious cluster organized around spiritual environmentalism became clear in Oregon's debate over physician-assisted suicide.

In November of 1994, by a 51 percent to 49 percent margin, Oregonians passed Measure 16, the Death with Dignity Act, making the state the first political jurisdiction in the country to legalize physician-assisted suicide. A similar measure had narrowly failed in Washington in 1991. Litigation delayed enactment of the measure until February of 1997 when the Ninth Circuit Court of Appeals dismissed the case objecting to the law. In a separate effort to block enactment, the 1997 Oregon legislature returned the measure to the ballot for reconsideration and repeal, but in November of that year Measure 51 was defeated by a 60 percent to 40 percent margin.

Catholics and conservative evangelical Christians funded the $4 million campaign for Measure 51. A coalition of moderates, liberals, and libertarians, organized as the "Don't Let 'Em Shove Their Religion Down Your Throat Committee" spent $1 million to oppose it. The campaign portrayed religion as an obstacle to individual freedom. That portrayal, and the newly inserted element of states' rights occasioned by federal efforts to block the initiative, contributed to Oregonians' re-affirming physician-assisted suicide by a 60 percent vote against Measure 51.

Controversy over the initiative did not end with the 1997 vote. The Pain Relief Promotion Act, designed to thwart the measure, failed to reach the floor of the United States Senate in 2000. In 2001 United States Attorney General John Ashcroft ordered the federal Drug Enforcement Administration (DEA) to track and prosecute doctors who prescribe lethal doses of drugs under the Oregon Law, which led to further litigation, this time between the state of Oregon and Ashcroft. On April 17, 2002 a three-judge panel of the Ninth

Circuit Court of Appeals ruled in favor of Oregon, and on May 24, 2002 the Justice Department appealed the decision to the full Ninth Circuit Court. Oral arguments in the appeal were held before the entire panel of Ninth Circuit judges on May 7, 2003. At this writing the Court's opinion had not yet been delivered.

Both the 1994 and subsequent debates over the Death with Dignity Act focused on definitions of death as a "natural process," and on what assisted suicide does to familial and civic bonds. Opponents argue that physician-assisted suicide amounts to "playing God" and so disrupts the natural processes of death. Proponents argue that physician-assisted suicide is no more disruptive of natural processes than the extraordinary measures taken to prolong life and chide opponents for viewing death as some kind of failure. Opponents express repeated concern that economic motivation will lead the poor, infirm, and other marginalized people to be pressured into ending their lives. Proponents argue that the law contains safeguards to protect against that and point to the economic status of those who have taken advantage of the law to support their claim.

Individuals with degenerative diseases who support the law portray physician-assisted suicide as a profoundly natural process. In a deposition posted on the Death With Dignity fund Web site, "Katherine L" wrote: "I know the level of participation in life—mentally, spiritually, physically, emotionally—that I believe I need to continue as a valuable and contributing member of earth's family. I feel very strongly about preserving the right to make my final, very private choice of leaving this beautiful planet in peace, with dignity."

Statements from family members of those who have chosen physician-assisted suicide portray it as a profoundly communal process. One family described their mother's assisted suicide in 2001 on the Compassion in Dying Web site: "We were able to gather as a family, each kiss her, and each tell her how much we loved her. She died peacefully, looking out over the Willamette River, in a room filled with love. . . .[Our mother] was proud to be an Oregonian, to live in a state less bound by convention and more open to independent and free thinking."

These statements resolve individual freedom, loving social relationships, and natural beauty into a moment of profound human dignity. Situated within an understanding of humans as part of larger natural processes, physician-assisted suicide becomes a moment of ethical choice by a fully free individual within a community. However much the statements may recast the events they describe, they point to an emerging aesthetic and theology that situates individuals within nature and human life within planetary life.

But this vision makes no sense to those for whom physician-assisted suicide signals a technologically and economically repressive society within which individuals are isolated and alienated, social bonds destroyed, and humanity assaulted because its subjection to transcendent powers is not acknowledged. The conflict on its deepest level is about the proper understanding of relationships among individuals, society, and nature.

The sentiments expressed by those supporting physician-assisted suicide locate them as part of a new religious cluster that is growing in strength, one rooted primarily in the secular but spiritual population, but also incorporating members of the mainline and Pacific Rim religious clusters as well. Organized around concern for the environment understood to include natural resources, human communities, and quality of life, this cluster provides the contrasting pole to evangelicals. Its theologians are Northwest writers, from poets like William Stafford to nature writers like Barry Lopez or James Mitsui, and authors of fiction such as Sherman Alexie, James David Duncan, and Ursula Le Guin.

As the evangelical and spiritual environmental clusters grow they define polarized boundaries for public debate. Environmental protection and sexual politics are about purity; the debate is over the natural relationship between land and souls. This is a debate that, if very preliminary data from the Bliss Institute is accurate, could shape public discourse in the region for some time. Of those surveyed, only 28.6 percent percent of high-commitment evangelical Protestants in the Pacific Northwest supported environmental protection, compared to 42.9 percent nationally. Among low-commitment evangelical Protestants, the results were 39.7 percent regionally and 56.1 percent nationally. While the region closely mirrors the nation when "pro-protection" and "moderate on protection" responses are combined, the smaller percentage of evangelicals in the Pacific Northwest clearly favoring environmental protection is striking. It also is congruent with the perspective of some regional evangelicals that a concern for environmental protection is idolatrous, displays lack of trust in God, and violates God's command to make the earth fruitful. Such comments locate these evangelicals squarely within the story of the Pacific Northwest as a place of abundance that is wasted unless developed. The "pro-environmental protection" population that is readily associated with godlessness, sexual deviation, and social disorder has become the "de facto" religious reference group against which many evangelicals in the Pacific Northwest define themselves.

By contrast, respondents who identified as secular or as high-commitment or low-commitment mainline Protestant were comparable to the nation on environmental protection. Non-Christians in the Pacific Northwest, however, were significantly more likely than non-Christians nationally to favor environmental protection, 83.3 percent to 62.6 percent.

Data on voter registration and religious affiliation also reveals tension between evangelicals and "Nones," many of whom are part of the spiritual environmentalist cluster. According to the American Religious Identification Survey (ARIS), 14 percent of "Nones" are Republican compared to 54 percent of Evangelicals; 31 percent are Democrats, compared to 15 percent of Evangelicals; and 46 percent are Independent, compared to 27 percent of Evangelicals. These numbers point to further conflict.

Sharp definition of boundaries between these two increasingly visible religious clusters changes the religious landscape for other clusters in the region. It creates a climate that pushes faith communities toward defining identity and articulating beliefs in ways that may be incongruent with their theological heritage and long-standing ethos and practice. It narrows space for discussion, making it more difficult for mainline Protestant, Catholic, and Reform and Conservative Jewish communities, Pacific Rim communities, and others to bring their theological perspectives into public discussion.

Further, the region's sharply joined debates over sexual politics and assisted suicide have alienated many outside churches who might have become allies on other issues. It also has contributed to others leaving churches because they could not reconcile themselves to what seemed to them an impoverished and impotent religious vision or senseless conflict in the face of more pressing matters.

Consequences for Other Clusters

It is unclear precisely how the current context, with its hardening poles of discourse and economic instability, including limited environmental resources, is affecting more ethnically grounded and sectarian religious communities within and beyond Christianity, both internally and in terms of their public activity and visibility.

Beginning with largely Christian groups, research remains to be done on the effects of the last 20 years of the twentieth century, of increasingly sharp and narrowly focused public debate on historically African-American churches in the Pacific Northwest. Into the 1970s these churches retained members better than other denominations, in part some think because they were havens from racism. They offered community to those away from family and emphasized local issues and the welfare of their members. The Pacific Northwest's openness to Pentecostal churches aided growth in some predominantly African-American denominations. Whether historically African-American churches today are keeping their younger members at rates better or worse than in other parts of the country remains a question.

The extent to which black churches are distracted from local issues by polarized debate on sexual politics is unknown. How these churches' traditions of organizing, networking, interacting with public institutions, and participating in public discourse are evolving needs to be pursued. The extent to which members or their children are joining the ranks of the unchurched or affiliating with Islam, which has a long history among African Americans, or with other Pacific Rim traditions, remains to be explored. The ways in which economic and social racism experienced by blacks in the Pacific Northwest shape their perspective on the issues posed by the evangelicals and spiritual environmentalists is not clear.

Similar questions remain for other dominantly ethnic denominations and sectarian groups. Research available for the Religion by Region project did not make possible fine discrimination on the views of religious families that, while very small, cumulatively make up an important segment of the region's religious adherents. Much remains to be done to understand how Pietist and Anabaptist groups such as Mennonites, Hutterites, Brethren, and Moravians perceive themselves in relation to the region and current debates. Groups in this family historically have valued western spaces for the isolation it has afforded them.

Fuller descriptions are needed to understand how denominations in the "Other Conservative Christian" category, such as the Seventh-day Adventists or Churches of Christ understand themselves today. These groups share concerns with the evangelicals, though their theological visions are not entirely compatible.

Denominations clustered under the "Congregational/Reformed/non-UCC Congregational" heading, such as the Christian Reformed Church in the United States of America and the Lutheran Church-Missouri Synod, have been grounded heavily in ethnicity, but the relative strength of ethnic-religious identification today is unclear. Understanding how these communities bring their theologies to bear on public issues in the Pacific Northwest today could provide an important perspective on the future.

Similarly, Mormons, the second-largest single religious body in the state, remain remarkably quiet in public debate. Public issues are discussed within Mormon congregations, but Mormons are reluctant to make themselves visible, in part because of their on-going experience of persecution and a desire to demonstrate their patriotism.

Pacific Rim communities are in some ways more visible than smaller ethnic Christian groups. Indigenous religious and cultural beliefs and practices have been intimately intertwined in Native Americans' assertion of treaty rights across the region and in conflicts over resource development in Alaska. The 1971 Alaska Native Claims Resettlement Act, the 1974 Bolt decision on treaty fishing rights with subsequent disputes over salmon fishing, the recent resumption of Makah whaling, and decades of work by some tribes to achieve federal recognition have all generated public debate. That debate often is intense and emotionally laden because it raises to consciousness the region's legacy of conquest and injustice.

It questions the legitimacy of European-American presence and dominance in this place.

The conflict is cultural as well as material. Most recently it has been played out over Kennewick Man, the 9,300-year-old skeleton found in 1996 on the Columbia River near Kennewick, Washington. Litigation over studying the skeleton or returning it to the Confederated Tribes for burial, in which many proponents for the former argued that the skeleton was not Indian, was a contest over to whom the Pacific Northwest really belongs.[6]

In the last two decades of the twentieth century debate also has focused on Native Americans' religious freedom. This became a national issue with the 1989 U.S. Supreme Court ruling in the Oregon Employment Division v. Smith case that involved the use of peyote in the ritual of the Native American Church. The ruling so severely circumscribed religious freedom that it prompted federal and state legislation to guarantee religious freedom to Native Americans.[7] Most citizens of the Pacific Northwest applauded guaranteeing Native Americans' religious rights in this case. Fewer, however, supported the right of the Makah Indians to hunt gray whale, an activity that is part of their religious and cultural practice. In a situation of increased pressure on natural resources, Native Americans' religion will continue to be pushed into the public sphere. Whether they will be recognized and their legitimacy acknowledged remains to be seen. That recognition is integrally related to the question of European-Americans' appropriation of Native American religious practices, continued cultural colonization, and exploitation.

For Pacific Rim immigrant communities the issues of public involvement are complex. Ethnic festivals, anti-immigrant hostility, and zoning conflicts over houses of worship in residential neighborhoods heighten their visibility. Religion evolves in these communities as they negotiate the Pacific Northwest context. How established immigrant religious communities assist their members to adjust to life in the United States and what consequence that has on religion in those communities remain to be studied. How religious beliefs of these communities are influencing their choices in the voting booth is not well understood.

Also important to the future is continued conversion of European-Americans and African-Americans to Islam, Buddhism, Hinduism, and other religions from across the Pacific. Such conversions increase the complexity of religion in the region. In some cases converts provide another theological strand for the region's spiritual environmentalists, for example Buddhism's influence on the writer Gary Snyder's thinking about the region.

Beneath all the recent changes, long-standing patterns in the region's religious environment continue. They both temper and drive religious conflict in the public realm. The Pacific Northwest will remain a relatively open religious environment. The larger and more vocal evangelical presence in the pool of adherents does not alter the fact that most people are outside of churches, synagogues, temples, or mosques. Influencing public policy will continue to require building alliances and appealing to the un-churched. But as ethnic identification with religious bodies and their theologies wane in this context of weak re-enforcement for religious affiliation, religious positions in public debate may carry increasingly less persuasive power.

The more sharply drawn poles in public religious debate between the strong evangelical and spiritual environmental clusters can be seen as part of a regional religious rhythm, cooperation across boundaries, and a pre-occupation with reinforcing boundaries of identity and belonging. In the past this rhythm has led to occasional consensus and to cooperation on the region's most significant issues. Whether it will again remains to be seen. This rhythm of cooperation across and pre-occupation with maintenance of boundaries historically has been intertwined with testing the limits of individual freedom and social control, another long-standing pattern that will continue.

That in 1970 Alaska and Washington followed New York to lead the nation in providing "abortion on demand" and that in 1994 Oregon became the first state to approve physician-assisted suicide are consequences, in part, of the region's religious environment—one in which testing limits of individual freedom and social control is intimately intertwined with the search for personal identity, freedom, and the meaning of this place.

The regional pattern of innovation in forms of religious organization and activity will influence the future. The desire to maintain religious institutions and to carry out ministry and care for the needs of the broader community in a context of low adherence, limited resources, and ambivalence toward religious institutions has driven innovation in organizational religious forms regionally. Ecumenical and inter-faith cooperation and organizations have a long history here. Businessmen's prayer breakfasts and women's organizations such as Women Aglow, both regional creations; youth-oriented para-church organizations such as Young Life and Intervarsity Christian Fellowship; and religiously inspired think tanks such as the conservative evangelical Discovery Institute, all are part of the religious landscape. Openness to innovative forms of organization and a penchant for continuing to work across the limits of denominational and congregational boundaries have been true across all the clusters of religious groups described in this volume.

Two newer ventures in ecumenical international Christian humanitarian relief and development, World Vision and Mercy Corps, carry on this tradition of innovation. World Vision International is headquartered in Federal Way, Washington, and Mercy Corp, originally in Seattle, now is in Portland, Oregon. These organizations are rooted in Christian theological visions, the former evangelical, the latter Quaker and Catholic, but they operate on models more akin to technology industries than denominational bureaucracies. These organizations and others that combine religious commitment and business acumen will continue to thrive in the region. Their growth and how they are changing the nature of congregations and human services, both regionally and locally, remain to be explored.

The continuing success regionally of the Jesuit Volunteer Corps and the much newer Lutheran Volunteer Corps is matched by opportunities for service provided by Habitat for Humanity, an array of environmental groups, and other organizations that engage in education, community service, and political activism. The region also is home to the Whidbey Institute and other newer organizations that seek to educate, create networks, and inform public policy in ways that will further a symbiotic relationship between people and nature in the Pacific Northwest. Retreat and spirituality centers sponsored by a wide range of individuals and religious communities abound in the region.

All of these organizations work beyond the confines of individual denominations and congregations. All draw on spiritual interests and a desire for community and connection in a population that is highly ambivalent about institutions in general and religious institutions in particular. The successful organizations draw on the reservoir of commitment present in religious communities while appealing to those beyond the doors of church, synagogue, temple, or mosque. All offer possibilities for community either in small groups or by becoming part of a much larger enterprise. They offer individuals the challenge to make sacrifices and thereby make their faith real and palpable in their own lives and in the world, but they invite people to make the sacrifice on their own terms.

These kinds of organizations and activities are not readily recognized as religious, yet they constitute the major way that religious commitment is generated and harnessed in the Pacific Northwest. Religious commitment here continues to be fluid, individualistic, egalitarian in structure, focused on results, and episodic. Community remains a problematic aspiration. What this regional religious ethos means for the ways that Pacific Northwesterners negotiate the challenges of public life in the twenty-first century remains to be seen.

Endnotes

1. Ann Swidler, "Saving the Self: Endowment and Depletion in American Institutions," in Richard Madsen, William M. Sullivan, Ann Swidler, and Stephen M. Tipton, ed. *Meaning and Modernity: Religion, Polity, and the Self*, edited by (Berkeley, CA: University of California Press, 2002): 41-55; Wade Clark Roof and William McKinney, *American Mainline Religion: Its Changing Shape and Future* (New Brunswick, NJ: Rutgers University Press, 1987).

2. Mark A. Shibley, "Religion in Oregon: Recent Demographic Currents in the Mainstream," *Pacific Northwest Quarterly*, 83/3 (July 1992): 82-87.

3. William M. Lunch, "The Christian Right in the Northwest: Two Decades of Frustration in Oregon and Washington," in John Green, Mark Rozell, and Clyde Wilcox, eds. *Marching Toward the Millennium: The Christian Right in the States 1980-2000* (forthcoming): 299-301; 316-319.

4. Robert Wuthnow, "Reassembling the Civic Church: The Changing Role of Congregations in American Civil Society," in *Meaning and Modernity*: 166, 171, 174-175.

5. William Kittredge, *Owning It All* (St. Paul, MN: Graywolf Press, 1987): 62-63, quoted in William G. Robbins, *Landscape of Promise: The Oregon Story, 1800-1940* (Seattle: University of Washington Press, 1997): 19.

6. Suzanne J. Crawford, "(Re)Constructing Bodies: Semiotic Sovereignty and the Debate over Kennewick Man," in Devon Mihesuah, ed., *The Repatriation Reader: Who Owns Native American Remains?* (Lincoln, NE: University of Nebraska Press, 2000): 211-236.

7. Garrett Epps, *To An Unknown God: Religious Freedom on Trial* (New York: St. Martin's Press, 2001).

APPENDIX

In order to provide the best possible empirical basis for understanding the place of religion in each of the religions of the United States, the Religion by Region project contracted to obtain data from three sources: the North American Religion Atlas (NARA); the 2001 American Religious Identification Survey (ARIS); and the 1992, 1996, and 2000 National Surveys of Religion and Politics (NSRP).

NARA For the Project, the Polis Center of Indiana University-Purdue University at Indianapolis created an interactive Web site that made it possible to map general demographic and religious data at the national, regional, state-by-state, and county-by-county level. The demographic data were taken from the 2000 Census. The primary source for the religious data (congregations, members, and adherents) was the 2000 Religious Congregations and Membership Survey (RCMC) compiled by the Glenmary Research Center. Because a number of religious groups did not participate in the 2000 RCMS—including most historically African-American Protestant denominations—this dataset was supplemented with data from other sources *for adherents only*. The latter included projections from 1990 RCMC reports, ARIS, and several custom estimates. For a fuller methodological account, go to *http://www.religionatlas.org*.

ARIS The American Religious Identification Survey (ARIS 2001), carried out under the auspices of the Graduate Center of the City University of New York by Barry A. Kosmin, Egon Mayer, and Ariela Keysar, replicates the methodology of the National Survey of Religious Identification (NSRI 1990). As in 1990 the ARIS sample is based on a series of national random digit dialing (RDD) surveys, utilizing ICR, International Communication Research Group in Media, Pennsylvania, national telephone omnibus services. In all, 50,284 U.S. households were successfully interviewed. Within a household, an adult respondent was chosen using the "last birthday method" of random selection. One of the distinguishing features of both ARIS 2001 and NSRI 1990 is that respondents were asked to describe themselves in terms of religion with an open-ended question: "What is your religion, if any?[1]" ARIS 2001 enhanced the topics covered by adding questions concerning religious beliefs and membership as well as religious switching and religious identification of spouses/partners. The ARIS findings have a high level of statistical significance for most large religious groups and key geographical units, such as states. ARIS 2001 detailed methodology can be found in the report on the American Religious Identification Survey 2001at *www.gc.cuny.edu/studies/aris_index.htm*.

NSRP The National Surveys of Religion and Politics were conducted in 1992, 1996, and 2000 at the Bliss Center at the University of Akron under the direction of John C. Green, supported by grants from the Pew Charitable Trusts.

Together, these three surveys include more than 14,000 cases. Eight items were asked in all three surveys (partisanship, ideology, abortion, gay rights, help for minorities, environmental protection, welfare spending, and national health insurance). The responses on these items were pooled for all three years to produce enough cases for an analysis by region. These data must be viewed with some caution because they represent opinion over an entire decade rather than at one point in time. A more detailed account of how these data were compiled may be obtained from the Bliss Institute.

Endnote

1. In the 1990 NSRI survey, the question wording was: "What is your religion?" In the 2001 ARIS survey, the phrase, "...if any" was added to the question. A subsequent validity check based on cross-samples of 3,000 respondents carried out by ICR in 2002 found no statistical difference between the pattern of responses according to the two wordings.

BIBLIOGRAPHY

Barlow, Philip L. and Edwin Scott Gaustad. *New Historical Atlas of Religion in America*. New York: Oxford University Press, 2001.

Buerge, David M. and Junius Rochester. *Roots and Branches: The Religious Heritage of Washington State*. Seattle, WA: Church Council of Greater Seattle, 1988.

Cone, Molly, Howard Droker, and Jacqueline Williams. *Family of Strangers: Building a Jewish Community in Washington State*. Seattle, WA: University of Washington Press, 2003.

Haycox, Stephen. *Alaska: An American Colony*. Seattle, WA: University of Washington Press, 2002.

Iwamura, Jane Naomi and Paul Spickard, eds. *Revealing the Sacred in Asian and Pacific America*. New York: Routledge, 2003.

Jones, Dale E., Sherri Doty, Clifford Grammick, James E. Horsch, Richard Houseal, Mac Lynn, John P. Marcus, Kenneth M. Sanchagrin, and Richard H. Taylor. *Religious Congregations and Membership in the United States 2000: An Enumeration by Region, State and County Based on Data Reported for 149 Religious Bodies*. Nashville, TN: Glenmary Research Center, 2002.

Killen, Patricia O'Connell. "The Geography of a Religious Minority: Roman Catholicism in the Pacific Northwest." *U.S. Catholic Historian* 18/3 (Sum 2000): 51-72.

Lowenstein, Steven. *The Jews of Oregon, 1850-1950*. Portland, OR: Jewish Historical Society of Oregon, 1987.

Loy, William G. and Stuart Allan. *Atlas of Oregon*. 2nd Revised Edition. Eugene, OR: University of Oregon Press, 2001.

Mitchell, Richard G., Jr. *Dancing at Armageddon: Survivalism and Chaos in Modern Times*. Chicago, IL: University of Chicago Press, 2002.

Nordquist, Philip A. "Lutherans in the West and Northwest." In Heidi Emerson, ed. *New Partners, Old Roots*. Tacoma, WA: J &D Printing, Inc., 1986.

North American Religion Atlas. Polis Center, Indiana University-Purdue University at Indianapolis. URL: http:// www.religionatlas.org

O'Connell, Nicholas. *On Sacred Ground: The Spirit of Place in Pacific Northwest Literature*. Seattle, WA: University of Washington Press, 2003.

Oleska, Michael. *Orthodox Alaska*. Crestwood, NY: St. Vladim ir's Seminary Press, 1992.

The Pluralism Project. URL: http://www.pluralism.org

Schoenberg, Wilfred P., S.J. *A History of the Catholic Church in the Pacific Northwest 1743-1983*. Washington, DC: The Pastoral Press, 1987.

Shibley, Mark. "Religion in Oregon: Recent Demographic Currents in the Mainstream. *Pacific Northwest Quarterly*, 83/3 (July 1992): 82-87.

Wellman, James K., Jr. "Religion without a Net: Strictness in the Religious Practices of West Coast Urban Liberal Christian Congregations." *Review of Religious Research* 42/2 (2002): 184-199.

INDEX

CONTRIBUTORS

PATRICIA O'CONNELL KILLEN is professor of religion at Pacific Lutheran University in Tacoma, Washington, where she chairs the Department of Religion and directs the Center for Religion, Cultures and Society in the Western United States. Among her publications on religion in the region, "Writing the Pacific Northwest into Canadian and U.S. Catholic History: Geography, Demographics, and Regional Religion" [*Historical Studies* 66 (2000): 74-91] received the Paul Bator Memorial Prize from the Canadian Catholic Historical Association. Currently she is working on a selected edition of the letters of A.M.A. Blanchet, Bishop of Walla Walla and Nesqually 1846-1879.

LANCE D. LAIRD teaches comparative religion at the Evergreen State College in Olympia, Washington. He holds a B.A. in religious studies and an M.Div. in Christian theology. He earned his Th.D. at the Harvard Divinity School in Islamic studies and Christian-Muslim relations. He and his students have engaged in research on religious diversity in Western Washington through the Pluralism Project at Harvard University.

MARK A. SHIBLEY is associate professor of sociology at Southern Oregon University where he coordinates a new interdisciplinary Social Science and Policy program in Environmental Studies. His book, *Resurgent Evangelicalism in the United States: Mapping Cultural Change Since 1970* (University of South Carolina Press, 1996), won the Distinguished Book Award from the Society for the Scientific Study of Religion in 1997. His recent publications include articles on the Christian Right and on the role of religious organizations in the contemporary environmental movement. His current work explores the spirituality of the un-churched in the Pacific Northwest.

MARK SILK is associate professor of Religion in Public Life at Trinity College, Hartford, Connecticut, and founding director of the Leonard E. Greenberg Center for the Study of Religion in Public Life at Trinity. A former newspaper reporter and member of the editorial board of the *Atlanta Journal-Constitution*, he is author of *Spiritual Politics: Religion and America Since World War II* and *Unsecular Media: Making News of Religion in America*. He is editor of *Religion in the News*, a magazine published by the Greenberg Center that examines how the news media handle religious subject matter.

DALE E. SODEN is professor of history and director of the Weyerhaueser Center for Christian Faith and Learning at Whitworth College in Spokane, Washington. He researches Protestantism in the Pacific Northwest and has published scholarly articles on the Women's Christian Temperance Union in the region as well as Billy Sunday's revivals. He is the author of Whitworth College's centennial history and of *The Reverend Mark Matthews: Activist in the Progressive Era* (University of Washington Press, 2001), which explores how Matthews built First Presbyterian in Seattle into the denomination's largest congregation in the United States and the significant role he played in the city's politics between 1902 and 1940.

JAMES K. WELLMAN, JR. is assistant professor of western religion in the Comparative Religion Program, Jackson School of International Studies at the University of Washington. His book, *The Gold Coast Church and the Ghetto: Christ and Culture in Mainline Protestantism* (Illinois, 1999), won the 2001 Francis Makemie Award from the Presbyterian Historical Society for the best book in American Presbyterian/Reformed history. It examines a 4,000-member downtown congregation in Chicago and its relation to class and race in the twentieth century. Recently he has published on urban, liberal, Protestant congregations on the West Coast. Currently he is pursuing research on Pacific Northwest evangelicals, including mega-churches, conservative ethnic congregations, new alternative worship churches, and parachurch organizations in the region.